King Edward's School at Bath

1552–1982

The Fall and Rise of the Grammar School

JOHN WROUGHTON

D1437851

KING EDWARD'S SCHOOL AT BATH

Table of Contents

List of Illustrations

Foreword

During the last twenty years King Edward's has been transformed from a small provincial grammar school to an Independent school of national standing with membership of the
Headmasters' Conference and a three-fold increase in size.
Against the background of the turbulent 1960's and the raging
inflation of the 1970's, when the family unit and traditional
values were crumbling fast, the School shook itself free from
the confines of Thomas Jelly's beautiful building in Broad
Street (happily still occupied by the Junior School) and
emerged onto the open spaces of North Road.

It was hardly to be expected that such a traumatic exchange could be achieved without some crisis of identity. The
School should be aware of its past as much as of the present,
for its entity is comprised of both elements. The magnum opus
of Katharine Symons (*The Grammar School of King Edward VI,
Bath and Its Ancient Foundation*) completed after a labour of love
lasting 14 years is no longer relevant to a generation equipped
with television sets and computers, and we are fortunate to
have in John Wroughton an historian of distinction prepared
to place his expertise at our service.

In this spirit I commend his volume to all Edwardians—
past, present and future—and to all our many friends, especially among the Citizens of Bath whom our School (despite
difficult periods) has served with pride and distinction for over
four centuries.

MARK RUTHERFORD

January 1982.   Chairman of the Board of Governors

Preface and Acknowledgements

When the Governors first commissioned me to write a new history of King Edward's School, I feared initially that it would be a rather dull and tedious assignment. How wrong I was! The more I dug into the past, the more I realised that I was dealing with a School of considerable stature. Characters of great national distinction quickly began to dominate the pages of its old admission registers. Their enterprise, coupled with the academic prowess of a series of outstanding Headmasters had, by 1800, made King Edward's universally famous. Then, almost without warning, the School plunged into sudden decline and almost total extinction—thanks to the mindless folly of various outside bodies. This human drama, which was enacted as the nineteenth century unfolded, was absorbingly tense, bitterly tragic and well worthy of weekly serialisation on any T.V. channel. Public protests, heartbroken Headmasters, interfering Trustees and 'ragamuffin' pupils all made their somewhat surprising appearance. Almost equally breathtaking has been the story of the School's revival to a place of fame and honour in our own times. Few schools in the country could have enjoyed such a rich and varied past. But it is perhaps worth noting that King Edward's School has only prospered when it has been left free to pursue with single-minded determination its old traditional aim of academic excellence. Political interference from outside groups determined to modify that aim has brought nothing but disaster.

I am most grateful to the Governors not only for giving me total freedom of access to all their records, but also for allowing me to write this history without the slightest pressure of any kind. In the first five chapters, therefore, I have viewed with a critical eye the considerable evidence which has lain before me. I have tried hard to analyse faults and failings as well as credits and successes. After all, the School has not always been at its best—nor have some of its major characters been entirely worthy of its long traditions. I hope that the reader will, however, spare a thought for my problems as I faced up to writing the final chapter. Contemporary history is always difficult. There is *too much* evidence. There is no possibility of standing back to put things properly into perspective. There is, above all, a very real danger that the unsuspecting historian (who is, after all, composed of flesh, blood and bones) will have his judgement clouded over by personal feelings—especially if, as in this case, he has been an active participant in the events he describes. Like all contemporary history, therefore, Chapter 6 must be regarded as a provisional and tentative effort to *narrate* the story of the years 1962–1982. Little attempt has been made to comment or to criticise—let alone to make judgements on personalities. This task must be reserved for the next historian of the School who will see things quite differently.

I should like to acknowledge the enormous debt I owe to Mrs. Katharine E. Symons, whose original history of the School, *The Grammar School of King Edward VI, Bath and Its Ancient Foundation,* has proved a mine of valuable information—especially in connection with Chapters 1 and 2. I am also particularly grateful to Mr. H. M. Porter, a former Headmaster of the School, for his comprehensive *Notes on King Edward's School, 1921–1961,* which were compiled with the aid of his personal diaries and placed entirely at my disposal. Unabated encouragement throughout the course of my research has been given by Mr. Mark Rutherford (the Chairman of Governors), Mr. Warren Derry (former Vice-Chairman of Governors) and Mr. B. H. Holbeche (the present Headmaster). One of the most enjoyable aspects of my task has been to receive reminiscences and early photographs from Old Edwardians and members of Staff (past and present). These include Mr. W. A. Bastin, Mr. L. R. Bence, Sir George Beresford-Stooke, Mr. R. H. Bradfield, Mr. H. C. P. Burden, Mr. T. L. Carder, Mr. I. L. Creese, Col. W. T. Currie, Mr. F. J. T. Dobbs, Mr. L. R. Hall, Mr. B. Henson, Dr. R. A. Henson, Mr. J. F. Langley, Mr. G. F. Laurence, Mr. J. W. A.

Lovell, Mr. F. H. C. Mills, Mr. G. H. Moore, Mr. W. Paterson, Mr. T. E. Rhymes, Dr. A. W. Spence, Mr. N. V. H. Symons, Dr. F. R. Thorn, Dr. J. B. Tucker and Mr. W. E. Willett. I am also indebted to Mr. J. Bryant of the Bath City Archives, Mr. C. H. Couchman Clerk and Receiver to the Bath Municipal Charities formerly known as the Bath Charity Trustees and the Staff of the Bath Reference Library for all their helpfulness in assisting me to locate information. Miss E. Holland and Mrs. M. Oliver, through their work on The Survey of Old Bath, enabled me to pinpoint the earliest site of the School. Three pupils—J. R. Brown, M. D. Calvert and T. D. Carter—usefully investigated certain manuscript material inside the School's own Archives Room, whereas Mrs. Susan Smith kindly provided information gleaned from the Census Returns. Two former pupils gave invaluable assistance with the final stages of the preparation of the book—Tim Dunn (proof-reading) and Philip Smith (compilation of the index). Finally, Mrs. Enid Underwood deserves full credit for her patient and accurate typing of the manuscript.

J.P.W.
1st February, 1982

Chronology

1552: School founded by the Royal Charter of King Edward VI

1552: Rev. John Short elected Master

1553: Nicholas Jobbyn bequeathed books to the School

1576: Rev. John Long, M.A. (King's College, Cambridge) elected Master

1582: Mr. Matthew Lloyd, M.A. (Jesus College, Oxford) elected Master

1583: School moved from Frog Lane to St. Mary's, Northgate

1583: Rev. Patrick Blere (St. Andrew's University) elected Master

1586: Rev. Richard Meredith, M.A. (New College, Oxford) elected Master

1587: Rev. Scott elected Master

1589: Rev. Alexander Hume, M.A. (St. Andrew's University) elected Master

1592: Rev. Arnoll, elected Master

1596: Rev. Henry Slyman, M.A. (St. Edmund Hall, Oxford) elected Master

1597: John Hales left School for Oxford

1600: The first Latin oration made by a pupil on Mayor-making day.

1604: Rev. James Sharpe, M.A. (Trinity College, Oxford) elected Master

1617?: Rev. Thomas Shrewsbury, M.A. (University College, Oxford) elected Master

1618: William Prynne left School for Oxford.

1626?: Rev. Bartholomew Man, M.A., (Corpus Christi College, Oxford) elected Master

1636: Rev. Francis Mynn, M.A. (Christ Church College, Oxford) elected Master

1644: School temporarily disbanded during the Civil War
1662: Rev. Francis Mynn sacked for negligence; replaced as Master by Rev. Richard Hoyle.
1663: Rev. Jones elected Master
1665: Rev. William Peake, B.A. (Magdalen College, Oxford) elected Master
1681: Rev. William Baker, B.A. (Brasenose College, Oxford) elected Master
1687: Mr. Francis Carne appointed Master on order of King James II
1688: Rev. William Baker reinstated as Master
1713: Rev. William Street, M.A. (Hart Hall, Oxford) elected Master but died shortly afterwards.
1713: Rev. Benjamin Wilding, M.A. (Balliol College, Oxford) elected Master
1720: Rev. Bartholomew Richards, M.A. (Balliol College, Oxford) elected Master
1721: Rev. Walter Robbins, LL.B. (St. John's College, Cambridge) elected Master
1735: Bath Corporation fined £500 for their 'terrible mismanagement of endowment funds'.
1754: Opening of the new Broad Street building.
1754: Dispute over the Mastership—Rev. Arthur Hele, M.A. (St. John's College, Cambridge) elected
1762: The revenues of Charlcombe Rectory became part of the Master's Salary.
1777: Admiral Sir Sidney Smith left School
1778: Rev. Nathanael Morgan, M.A. (King's College, Cambridge) elected Master
1778: Richard Laurence left School
1780: Major-General John Gaspard Le Marchant left School
1795: Gathering of Mr. Morgan's Old Boys at the White Hart Inn
1799: Thomas De Quincey left School
1807: Rear-Admiral Sir Edward Parry left School
1811: Rev. Thomas Wilkins, M.A. (Worcester College, Oxford) elected Master
1818: Visit of the Charity Commissioners to King Edward's
1822: Election of the School's first ten free Foundationers; resignation of Mr. Wilkins in protest.

1823: Rev. James Pears, M.A. (New College, Oxford) elected Master

1830: Public protest by some parents about the methods and attitudes of Mr. Pears.

1832: Commencement of a suit, brought by parents, in the Court of Chancery against the Bath Corporation for its mismanagement of the School.

1834: End of tradition requiring Head Boy to make Latin oration on Mayor-making day.

1836: Management of School transferred from Bath Corporation to Bath Charity Trustees.

1849: A New Scheme issued for the management of the School.

1852: Election of 40 additional free Foundationers

1853: Rev. Arthur Macleane, M.A. (Trinity College, Cambridge) elected Headmaster

1853: Rev. J. G. M. Carey, B.A. (Trinity College, Cambridge) appointed Second Master

1853: The Tercentenary Festival

1854: The Brodrick Prize Fund established

1856: Controversy over the Headmaster's right to flog boys

1856: Rev. E. Bartrum, M.A. (Pembroke College, Oxford) appointed Second Master

1858: Rev. Henry Fagan, M.A. (Pembroke College, Cambridge) elected Headmaster.

1861: Establishment of the first university leaving Scholarship

1862: Cricket first introduced

1863: Mr. O. H. L. Packman, M.A., appointed Second Master

1864: Public dispute between Headmaster and Second Master over discipline.

1865: Rev. G.L. Topping, M.A. (Brasenose College, Oxford) appointed Second Master

1867: School inspected by the Schools Inquiry Commission

1870: School officially classed as a 'School of Second Grade'

1870: Rev. John McDowell, M.A. (Trinity College, Dublin) elected Headmaster

1872: The New Scheme came into operation; management

of the School passed from the Charity Trustees to a Board of Governors.

1874: Rev. Henry Sanderson, M.A. (Sydney Sussex College, Cambridge) elected Headmaster

1876: A playing field rented for the first time.

1878: Annual Leaving Exhibitions awarded for use at University

1890: Edmund White Prize Fund established

1891: J. S. Turner Prize for French and German established

1892: The School Cap first introduced

1896: Mr. Edward Symons, M.A. (University College, Oxford) elected Headmaster after the dismissal of Mr. Sanderson.

1896: Mr. R. S. Crump, M.A. (Queen's College, Oxford) appointed Second Master

1897: The School Song introduced

1897: A Science Laboratory established

1898: Physical Training lessons commenced in the Y.M.C.A. Gymnasium

1898: Establishment of a Preparatory School

1899: The new Board of Education took over ultimate responsibility from the Charity Commissioners for schools like King Edward's

1899: No. 20 Belmont purchased as a residence for the Headmaster.

1900: A School Flag purchased

1900: Mr. E. A. Eden, M.A., B.Sc. appointed Second Master

1900: Formation of the Cadet Corps.

1904: Official Board of Education Inspection and Report

1904: School Library established

1905: Swimming classes commenced at the Cleveland Baths

1906: The Old Edwardians' Association formed

1906: Rev. W. T. Underwood, M.A. (St. John's College, Oxford) appointed Second Master

1906: The Robert Dyer Commans Exhibition Fund established

1908: The Cadet Corps restyled the Officer Training Corps

1908: The Tudor Rose adopted as the School Badge; a new maroon and blue cap introduced

1909:   *The Edwardian* first published
1910:   A Shooting VIII formed by the O.T.C.
1912:   Official Board of Education Inspection and Report
1913:   Formation of O.T.C. Band
1913:   Boarding House established at 19 Portland Place
1914:   Annual O.T.C. Competition Day commenced on the Recreation Ground
1914:   A New Scheme restored the School to First Grade Status
1914:   The Tutell Science Prize established
1915:   Capt. E. T. Langley, B.Sc (London) appointed Second Master.
1919:   The Nahum Nurnberg Prize Fund established
1920:   Official Board of Trade Inspection and Report
1920:   School granted 'Recognised Status'
1921:   London Association of Bath Old Edwardians formed
1921:   The Laurence Cook Prize for High Endeavour established
1921:   Capt. Archibald Annand, M.C., M.A. (Pembroke College, Cambridge) elected Headmaster.
1921:   Direct Grant Status conferred on the School
1921:   End of the Form Master System—start of specialised Departments
1922:   Preparatory School moved into No. 20 Belmont
1922:   The House System introduced; inter-House Cross-Country began
1922:   Rugby introduced in place of Soccer as the major winter game
1923:   Annual Athletic Sports first established
1925:   Inter-House Swimming Sports commenced
1926:   Old Edwardians' Rugby Club formed
1927:   Official Board of Education Inspection and Report
1939:   Boarding House closed down.
1940:   Officer Training Corps restyled Junior Training Corps.
1945:   Mr. Maurice Porter, M.A. (Trinity College, Cambridge) elected Headmaster
1945:   Struggle to retain Direct Grant Status
1945:   Games became compulsory
1945:   Formation of Dramatic Society

1945: Mr. E. O. Jago, B.A. (Cantab.) appointed Second Master
1946: School Dinner provided
1946: Hockey first introduced
1947: School Medical Inspection first began
1948: Sixth Form divided into Lower and Upper Sixth
1948: Junior Training Corps restyled Combined Cadet Force
1949: Founder's Day Service in the Abbey first held
1950: Mr. W. E. Willett, B.A. (London) appointed Second Master
1950: St. Michael's School Buildings leased
1952: Full School Uniform introduced
1952: Bathampton Playing Fields first used
1952: Fourth Centenary celebrated; War Memorial Library established
1956: Official Ministry of Education Inspection and Report
1959: The North Road site purchased
1959: Development Appeal launched; formation of the Ladies' Committee
1959: Second stream of entry admitted
1961: Senior School established at North Road; Junior School at Broad Street
1962: Mr. Brian Holbeche, M.A. (St. Catharine's College, Cambridge) elected Headmaster
1962: Regular Parents' Meetings commenced; Careers' Room established
1963: Formation of the Fathers' Committee
1964: Lecture Theatre opened
1964: Formation of The Friends of King Edward's School
1964: Headmaster elected onto the Headmasters' Conference
1965: Biology Laboratory opened
1966: Official Ministry of Education Inspection and Report
1969: Saturday morning school ended
1970: Sixth Form Tutor Groups formed
1971: Geography Block opened
1971: Development Appeal launched
1972: Third Stream of entry admitted
1974: Mr. J. P. Wroughton, M.A., F.R. Hist.S. (Hertford College, Oxford) appointed Second Master.

1974: Sixth Form Centre opened in Nethersole
1974: Multi-Purpose Hall opened
1975: All-weather Pitch opened
1975: C.C.F. celebrated its 75th Anniversary
1976: School became fully independent with the abolition of the Direct Grant System
1977: Mathematics Block opened
1978: Restoration of the Broad Street facade
1979: Opening of the Stewart Building
1980: Major structural changes to interior of Junior School
1981: Formation of Former Parents' Association
1982: Development Appeal launched
1982: Death of Mr. Holbeche while still in office.

CHAPTER ONE

St. Mary's—Years of Foundation, 1552–1754

'. . . *that for the future there should be and will be one grammar school in the said City of Bath which will be called the free grammar school of King Edward VIth which is for the teaching, education and instruction of boys and young men in grammar, to continue for ever.'* (Letters Patent granted under the Great Seal by King Edward VIth on 7th July, 1552.)

City and State in the Sixteenth and Seventeenth Centuries

At the time of the School's foundation in 1552, Bath was a compact medieval city surrounded by green fields and meadows. Apart from an overspill outside the North and South Gates, its two thousand inhabitants lived chiefly in the small area protected by old stone walls. Cramped conditions and narrow streets were a constant hazard to health. Foul-smelling rubbish accumulated on every footpath to rot away slowly in the still and humid air of Bath. Payments were occasionally made by the Chamberlain for 'shovlinge upp the Durte in Westgate Street' or 'cleansing ye way by the Bridge'. But even as late as 1654, John Evelyn described the streets as 'narrow, uneven and unpleasant'.

The citizens did, however, enjoy one vital asset—an abundant supply of fresh water. As early as 1530 Leland had noticed that Bath was favoured with 'many springs of pure water, that be conveyed by divers ways to serve the city . . . and many houses in the town have pipes of lead to convey water from place to place'. People who could not afford the luxury of their own piped supply were able to obtain fresh water by taking buckets to the several public conduits erected at points around the city.

Bath became a prosperous city in the sixteenth century thanks chiefly to its close involvement with a flourishing cloth

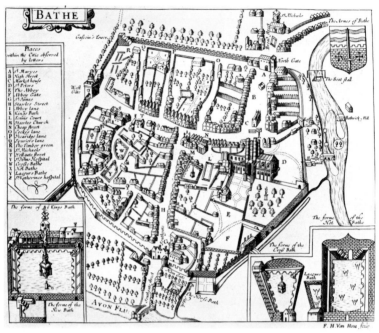

Early 17th century map of Bath, based on that by John Speed.
Avon County Library (Bath Reference Library)

industry. It was, in addition, a health resort which attracted
large numbers of visitors seeking the healing qualities of its
hot water springs. Dr. Thomas Venner, a physician at the
Baths, claimed in 1628: 'They be of excellent efficacy against
all diseases of the head and sinews, proceeding from a cold
and moist cause, as rheums, palsies, epilepsies, lethargies,
apoplexia, cramps, deafness, forgetfulness, trembling or weakness of any member, aches, and swellings of the joints.' He
also invited 'those that fear obesity, that is, would not wax
gross . . . to come to our baths'.

An increasing number of inns and lodging houses consequently sprang up to cater for the needs of this profitable
tourist trade. The leading citizens of Bath were, therefore, a
mixture of clothiers, farmers, merchants, shopkeepers, doctors, lawyers and innkeepers—all enjoying higher standards of
living than the residents of even such places as York. Afflu-
ence was readily apparent in the splendid stone houses which

The Abbey House (home of Dr. John Sherwood whose son attended the School in 1600).

Taken from Guidot's Map, 1731

dominated its streets. Not until after 1725 did the face of this wealthy medieval city change. Only then did physical expansion take place with the development of Georgian crescents and the establishment of a fashionable society.

Thus during almost the first two hundred years of its existence, King Edward's School developed under ideal conditions of local stability and prosperity. City affairs were controlled by the Corporation, a self-perpetuating body which consisted of the Mayor, Aldermen and Common Councillors. Together they elected two Members of Parliament, maintained law and order and regulated trade. The Guildhall, which stood in the centre of the High Street, also housed the Market (which met twice a week on Wednesdays and Saturdays) and the armoury. The Bath Regiment of Trained Bands paraded regularly from 1573 as a defensive measure against possible Spanish invasion. Local security after curfew, however, was the responsibility of a bellman and two watchmen who patrolled the streets in search of fire or felon. The stocks and pillory, which had been erected outside the Guildhall, served as a timely reminder that justice could be both swift and appropriate.

These were exciting years for the nation as a whole. Edward VI, who died in his teens just one year after the foundation of the School, was succeeded by the turbulent rule of 'Bloody' Mary. The 'spacious days' of Queen Elizabeth I saw England's rise to fame as a trading and sea-faring country with the glorious defeat of the Spanish Armada in 1588. But the simmering dispute between Crown and Parliament eventually ended with Civil War and the execution of Charles I in 1649. Cromwell's regime, the Restoration of Charles II, the Glorious Revolution of 1688 and the establishment of the Hanoverian dynasty in the form of George I (1714) were events that did not go unnoticed in Bath or in its newly-founded Grammar School.

Foundation

By 1552, however, one feature of the original medieval city had already been deliberately destroyed. The fine old Benedictine Priory, which had dominated the South-eastern corner of the city since its foundation by King Offa in 775, now lay in ruins. Sharing the fate of all monasteries throughout the country, it had finally fallen victim to Henry VIII's Reformation of the English Church. Monks in general had long since acquired a bad reputation for idleness, ignorance and immorality. This seemed to be confirmed by Dr. Richard Layton's official visitation to Bath in 1535.

Although he found Prior Holleway to be 'a right vertuose man', his monks in sexual matters were 'worse then I have any fownde yet' and his monastery 'four hundred powndes in dett'. Although Layton's report was heavily biased and largely unjustified, Bath Priory could not be saved. Bowing to considerable government pressure, a voluntary surrender was eventually made on 27 January, 1539. Its vast estates and treasure store were seized by the Crown; its seal smashed to prevent further use; its twenty-one monks pensioned off; its main buildings—church, dormitories, refectory and cloister—sold to individuals and stripped of their materials.

The dissolution of Bath Priory, unlamented by the majority, was nevertheless of considerable importance. It was in fact directly responsible for the foundation of King Edward's School. A claim made to the Court of Augmentations in 1543 by John Pytt served to underline just exactly what had been lost to local people by the dissolution. Pytt had previously received a pension of £9 per annum for surrendering his position as Sub-Prior. He now successfully claimed a further £4 for his loss of the office of Master of the School within the Priory. Each medieval monastery had traditionally set up a school to teach Latin to intending monks and clerics, as well as to others who needed it for secular purposes.

It has been estimated that between 300 and 400 of these Grammar Schools were in existence by 1539, the majority of which ceased to function after the dissolution of the monasteries and chantries. This considerable loss to the country's education did not go unnoticed. Henry VIII himself, in the Chantries Act of 1545, decreed that charitable funds associated with religious houses should be made available for the re-establishment and development of these old monastic Grammar Schools. It was not, however, until the reign of Edward VI that anything was actually done. Thanks largely to impassioned pleas made in sermons at Court by Bishop Latimer and Thomas Lever, the young King's conscience was eventually awakened to halt 'the putting down of Grammar Schools' and 'the devilish drowning of youth in ignorance'. As a result thirty schools were re-established with endowments drawn from old monastic lands after petitions received from local inhabitants.

On 28 June, 1552 the Mayor (Edward Ludwell) and Citizens of Bath made a humble petition to the King for a grant of the lands in the Bailiwick of Bath for the dual purpose of setting up a Grammar School and supporting ten poor people. It must be added, however, that the motives of the Mayor and Corporation were only in part educational. It is true that Bath was the only Cathedral City in England left without a school. But a panic had suddenly gripped the local citizens that King Edward was considering selling off all the former monastery land still in his possession to settle his vast debts. This would have created serious problems for the Corporation in Bath.

King Edward VI; portrait in the possession of the School.
Photo by C. T. Leaman

Although the Crown had, by 1552, already sold to individual buyers the wealthy monastic estates which lay outside the city, confiscated property *inside* the City had remained unsold. In fact the Crown had earlier agreed that the Corporation, which had originally paid 'fee-farm' rents for this

King Edward VI presenting a Charter.

School Archives

property to the Priory over a long period of time, could continue to do so to the Crown. This enabled the Corporation to continue to manage and develop the property as it liked. All the rights and benefits associated with lordship, including considerable profits obtainable from sub-letting, could still be enjoyed. As rumours increased of the likelihood of a sale the Corporation, banned by the Statute of Mortmain (1279) from actually purchasing the land itself, feared inevitable complications and horrible consequences of purchase by outside individuals.

It was, therefore, partly to offset this possibility that the City rather cleverly presented its petition to the King listing a total of 102 properties requested. This schedule of lands with their values was drawn up by the Mayor himself, Edward Ludwell who, as Deputy Crown Bailiff, was extremely familiar with Crown property within the City. It consisted of all the Priory property originally rented together with a few additions gained by the Crown at the Dissolution (with the exception of Ham Meadow, Ambury Meadow and the Priory buildings, which had been sold in 1542). Although some land within the City walls and immediate suburbs was owned by churches, hospitals, almshouses, guilds or private individuals, a substantial proportion of Bath was contained in the schedule submitted by the Corporation. The petition, which was presented by the Mayor, who was also M.P. for Bath, was granted by Letters Patent under the Great Seal on 7 July, 1552.

This 'Charter' (still in the possession of the School and reproduced here) granted 'that for the future there should be and will be one grammar school in the said city of Bath which will be called the free grammar school of King Edward VIth which is for the teaching, education and instruction of boys and young men in grammar, to continue for ever'. For the upkeep of the school, the Mayor and Citizens of Bath were granted 'all and each of our messuages,[1] lands, tenements,[2] lofts,[3] cottages, orchards, gardens, pastures, mills, shops, cellars, rooms and other privileges . . . situated both within the City of Bath and in the Suburbs of the same city in our said county of Somerset, which is the late portion of the lands, possessions and revenues of the priory of Bath in the same county of Somerset which has been recently dissolved but which used formerly to exist.'

They were given the privilege of holding this property 'in free socage or burgage', thus releasing them from normal services and rents due to the feudal lord. Instead, a nominal

1 A portion of land intended as a site for a dwelling.
2 Land which is held by any form of tenure.
3 The site of a house with its outbuildings.

sum of £10 a year 'of good and lawful money of England' was to be paid to the Court of Augmentations. According to the property schedule submitted by Ludwell the gross annual value of the property granted was estimated at £54 5s. 4d. However, largely because some of the tenements and cottages were in a delapidated condition, the cost of repairs had 'yearlie growen to greate sommes' and was 'very ruinouse'. Consequently, the net revenue passing into the King's hands had not exceeded £25 per annum. This figure, which represented only the fixed or 'assized' rents payable in place of ancient feudal services, rather conceals the real value of the land even in 1552.

The Corporation had been perfectly entitled to 'farm' or sub-let the property, retaining all the profits except the 'assized' rents, which had previously been paid to the Priory and later (from 1539) to the Crown. The Edwardian Charter enabled the City to enjoy all these profits together with the considerable 'fines' imposed when sub-tenants wished to erect buildings or make alterations. Furthermore, they were granted the right of 'reversion' to all the property, enabling them to claim back the land and buildings after the termination of the lease (often granted for a specified number of lives). They were also permitted in future to purchase additional lands to the value of £10 per annum (in spite of the Statute of Mortmain).

Out of this considerable wealth, both real and potential which included ownership of the Hot Spring Baths, the Mayor and Corporation were required to find 'one suitable, able and educated person, who is well instructed and learned at least in Latin and who is to serve in the aforesaid free grammar school and will receive ten pounds a year for his salary'. No further educational restrictions were placed on them, although they were empowered 'to name and appoint a teacher for the aforesaid free grammar school as often as the same free grammar school lacks a teacher' and (with the advice of the Bishop) to make statutes concerning 'the ordering, governing and directing of the teacher and undermaster or assistant teacher, and of the students of the aforesaid school'. They were, in addition, required from the same funds to 'help, relieve and comfort for all time for ever ten poor persons

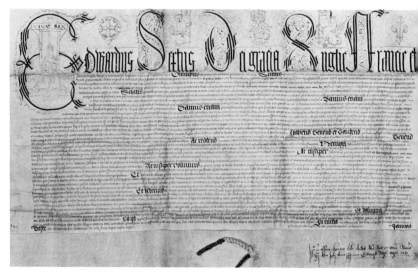

The School Charter, 1552.
School Archives. Photo by C. T. Leaman

dwelling and staying within the aforesaid city of Bath.' This
was to become known as the Black Alms or St. Catherine's
Charity.

The Charter concludes by emphasising that the Mayor and
Corporation should spend 'the profits, incomes, rents and
revenues' of all the listed property 'henceforward, forever,
totally and entirely for the continuance and maintenance of
the free grammar school . . . and for the relief and support of
ten poor persons'. The story of what follows is partly the story
of their failure to meet these obligations. King Edward's
School had been founded on the heritage of Bath Priory. Its
intellectual and spiritual endowment had been drawn from
the monastic grammar school latterly run by John Pytt; its
material endowment had been drawn entirely from lands
granted to the monastery in earlier times by King Osric, King
Offa and other eminent benefactors.

Life in a Sixteenth Century Grammar School

The absence of many early records or precise instructions for
the government of King Edward's School during the sixteenth

and seventeenth centuries makes it somewhat difficult to build up a detailed picture of life in the 'free' Grammar School at Bath. It will be helpful, therefore, to consider first a typical Grammar School of this period, because teaching methods, curriculum and daily routine varied little.

The Grammar Schools took boys from all social backgrounds (unless they were Catholics)—the sons of lesser nobility, squires, clergy, traders, yeomen, lawyers, doctors or craftsmen. But although King Edward's was styled a 'free' Grammar School in the Charter and although it was locally called 'The Free School' until the nineteenth century, education was certainly not free of charge. Indeed, the first election of ten free scholars did not occur until 1822. Furthermore the city records fail to reveal any payments for the provision of uniform (which was normal in free Charity Schools) or any instructions to the Master regarding free tuition (until 1823). The term 'free' school (based on the word *libera* in Latin) should, therefore, be taken to mean a school open to all boys and free from hampering restrictions. Fees were payable to the Master. Writing in 1647, James Howell emphasised the personal sacrifice that many parents were willing to make in the cause of education—a theme often repeated throughout the history of King Edward's School:

> Every man strains his fortunes to keep his children at school. The cobbler will clout it till midnight, the porter will carry burdens till his bones crack again, the ploughman will pinch both back and belly to give his son learning, and I find that this ambition reigns nowhere so much as in this island.

Boys normally entered the Grammar School at the age of seven or eight, leaving at fifteen for University (or perhaps earlier if other jobs or professions were to be followed). Before attending the Grammar School, the child would already have learnt to read and write in English at one of the 'petty' schools run by elderly dames. Instruction there was based on the 'horn-book' which consisted of a sheet of paper printed with the alphabet and the Lord's Prayer. It was pasted on a simple board with a handle and covered with a piece of transparent horn for protection.

Once at the Grammar School, however, boys were expected

to concentrate on Latin (with perhaps some religious instruction, a little Greek in the higher forms and a smattering of Hebrew). Latin was still very much the 'official' language of the day used by diplomats, lawyers, doctors, civil servants and clerks. It was a basic requirement for entry to University and to all the leading professions, including the Church. No place, therefore, would have been found at schools like King Edward's, during the sixteenth and seventeenth centuries, either for English or for the increasing range of 'new subjects', science, mathematics, geography, history and modern languages.

A vivid picture of life and conditions in a typical Grammar School of this period is given in the 'Statutes and Orders for the Government of the Grammar Schoole of Ashby-de-la-Zouche' (founded in 1567). The School was divided into five forms (all, of course, housed in the same large schoolroom with the one Master presiding). The boys in the lowest form were to be taught both the basic rules of Latin Grammar and the Church catechism by a senior scholar chosen daily by the Master. He would also ensure that these *petties* (or juniors) could properly read and write. Boys entering the second form devoted their time to learning rules for sentence construction, whereas third formers concentrated on the Latin rules for nouns and verbs. In the fourth it became possible for the pupils to write 'a Lattin of their own makeing' (i.e. to translate into Latin sentences set by the Master). The most senior scholars in the fifth form were set two 'themes' a week to develop their style in writing Latin prose or verse. They were also expected by then to be able to converse freely and fluently in Latin. To encourage this, the Statutes ruled that 'none of the chiefest fformes shall speak English one to another'.

This rather precise and unvaried programme of work was implemented by means of somewhat basic teaching methods. Constant repetition, endless testing, frequent note-taking and nightly homework of the memorising kind were apparently the main ingredients:

> The Schoolmaster shall give them lessons in the morning the which lessons shall be examined in the afternoon the same day. And on the next morning after shall be perfectly repeated without ye booke ... Upon ffryday in the afternoon the

schollers shall repeat and say without books and construe their lessons learned the same weeke . . . And every scholler shall write the notes . . . in paper bookes prepared for that purpose which notes the Master shall deliver to them in his reading . . . And what time they have vacant on ffryday or on Saturday they shall bestow in writeing of Llatines and such like exercises of writeing.

Grammar text-books were used to assist in the process of learning, notably William Lily's *Grammatica Latina*, Cato's *Disticha de Moribus*, and an introductory phrasebook, *Pueriles Sententiae*. The Master would also read extracts from the classics, especially to the higher forms. These included Tully's *Epistles*, *Aesop's Fables*, Ovid's *Metamorphoses*, Caesar's *Gallic War* and Livy's *History of Rome*.

Boys were expected to work hard for six days a week. In summer they reported at six o'clock in the morning (7.30 a.m. in winter). Morning school lasted until eleven o'clock with one half-hour break at about nine o'clock (to enable the boys to eat their packed breakfast). After going home for lunch, they would return at one o'clock, working on until five o'clock (again with a break of half-an-hour in the middle of the afternoon). Thursday afternoon, however, was 'games afternoon'. The regulations stipulated that:

In their play they shall use honest games, they shall keep themselves together, they that exercise shooting shall be in a place meet for that purpose, they shall not play in the streets. Nor goe to alehouses. Nor any unlawful games or breake into orchyards or rob gardens.

Holidays were taken on Saints' Days in the Church calendar, with longer breaks at Christmas (18 days), Easter (12 days), and Whitsuntide (7 days).

A very high standard of behaviour was expected from the pupils of the Grammar School both inside and outside the premises. They were not to 'swear or ffight with another or abuse or disturb one another or steale from any'. In particular, they were to show courtesy and respect for visitors to the School and local people generally. 'When any stranger cometh into the Schoole ye schollers shall arise stand and salute them and likewise civilly give the upper hand to those whome they doe meet in the streets and courteously salate as it becometh schollers.' Great stress was placed on discipline. Unjustified lateness and absenteeism were severely punished. If a boy was absent for fourteen days in a period of three months (except for illness), 'hee shall be expell'd from the schoole and his name blotted out.'

Trustworthy boys, forerunners of our later Prefects, were given responsibilities to assist in the control and discipline of the School. 'In every fforme one Monitor shall be appointed weekly to note such schollers as in every fforme shall be either absent or come late after the hours before appointed.' These Monitors were also responsible for gathering in written work from the boys in their form and for collecting from the Master their weekly work assignments. A 'Custos' was appointed to report to the Master any boy in the fifth form who had been heard speaking in English. Two 'Prepositors' were given the task of keeping an eye on the behaviour of the boys when they went to church. They were to 'note them which be absent, and which doe breake any of these orders'. Two additional 'Prepositors' were similarly to keep a watch on the boys during their games afternoon, passing the names of trouble-makers to the Master on 'the day of Correction'.

There were, in fact, two occasions during the week set aside for the punishment of offenders—Monday morning and Friday afternoon. These times, needless to say, were dreaded. Punishment could take a number of forms. According to John Brinsley (Headmaster at Ashby-de-la-Zouche) rebukes, loss of privilege, loss of place in the form and detention on games afternoons, could all be tried before resorting to the rod. But corporal punishment was nevertheless frequently employed. Brinsley gave detailed advice on its use:

> When you are to correct any stubborne or unbroken boy, you make sure with him to hold him fast . . . appoint 3 or 4 of your schollers, whom you know to be honest, and strong enough, or more if need be, to lay hands upon him together, to hold him fast over some forme, so that he cannot stirre hand nor foot; or else if no other remedy will serve, to hold him to some post(which is farre the safest and free from inconvenience) so as he cannot any hurte himself or others, be he never so peevish.

Brinsley and many other schoolmasters of the period believed that God had 'sanctified the rod . . . to drive out that folly which is bound up in their hearts, to save their soules from hell, and to give them wisdome'. It was, therefore, their duty to use it. If, however, it failed to work and any boys were found 'to be very disordered or not to profitt in learning', the Visitors (who inspected twice a year) 'shall expell out of the Schoole'. Standards were to be maintained at all costs.

The First Schoolroom in Frog Lane

It was a school very similar to the one described above that started its life as the free Grammar School of King Edward VI at Bath in 1552. Although it was originally thought that the schoolroom was first located in accommodation above the West Gate of the City, there now seems little evidence to substantiate this theory. Indeed, the legend would appear to be based almost entirely on the speculation of John Wood the Elder (a fine builder, but not the most reliable of historians) in his *Essay on Bath* (1742). Surviving leases and other documentary material associated with Westgate House give absolutely no hint of the School's earlier residence on that site.

Recent research,[1] however, has shown that King Edward's School was almost certainly based during this initial period in a house at the end of Frog Lane (see map). Situated on the site of the present New Bond Street, Frog Lane ran parallel to and just outside the City Walls. Access to the lane was gained through a narrow passage beneath a house which fronted onto Broad Street. The School House itself was fairly spacious with a garden attached, looking out to the rear over a plot of ground known as the Rack Close.

As early as 1631 this property was being referred to in leases as a 'tenement . . . heretofore known by the name of the Schoole House'. This description continued right through the eighteenth century. Bearing in mind that King Edward's was the *only* school which existed in Bath during this early period, it is safe to assume that the house at the end of Frog Lane, known locally as 'the School House', was indeed its original site.

1 Undertaken by Miss E. Holland and Mrs. M. Oliver as part of the Survey of Old Bath.

Almost immediately after its foundation, the School benefited from the generosity and interest of one of the former
monks, Dom Nicholas Bathe, who had been pensioned off
from the Priory in 1539 to become the Vicar of St. Mary
Stalles, at that time the main Parish Church in Bath. A
scholarly man, he became a Chaplain to the Mayor and
Corporation, Accountant to the City and a close friend of

Extract from the Survey of 1641.

'John Simons Mayor and his wife and Walter Symons their Sonne doe hold
for their lives by Indenture and dated by the Tenth day of October Anno of
the Raigne of Kinge Charles the Seveanth (1631) one Messuadge or
Tenement with a garden thereunto adjoininge situate in Frogg Lane
heretofore called the Schoolehouse between a garden now in the Tenure of
John Crissel on the North side the way leadinge by the Burrowalls on the
South side and a garden in the tenure of John Allen on the East side and
abutteth backward upon a ground called the Racke Close on the West side.
Rent *xs* not to be lett without licence.'

Bath City Archives

Edward Ludwell himself (Mayor in 1552). It is extremely likely therefore, that Sir Nicholas Jobbyn (as he now became known) worked closely with Ludwell in organising the petition for the foundation of the school.

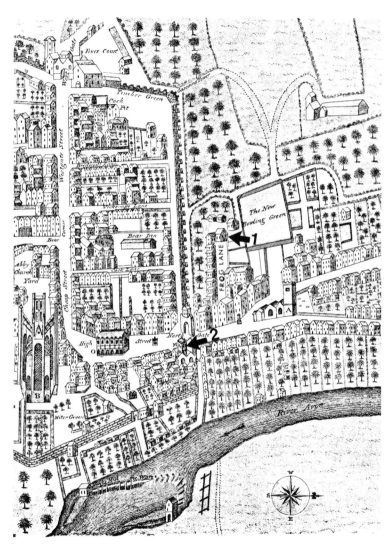

17th Century map showing the location of the School's first two sites in Frog Lane (1) and St. Mary's, North Gate (2).

Just before he died in 1553, Nicholas Jobbyn made a will in which he bequeathed 'for the use of the free gramer schole, certyne books of gramer and learning, for the use of the scolemaster and the scollers there'. Nor was the Schoolmaster himself forgotten, because he left 'to John Shorte my second best gowne, and if he contynue at the free gramer scole he shall have some of my gramer bookes'. Furthermore, with the school's property endowment in mind, he added: 'To the meyntening of the tenements belonging to the free scole of Bathe, all my tymber.' In view of the dilapidated state of some of the cottages involved and the high cost of repairs, this was undoubtedly appreciated by the City Corporation.

At least the school could now make a start with its instruction in Latin grammar from the books donated by Jobbyn. It was also obliged from 1553 to teach a catechism to its pupils. This was on instructions from no lesser a person than the Founder himself (Edward VI), who wrote to all Bishops ordering them to cause all schoolmasters to teach the new Greater Catechism. Compiled in Latin by Dr. Alexander Nowell, Master of Westminster School, this more lengthy catechism expounded the doctrines of the Reformation. Religion was to continue to play an important part in the life of boys at King Edward's School—just as it had done at the Latin grammar school in the days of the Priory.

The School at St. Mary's, Northgate

In 1583 the school moved to new premises—the nave of the disused Church of St. Mary's by the North Gate. The Chamberlain's Accounts for that year bear witness to the feverish activity undertaken to convert the Church into a schoolroom. For instance, a thousand planks and boards were sawn up to make 'planking' for the school at a cost of 15 shillings. The school, therefore, was now situated in the north-east corner of the city, just inside the North Gate (see map). St. Mary's Church, which had been rebuilt in 1180 and was now in a state of disrepair, was soon to house other occupants quite apart from the boys of the free Grammar School. The tower was shortly to be converted into the City gaol from which, apparently, the prisoners shouted insults at

The School—St. Mary's Church, North Gate.
Line drawing by P. S. W. Beck.

travellers as they made their way through the North Gate.
History does not record what verbal contact was enjoyed
between the prisoners and the boys at the School! But the
prison was not the only source of interest to the pupils of King
Edward's. The school was now located in that sector of the
city which fairly bubbled with life and activity. Not far away
were the Guildhall and Market, the stocks and pillory, the
public water fountain or conduit (where travellers watered
their horses and citizens did their washing), the North Gate
itself and the ferry across the river.

Evidence from the Chamberlain's Accounts suggests that
the Schoolroom, the school yard and the schoolmaster's
house, garden and stable were enclosed, partly by the City
Wall and partly by a wall built parallel to the street. Access to
the school premises was gained through a door set in this wall.
When Antony à Wood visited Bath he noted in his diary that:

Over the dore, next to the street, leading into the said schoole is
this engraven on a freestone table—Schola Libera Grammati-

calis and institutionem puerorum Bathon. in lingua Latina
instructa ex institutione Edwardi Sexti quondam Regis Angliae
anno regni suit sexto Anno Domini 1552.[1]

Inside the enclosure there was, in addition, at least one other
dwelling place, the occupants of which paid an annual sum of
six pence for the right to cross the school yard. One subsequent tenant, Hester Horler, for easier access to her house,
persuaded the Corporation to allow her to knock a doorway
through the City Wall 'into the ffreeschoole courte' on payment of an annual rent of six pence. Presumably she had
found crossing the school yard too hazardous a business! An
earlier occupant of the house, George Matthews, had caused
something of a stir in 1633 when he set up a workshop there
overlooking the window at the east-end of the schoolroom.
The noise proved such a nuisance to the schoolmaster, Mr.
Man, and his pupils that he lodged a formal complaint with
the Corporation. As a result George Matthews was forced to
close his workshop. Beyond that house was a garden which
was leased in 1682 by George Collibee for one shilling a year,
plus the usual payment of six pence for the right to cross the
school yard.

Further structural work on the school took place in 1685 as
the School started to grow. The Accounts reveal payments for
such items as 'takinge downe of the leade of the schole and
newe tylinge of hit', '4 days sawinge of timber for the Roff',
'caringe of robbell out of the scholmasters house', 'makynge of
the doores in the scholemasters houses' and 'makinge uppe of
the towne wall in the scholemasters garden'. The improvements made to the schoolmaster's house suggest that accommodation was probably being provided for a few boarders.
This was normal practice in grammar schools of this period
and provided a welcome method of supplementing the salaries
of schoolmasters. Another major development occurred in
1589 when the school was extended into the chancel of the old
church. This entailed building a completely new roof and
inserting a window into its gable end.

---

1 Free Grammar School provided for the education of Bath boys in the Latin
language, by the foundation of Edward VI, formerly King of England, in the sixth
year of his reign, A.D. 1552.

In spite of the new window, the schoolroom would undoubtedly be dark and cold, especially in winter. It would
appear from the Chamberlain's Accounts that no provision at
all was made by the Corporation for heating and lighting.
Most schools at this time were heated by means of a fireplace
and chimney built along one side of the room. Thus, in
common with normal practice, the boys of King Edward's
were probably expected to provide their own share of firewood
and coal, and to bring candles for their personal use in school.
But conditions would certainly be somewhat spartan.
Elizabethan schoolrooms on average measured 50 feet long
and 25 feet wide, catering for about fifty or sixty boys.

Improvements and repairs to the fabric continued throughout the seventeenth century. The problem of lighting was
again raised in 1614 when 3s. 10d. was paid 'for a glass light
set up in the Schoole laufte window'. Any increase in the
number of windows, however, was a mixed blessing to the
schoolmaster—and to the Corporation which footed the bills!
With curious regularity the glazier visited the school to repair
broken windows (presumably those that faced out on to the
school yard!) The roof was retiled in 1614 and again in 1640;
the walls were plastered and painted white in 1640; the 'outer
door' to the street, inevitably subjected to rough daily treatment, was constantly in need of repair. In 1665 Goody Cole
was paid one shilling 'for cleansing ye ffree Schoole yard'.

Inside the schoolroom, the Master presided over the whole
school from a large chair and desk set on a dais at the end of
the room. The boys normally sat on benches or forms,
working with the books on their knees. The forms were
arranged in rows down the sides of the room with a writing
table in a large space in the centre (see illustration). This is
perhaps substantiated by payments made in 1628 'for a short
table bord for the Schoolhouse' and in 1633 'for a table frame
at the Schoolehouse'. At the same time William Holway was
paid 8s. 6d. 'for 3 daies worke at the Schoole-house and for
timber and nails to mend the fflower (floor) and the seates'.
Some schools, such as the grammar school at Stratford-upon-
Avon, boasted desks for their pupils. King Edward's School,
Bath certainly possessed *one* desk, for some of the earliest
entries in 1583 included six pence spent on 'slyttynge of ii

The Schoolroom inside St. Mary's.
Line drawing by P. S. W. Beck

jyrsts (joists) for posts for the Skole deske' and fifteen pence
for 'a borde for the desk'. This almost certainly was reserved
for the exclusive use of the Master.

It is possible that desks were also used, as in other schools,
for housing valuable books which were literally chained to
them. Some schools, such as Eton, gradually built up large
chained libraries. The books donated by Sir Nicholas Jobbyn
(see above) would probably fall into this category. It is,
therefore, significant that when, in 1594, the Corporation
purchased two Latin dictionaries for the School, costing £1 3s.
4d. and 19s. 0d. respectively, a directive against one of them
read: 'to remain in the freeschole'. The possibility of chains
could not be ruled out. In the same year a joiner was paid 4s.
6d. for 'a writinge board for the scole'. Blackboards such as
these were strongly recommended by educationalists of the
day, like John Brinsley, for teaching a pupil to write.

But even greater attention was given to training a boy in the art of speaking Latin both fluently and stylishly. This was partly achieved through the performance of plays in Latin. Ben Jonson felt that this was being overdone in the country's grammar schools: 'They make all their scholars play-boys . . . Do we pay our money for this? We send them to learn their grammar and their Terence, and they learn their play-books'. It is true that schoolmasters wrote plays for their pupils to perform for local citizens. In Bath, for example, John Long received payments of 6s. 1d. and 3s. 4d. from the Corporation for two plays he wrote in 1583. The Corporation also paid in 1602, 6s. 8d. to 'the younge men of our cittie that played at Christmas' and 5s. 0d. to 'the children that played att Candellmas'—almost certainly the scholars of King Edward's School.

Fluency was also achieved by composing and delivering oration in Latin. As early as 1600 the City gave a reward of five shillings to 'Doctor Sherwoodes son for pronouncing an oracion'. He was a scholar of King Edward's School and the first in a long succession of boys chosen to make a Latin oration to the mayor on Mayor-making day. At least from 1709 this was done almost annually until 1834 when the tradition ceased (see below).

Masters of the Free School

A complete list of the known Masters of the School (or Headmasters as they became called from 1837 when management of the School was transferred from the Corporation to the Charity Trustees) is given in the Chronology. From the start they seem to have had two things in common—they were all men of considerable scholarship and they were, with a few exceptions, ordained ministers of the Church of England. Indeed, of the thirty-four identifiable men who have been Headmasters from the foundation to the present day, only six have not been clergy—Mr. Lloyd (1582), Mr. Carne (1687), Mr. Symons (1896), Mr. Annand (1921), Mr. Porter (1945), and Mr. Holbeche (1961).

The Anglican connection, of course, is hardly surprising—especially in the earlier years when the Master was required to obtain a licence from the Bishop before commencing his duties. Throughout the period from the School's establishment in 1552 to its removal to Broad Street in 1754, various Acts of Parliament continued to control the appointment of schoolmasters. Governments were determined to prevent the corruption of youngsters by heretical, subversive or immoral masters. Much legislation, like the Act of 1665, was concerned to ensure that teachers 'do themselves frequente the public prayers of the church and cause their scholars to do the same' and 'appear well affected to the government of his Majesty and the doctrine and discipline of the Church of England'. Catholics and Dissenters were totally excluded. Other action like the Parliamentary Ordinance of 1654 during the Protectorship of Oliver Cromwell, gave power to eject schoolmasters who were 'ignorant, scandalous, insufficient, or negligent'. Scandalous behaviour included blasphemy, swearing, holding 'popish opinions', adultery, the haunting of taverns, the frequent playing of cards or dice and the countenancing of wakes, morris-dancing and stage plays.

There is no evidence to suggest that any of the early Masters of King Edward's School were 'ignorant, scandalous or insufficient', or that they were guilty of adultery and the haunting of taverns, but at least one of them was sacked for negligence. Francis Mynn, an Oxford Graduate, had been appointed to the job in 1636 at the age of thirty-two. He had survived the turmoil of the Civil War and the political pressures imposed on him by successive armies of occupation, both Parliamentarian or Royalist. He had survived the inevitable disruption to school life which had caused one of his pupils, Thomas Rosewell, to leave in 1644 when 'the School was broke up'. But, on 22 September, 1662, he was dismissed after twenty-six years' service. The Council agreed:

> that Mr. Francis Mynn, Master of the ffree school in the Cittie shall be dismissed because from tyme to tyme he neglected his dutys therein, and his scholars by reason thereof have have generally departed to the sd school so that the same is now come almost to nought. He is to continue Master until Michaelmas next.

This amounted to one week's notice. However, in spite of neglect which had virtually caused the collapse of the school, the Corporation were soon to show considerable compassion. A month later, taking account of his unemployment, they agreed to give a pension, which amounted to one third of his salary:

> that whereas Mr. ffrancis Mynn, late school master of the ffree schole within the City hath resigned his said place But is not yet sufficiently provided for else where, Therefor on the request and desire of Dr. William Pearce, Bishop of this diocesse, and in consideration of his condition, It is agreed that Six pounds and thirteen shillings and ffower pence be allowed the Mr. Mynn for this year and so from year to year untill he shall be otherwise reasonably provided for, the same to be paid quarterly.

The pension continued for a year until he was appointed Vicar of South Stoke in 1663.

At least two other Masters were also affected by changes in government attitudes. It is highly probable, for instance, that the first Master (John Short), who had survived the Catholic inquisition of Queen Mary's reign (1553–1559) fell foul of Queen Elizabeth's measures 'for removing corrupt schoolmasters'. His apparent Catholic sympathies were enough for him to lose his job to John Long. The situation, however, was very much reversed in 1687 when King James II, a known Catholic, visited Bath. He insisted that William Baker, who had been Master since 1681, should be dismissed and that Francis Carne, a member of a prominent local Catholic family, should take his place. The Corporation, with no alternative but to comply, recorded its decision in the Council Minute Book—'Mr. Francis Carne elected Schoolmaster of the free school. He had full possession granted him of the School (By His Majesty's Command)'. The King's attempts to fill all important offices with Catholic sympathisers were short-lived. The Glorious Revolution of 1688–1689, which swept him into exile, brought the Protestant William of Orange over from Holland to rule as William III. By 1689, William Baker had been re-instated as Master of the School.

Schoolmasters of King Edward's were paid a basic salary by the Corporation which amounted to £12 in 1568 (when Chamberlain's Accounts first became available. This seems to be well below the average paid in schools of this kind. Furthermore, in spite of soaring inflation during the late 16th and early 17th centuries, it was only raised to £20 in 1631 and remained at that figure until 1762 (by which time, of course, the School had moved to Broad Street). Actually the Council once paid more (£30 to Mr. Jones in 1664), but soon reverted to their former miserly scale when he left the following year. Indeed, when one of the candidates for the vacant job in 1665 had the cheek to demand a salary of £25, they quickly sent him packing and appointed Mr. Peake who was quite content with £20.

The salary, which was paid quarterly, was supplemented by fees charged to pupils and boarders. Most Masters seem to have taken a few boys from neighbouring towns and villages as lodgers in the schoolhouse. All scholars would be required to pay 'quarterages', which usually amounted to six pence a quarter for 'grammarians' and threepence or fourpence a quarter for 'petties' or juniors (some of whom would still be polishing up their reading and writing and would be instructed by senior pupils). In spite of these additional payments and the rent-free occupation of the schoolhouse, the position was not at all attractive financially. Many scholarly young schoolmasters, therefore, tended to regard King Edward's as a stepping stone to more lucrative employment elsewhere—like Alexander Hume who eventually became Rector of the High School, Edinburgh, in 1597 and Benjamin Wilding who moved on to become Headmaster of Sherborne in 1720.

It is certainly true that the Corporation, at least over the first two hundred years of the School's history, adopted the policy of appointing young men as Masters of the Free Grammar School. This meant, of course, that they would have few qualms about paying them low salaries. Of those whose ages are traceable during this period, it is interesting to notice that the vast majority were in their twenties or early thirties— William Peake (21), Henry Slyman (23), James Sharpe (26), Bartholomew Man (26), Richard Meredith (27), John Long (28), Walter Robbins (29), Francis Mynn (32), Benjamin Wilding (32), Arthur Hele (42), William Street (44), Thomas Shrewsbury (45). But, very much to their credit, the Corporation did not cut down on quality.

There is real evidence that they took time and trouble to

recruit outstanding scholars from far and wide. Ability rather than local influence was the ruling factor in making appointments. Only two Masters, Matthew Lloyde and Francis Carne, were born and bred in Bath—but in each case they were elected under unusual circumstances. Lloyde was merely used as a temporary stop-gap for six months (see below), whilst Carne was forced on the Corporation during the visit of James II (see above). Throughout the whole history of the School the connection with' Oxford and Cambridge in the appointment of Headmasters has been extremely strong. Of the 28 Headmasters, whose universities are traceable, 16 have been graduates of Oxford, 9 of Cambridge, 2 of St. Andrews and one of Trinity College, Dublin. Gradually an 'Usher' or 'Under Master' was also appointed as the Master's assistant. At least one of these, William Street (who had been Usher to William Baker) was eventually elected Master by the Council in 1713. It was somewhat tragic that he died a few months after his appointment and shortly after his own son had given the Latin oration at the Mayor-making in 1712.

Two of the other Masters of the School, before its move to Broad Street, are worthy of more detailed mention as examples of the type of scholar recruited by the Corporation. John Long, educated at Eton and King's College, Cambridge, had already acquired an academic reputation by the time of his appointment to King Edward's School in 1576. Even at the age of fifteen he had contributed four Latin epigrams to a collection of verses presented by Eton Scholars to Queen Elizabeth in 1563. He quickly made his mark in Bath both as a schoolmaster and as a preacher. During his term of office he also devoted much of his time and energy in helping the Corporation to bring about the consolidation of Bath's Churches into one parish, based on the re-built Abbey Church of St. Peter and St. Paul. That this was finally accomplished in 1583 is due in no small measure to John Long. He was actually given six months' leave of absence from the School in 1581–1582 to concentrate on the final stages of the unification (during which time his Usher, Matthew Lloyde took over temporarily as Master).

He resigned shortly afterwards to be appointed first Rector of Bath in 1583. By the end of 1584 his undoubted ability had been rewarded by further promotion, when he left to become Bishop of Armagh and Primate of All Ireland. A man of complex character, he was warmly commended for his work in Ireland on his nomination for membership of the Privy Council—'he discharged the place with credite and the good lyking of those under hym, amongst whom, both by preaching and governing otherwise, he did much good, and won many'. Nevertheless, after his death at the early age of forty, other aspects of his nature emerged. He was, for instance, always in debt. His old colleague Matthew Lloyde lent him £30 which was never returned and, according to the Lord Deputy in Ireland: 'His lordship died £1,000 in debt and left scarcely enough to bury him'. The Cathedral Church in Armagh was apparently 'in great ruin' and many of its assets squandered. A clue to the reason behind this state of affairs was perhaps given by the Lord Deputy who commented: 'The late John Long, Archbishop of Armagh, loved good cheer but too well.' Scholars, Schoolmasters and Archbishops were occasionally human.

Alexander Hume, who was Master of the School between 1588 and 1591, was a completely different character. A Scotsman through and through, he had been educated at Dunbar School, St. Andrew's University and Oxford. After leaving Bath, he was eventually appointed Rector of the High School, Edinburgh, Master of Prestonpans Grammar School and finally Master of Dunbar Grammar School. During this period he made a reputation for himself as an outstanding scholar. The speech he made in Latin to welcome King James I to Dunbar in 1617 added to the fame he was already acquiring as an author. His book, *Of the Orthographic and Congruitie of the Britan Tongue*, was the first Grammar ever attempted in English. In it he had tried to reconcile the differences in speech and spelling between English and Scottish and thus produce a 'Britain Tongue'. His most famous work, however, was the Latin Grammar, *Grammatica Nova* (published in 1612) which was ordered to be taught in all Scottish schools. King Edward's School at Bath[1] had indeed been fortunate to have enjoyed the services of such an able teacher of both Latin and Greek at the outset of his career.

1 This is the School's official title.

Distinguished Pupils

Entry to the Universities of Oxford and Cambridge was by no means easy for Grammar School pupils in the sixteenth and seventeenth centuries. Most of the fully-fledged Colleges were closed Corporations, restricting their entry to Founder's Kin, to those who satisfied the birth qualifications of their Closed Scholarships and to a few hand-picked Commoners and Exhibitioners. It was, therefore, quite usual for a young student to gain entry first of all into one of the unendowed Halls of Residence, where he would matriculate as a member of the University and wait for possible later openings into one of the Colleges. Examples of these Halls in Oxford were Hart Hall (which at a later period became Hertford College) and Broadgates Hall (later Pembroke College). Boys, therefore, with a sound knowledge of Grammar School Latin and with parents who could pay the fees often found places there. Fees were charged by the University, at various stages of the course, according to the social rank of the pupil. For this reason, boys who did not need a qualification, but who intended to return to family estates or family business, very often left before taking a degree.

King Edward's School had established close connections with two Oxford Colleges. At Corpus Christi College it was possible for boys to apply for two Closed Somerset Scholarships founded by Bishop Foxe. Similarly at Oriel College there was a Somerset Fellowship founded by Archdeacon John Frank in 1441 and some Open Exhibitions and Fellowships founded by Dr. Richard Dudley in 1525, who had bequeathed the Manor of Swainswick, near Bath to provide the necessary financial support. Colleges frequently gave preference in the award of such scholarships to the able sons of tenants living on their estates. Bright Swainswick boys like the Prynnes, the Webbes and the Clarkes, who had learnt their Latin at King Edward's, found entry to Oxford easier than most.

One other College possessed property near Bath. New College which, together with Winchester College, had been founded by William of Wykeham, Bishop of Winchester, owned the Manor of Colerne. Some degree of priority was given with the election of scholars to both these Foundations to residents of places like Colerne, where their estates were located, and to inhabitants of Wiltshire and Somerset. Thus many boys from King Edward's, who lived either in the City or in outlying parts, went on first to Winchester College at the age of thirteen before transferring to the richly-endowed New College two or three years later. Amongst pupils who followed that course were Richard Meredith of Bath (1573), Henry Tapp of Newton St. Loe (1573), Robert Pierce of Combe Hay (1635), Thomas and William Harris of Colerne (1666).

The University records clearly reveal that a continuous flow of boys from Bath and district reached Oxford throughout the first two centuries of the School's existence. These were almost certainly pupils of King Edward's—then the only Grammar School in this part of the country. It is, however, interesting to notice that hardly any boys from this area attended Cambridge during the same period. Nevertheless, the school contributed most handsomely to the revival of learning within the city and to the general enrichment of economic, social and intellectual life. Boys, who had left the School for Oxford often returned later to take up positions of responsibility and leadership—Doctors, such as John Sherwood who had attended Trinity College Oxford in 1564 and Thomas Bayly (Magdalen Hall, 1631); Barristers, such as John Adams (Magdalen College, 1571) and Thomas Harris (New College, 1660); Educationalists, such as John Rosewell (Corpus Christi College, 1653) who eventually became Headmaster of Eton; and Clergy, such as Alexander Rosewell (Broadgates Hall, 1580) who became Rector of Combe Hay in 1596, Richard Hadly (Queen's College, 1600) who became Vicar of Twerton in 1623, Theophilus Webbe (Merton College, 1623) who became Rector of Bath in 1624 and James Masters (St. Alban Hall, 1627) who also became Rector of Bath in 1639.

Others came back to play a full part in local government— such as William Prynne (Oriel College, 1618), who later became Recorder of Bath (1647) and then its Member of Parliament (1660–1669); John Health (New College, 1605), who was elected Freeman of Bath in 1608; and Walter Chapman (Broadgates Hall, 1583) who eventually became Alderman and Mayor. Indeed, virtually the whole of the

John Hales (Old Edwardian): Regius Professor of Greek at Oxford University, 1615–19.

National Portrait Gallery

remarkable Chapman family, which made such a notable contribution to the professional and business life of the city, seem to have attended the school—although comparatively few of them during this period went on to Oxford. University records show that the majority of parents from Bath who educated their sons at King Edward's School and Oxford, were drawn from the ranks of the middle class—clergy, lawyers, doctors, Mayors, Aldermen, Freemen, Town Clerks and farmers. Some, nevertheless, were poor scholars from humble homes.

Four pupils are worthy of more detailed attention in view of the national fame they earned for themselves, their city and their school. Robert Pierce, the son of the Rector of Combe Hay, attended King Edward's before going on to Winchester College and Lincoln College, Oxford (1638). A student of medicine, he was elected Fellow of the College of Physicians in 1689. He entertained Charles II at the Abbey House in Bath, attending him also as personal physician. Perhaps more than anyone, he firmly established the medicinal value and prestige of the city's hot springs.

The 'ever-memorable' John Hales, son of the City's Attorney, had perhaps the most distinguished academic career of all. A Scholar of Corpus Christi College, Oxford (1597) at the age of thirteen, he was subsequently elected Fellow of Merton, Fellow of Eton and Canon of Windsor before his appointment as Regius Professor of Greek at Oxford (1615–1619). He later became Chaplain to Archbishop Laud. A friend of Milton, Ben Jonson and other eminent scholars, he was described by Bishop Andrew Marvell as 'one of the clearest heads and best prepared breasts in Christendom'. Lord Clarendon paid his own tribute by saying that 'he was one of the least men in the Kingdom, and one of the greatest scholars in Europe'. He died in 1656 and is buried at Eton College.

William Prynne, son of the farmer Thomas Prynne of Swainswick, became Barrister-at-Law at Lincoln's Inn in 1628 after graduating at Oriel College, Oxford. He became nationally famous in the 1630's for a series of pamphlets attacking both the Court and the bishops. He was twice tried in the Court of Star Chamber, being sentenced on each occasion to life imprisonment, a fine of £5,000, loss of his degrees and loss of his ears. On the second occasion he was also branded with the letters 'S.L.' (seditious libeller). Released from the Tower by the Long Parliament in 1641 just prior to the outbreak of Civil War, he played a leading part in the trial of Archbishop Laud (1645). He continued to write a stream of pamphlets, later compaigning against the Army, against the trial of Charles I and against the new Commonwealth. After his return to Swainswick, he eventually became

William Prynne (Old Edwardian): Member of Parliament for Bath, 1660–69.

School Archives

Recorder of Bath (1647), M.P. for Bath (1660–1669) and collector of its records. He was also Keeper of the Records of the Tower of London from 1660 until his death in London in 1669.

Thomas Rosewell, the orphaned son of a gentleman from Dunkerton, was born in 1630. According to an account of his life written later by his own son:

Soon after his father's death, Mr. Rosewell was by his guardian sent to school at Bathe. There he was taken ill of the small-pox, in the year 1641 ... Here he continued some time and made considerable progress in learning; till the Civil Wars began to rage: And the King's Army taking that garrison, their school was broke up, and the youth were scattered ... About this time, travelling a little from home, he accidentally saw King Charles the First, in the fields, sitting at Dinner under a tree, with some few persons about him. This made such deep impression in his young and tender mind, as disposed him the greater compassion and loyalty towards that unhappy monarch.

After gaining his degree at Pembroke College, Oxford, he later became Rector of Rode in Somerset and Sutton Mandeville in Wiltshire. He was eventually ejected from his living under the terms of the Uniformity Act (1662) and was forced to preach to non-conformist gatherings in private houses. It was, however, his arrest in 1684 on an absurd charge of treasonable preaching that made him nationally famous. He was tried and found guilty by the notorious Judge Jeffries, only to be pardoned by the personal intervention of King Charles II. 'If your Majesty suffers this man to die,' pleaded Sir John Talbot, 'we are none of us safe in our houses.'

CHAPTER TWO

Broad Street—Years of Success, 1754–1811

'The Mayor and Citizens have . . . . notoriously misapplied the revenues of the lands given to them by King Edward VI . . . . and have constantly applied the same to their own or other private uses'. (Commission of Inquiry into the management of the School's Endowment, 1735.)
'If, then, you let me go to any public school, what can be better than the Bath one? It is a very great improvement, I think, on the Eton method.' (De Quincey's letter to his mother, 1799.)

City and State in the Eighteenth Century

The eighteenth century witnessed dramatic changes in the local setting. Bath, somewhat belatedly, burst out of its medieval seams. A remarkable physical transformation took place. No longer confined to cramped conditions within its old walls, the city spread outwards into the fresh air and green meadows beyond. Under the influence of the Palladian school of architecture, John Wood and his son had, by 1774, built Queen Square, Prior Park, North Parade, South Parade, the Circus, the Royal Crescent and the Assembly Rooms. Meanwhile, Daniel Milsom had created Milsom Street as a new residential area and Thomas Baldwin had re-built the Guildhall. This young architect then went across the river to develop the Bathwick estates, owned by the Pulteney family. The new Pulteney Bridge, (completed in 1774) had already made the old medieval ferry obsolete by the time Baldwin had constructed Laura Place, Pulteney Street and the Sydney Hotel. Baldwin's re-development of Bath, including the new Pump Room, was completed by John Palmer who, by the end of the century, had also built St. James's Square and the Lansdown Crescent. New premises for King Edward's School, designed by Thomas Jelly and opened in 1754, fitted very much into this pattern of planned development in a common style. The sense of unity was furthered by the use of a common building material—Bath Stone quarried by Ralph Allen on Combe Down.

But this golden age in Bath's history meant much more than physical expansion and beautiful buildings. The fame which the city acquired during the eighteenth century was based largely on its reputation as the social centre of society. The designs of John Wood and Thomas Baldwin were but a backcloth for the activities of Richard 'Beau' Nash, appointed Master of Ceremonies by the Corporation in 1706. For over fifty years he presided over the annual gathering of people of fashion who, following the example of Queen Anne in 1702, flocked to Bath to enjoy its balls, its coffee-houses, its gambling, its medicinal waters, its walks and its intellectual activities. This uncrowned 'King of Bath' brought order and dignity to social activities by his uncompromising rules for behaviour. He also brought virtually every famous personality to the city to enjoy its splendour and enrich the purses of its citizens. King Edward's School increasingly catered for the needs of such a society.

Nationally, the eighteenth century was a century of war—a century which enabled some Old Edwardians to make their names on the field of battle. Most wars involved Britain, increasingly anxious to protect her trading interests, in fierce opposition to the French. The War of Spanish Succession (1700–1713), the War of Austrian Succession (1740–1748), the Seven Years' War (1756–1763), the War of American Independence (1775–1783), the French Wars (1793–1815), all took their toll in blood and taxes. But eighteenth century war was not total war. There was no conscription. Life in Bath continued much as normal. Because the city had acquired national prestige, however, the heroes of war came in turn to claim its applause—Clive of India, Wolfe of Quebec, the Elder Pitt (M.P. for Bath in 1757), Admiral Nelson, the Younger Pitt and King Edward's own Sir Sidney Smith. There they mixed with a glittering society of poets (Pope, etc), artists (Gainsborough, etc), preachers (Wesley, etc), nobility (Lord Chesterfield, etc), authors (Fielding etc), musicians (Herschel, etc,) and royalty (Frederick Augustus, Duke of York, etc). It is perhaps not altogether surprising that, in this spectacular setting, King Edward's School developed an unparallelled reputation for excellence.

Grammar Schools in the Eighteenth Century

Grammar School education saw little change in the eighteenth century. Although by then there was less vocational need for boys to write and speak fluently in Latin (as, indeed, had been the case in earlier centuries), the study of classical languages was defended as a mental discipline. By it a pupil would be trained to tackle the variety of problems which later in life he would be obliged to face. 'Classical studies are for all boys a gymnastic of the very best kind', said one headmaster.

Not every locality, however, was appreciative of the virtues which the traditional curriculum of the English Grammar School claimed to offer. By the end of the century many such schools, especially in country districts, were suffering a noticeable decline. Lord Chief Justice Kenyon referred to the grammar schools in 1795 as 'empty walls without scholars and everything neglected except the receipt of salaries and emoluments'. This was not, however, the situation in Bath where, as we shall see, an affluent and discriminating population set great store on the excellence attained by its own Free School. It paid little heed to mounting national criticism, sparked off by Locke and other philosophers at the end of the previous century, which condemned the neglect of English, Arithmetic, Geography and Modern languages.

'Progressive' schools, such as Leeds Grammar School, which attempted to introduce these new subjects, were actually prevented by law from doing so. In 1805 Lord Chancellor Eldon ruled that any move to teach anything other than the classics would be illegal because the school had been specifically founded as a 'grammar' school. Instruction in other subjects would be seen as blatant abuse of original endowments. This court judgment survived until it was reversed in the Grammar Schools Act of 1840. Masters who wanted to offer a wider range, therefore, were obliged to describe them as 'extras' to be taught outside normal school hours.

Schools were also condemned during this period for their harshness of life. Many boarding schools suffered from poor food and atrocious facilities. At least in Bath the splendid new premises in Broad Street offered comparatively comfortable accommodation. At Eton, however, boys were obliged to wash outside at the pump. Discipline, too, was frequently brutal. The Headmaster of Eton was reputed to have flogged eighty boys on one day in 1832. But, with the whole school taught in the same large schoolroom, a reign of terror was almost essential. This was not always accepted with good grace by eighteenth century scholars. Partly inspired by the French Revolution, boys at Winchester staged a number of rebellions. One, in 1793, saw a two-day seizure of school buildings under the red flag of liberty. Another, in 1818, ultimately required intervention by soldiers with fixed bayonets. Meanwhile, the boys of Rugby School used gunpowder in 1797 to blow open the door of the headmaster's study. Such drastic action was apparently not necessary in Bath.

It will be seen, however, that King Edward's School did suffer, in the way that most schools suffered during this period, from the curse of all sensitive boys—bullying. In the absence of organised games (which did not really make their appearance until the second half of the nineteenth century), pupils expended their energies in ways vividly portrayed in *Tom Brown's Schooldays*. Fighting was common. Only the fittest survived happily in the setting of the grammar school yard. The essayist, Sydney Smith (not, of course, the Old Edwardian by the same name) believed that such schools 'only prevent men from being corrupted by the world by corrupting them before their entry into the world'.

By the end of the century, grammar schools were beginning to face competition in secondary education from an increasing number of private schools. These tended to cater for the growing demand from businessmen and industrialists for a more useful type of education. Although many such schools retained classics on the curriculum, they were not bound by the restrictions of ancient charters and were therefore free to introduce new subjects. Several schools of this type began to advertise in the local Bath newspapers during the Mastership of Mr. Morgan. In 1808, for example, a new boarding and day school was established in Guinea Street, Bristol for 'Classical and Commercial Education'. It was to be run by Mr. Durban 'who has taught English grammar, geography and the use of the globes, writing in various hands, arithmetic by short and early methods; fractions vulgar, decimal and duodecimal; mensuration, gauging, navigation and book-keeping by single and double entry'. He promised, in addition, to pay great attention 'to orthography, and to the position of his pupils while they are writing . . . and to promote the comfort, health and improvement of the young gentlemen, who will be carefully examined in geography, the problems of the globes, arithmetical tables, etc. every Saturday'. The eighteenth century grammar school had no truck with such ideas or such methods.

The Corporation Scandal

In 1721 Mr. Walter Robbins became Master of the School. A native of Salisbury and a graduate of St. John's College, Cambridge, he had been appointed Curate of Charlcombe and Swainswick in 1719. Throughout his teaching career, he continued to maintain his responsibilities to the Church, becoming Rector of Charlcombe in 1728 and remaining Curate of Swainswick until 1749. A man of property, he had already acquired the advowson[1] of Swainswick shortly after his arrival in Bath. This was apparently put to good use in securing the Mastership of the School by what could only be construed as an act of bribery. The Council Minutes reveal the nature of his offer:

> November 22. Walter Robbins, Clerk, chosen Master of the Latin Free School, provided he make a settlement to Trustees in fee as Council shall advise of the Perpetuity of the Advowson of Charlcombe.

Thus the profits of the Charlcombe Rectory, estimated at £140 per annum, were to be set aside to supplement the salaries of future Masters of the School.

During his term of office, the range of subjects taught was slightly extended, judging by an advertisement in the *Bath Journal* in 1748:

> Advertisement, Grammar School near the North Gate. The Latin and Greek Classicks are faithfully and expeditiously

1 Ownership of the right to nominate the holder of a church living.

taught. By Mr. Robbins, from St. John's Col., Cam. Such as please may learn French at the said School.

However, his main claim to fame was not the introduction of French into the curriculum, but the peace-shattering confrontation he had with the Corporation in 1734. The Churchwardens of St. Michael's Church were already employing Mr. William King, a Bath attorney, to petition Chancery for an enquiry into the misappropriation of Church lands by Bath Corporation. Mr. Robbins had noticed, in the evidence raised during the course of that case, mention made of the property granted by King Edward VI for use of the School and the Charity. His curiosity aroused, he obtained a copy of the original grant, translated it into English and was horrified at the total failure of the Corporation to observe the stipulations of the Charter.

He therefore submitted a Petition to the Crown, requesting a full-scale investigation into the management of the Trust. Summarizing the terms of the Charter, he emphasised that the Founder's intention in granting the property had been that the Trustees 'should for ever thereafter wholley and solely convert and consume the profits to the continuance and Maintenance of the said free Grammar School . . . and in the Relief of Ten poor persons!' Furthermore, he continued, the value of the lands had now appreciated to over £500 per annum, thanks to recent building developments, whereas 'the Sallary of your Petitioner is advanced to no more than Twenty pounds a year and nothing more of the Revenues of the premises so Granted hath been Applied for the benefit of the said School or for the Relief or Comfort of any poor persons'. In other words, what had happened to the profits of the endowment over the last two hundred years? It was certainly true that comparatively little had been spent on the School since the conversion of St. Mary's, North Gate into a School-room in 1584.

This was exactly the question that the Chancery Commissioners were to investigate when they opened their inquiry on 20th September, 1734. The Corporation were in a somewhat defenceless position. After such a long lapse of time, its present members had no knowledge of the lands originally granted and no accounts to show how the funds had been administered. They did not even realise that the 'Black Alms' or St. Catherine's Hospital was being maintained (at least in theory) out of the endowment granted by Edward VI. They were certainly unable to show that the Grammar School had been properly and fully supported out of the same endowment since its foundation. The Commissioners clearly found the Mayor somewhat obstructive in failing to produce the necessary records. He was subsequently threatened with imprisonment. In view of this lack of co-operation and lack of immediate evidence, it is not surprising that the investigation failed to reveal the true identity of the lands originally specified in Edward's Grant. The Commissioners were finally able to name just five properties in eighteenth century Bath (out of the 102 in question) which were apparently part of the endowment—The Harte; The Bell; Monk's Mill and land by Eastgate; a tenement on Westgate; and St. Werburgh's Church (later Fountains Buildings).

Eventually, on 10 June, 1735, a Decree was issued which found in favour of Mr. Robbins and awarded him £50 towards the expenses of presenting his Petition. It was totally damning of the Corporation and its conduct over two hundred years. Not only had the Mayor and Citizens 'notoriously misapplied the revenues of the lands given to them by King Edward VI, but, even worse, they had 'constantly applied the same to their own or other private uses'. This embezzlement had been partly obscured by the failure to keep proper accounts. Nor had the lands of the endowment been kept separate, but had been 'so mixed and blended' with their other holdings that they could no longer be clearly distinguished. The Mayor came in for particular indictment 'having absolutely refused to produce any rental or survey . . . pretending that they had none'. There was a real suspicion, too, that some charity account books had been tampered with—'several leaves are cut out', the Commissioners complained.

As a result of all these findings and 'for many other notorious offences in breach of the said great trust!' the Corporation were fined £500 for their terrible mismanagement of endowment funds and were 'for ever more absolutely removed and displaced from the said Trust'. This was to be taken over by a group of specially-appointed Trustees, including the Bishop. Furthermore, the Corporation, within six months, were to survey and account for all the property granted by Edward VI, or be subject to a £5,000 fine which would be used to benefit the School and the Charity. Then, over a period of thirty-five years, funds would be allowed to build up from the revenues of the newly-identified property. During this time, the Master of the School would be given a salary of £20 per annum and a rent-free house—on condition that he educated, without charge, ten sons of freemen or inhabitants of Bath. Then, after thirty-five years, the Trustees were 'to purchase a piece of land and thereon build a schoolhouse and house convenient for the Master' (whose salary would be increased to £50 per annum—on condition that he taught even more poor boys free of charge.)

In spite of the clarity of its provisions and a Writ of Execution issued in 1736, the Decree was never put into effect. There were several reasons for this. The nominated Trustees refused to accept their appointment. Mr. William King, the main driving force in the prosecution who had also been appointed 'Steward' of the endowed property, died in 1738. Mr. Robbins lost interest when he read the conditions requiring him to take in poor boys free of charge—provisions which would have inevitably changed the nature of his 'Grammar' School. Consequently, the Corporation remained in control over the school until 1835.

The New School

Although the harshly worded Decree issued by the Chancery Commissioners in 1734 had proved to be ineffective, it had nevertheless given something of a rude awakening to the consciences of Mayor and Corporation. They could no longer ignore the fact that they were Trustees of a considerable endowment intended for the exclusive benefit of the Edwardian Grammar School and Charity. It is not wholly surprising, therefore, that on 6 August, 1742 they appointed a Committee, consisting of the Mayor, two Justices of the Peace and four senior Councillors 'to find out a piece of ground necessary to erect a free school'. There is no doubt, however, that this sudden interest in building decent premises for the School owed more than a little to the enthusiasm with which Ralph Allen (the Mayor) and John Wood were tackling the re-development of Bath then in progress.

The Committee eventually chose a large garden called The Town Acre (which stood at the top of the present Milsom Street on a site now occupied by Edgar Buildings). They set aside £3,150 for the cost of the building and commissioned John Wood to design it. In his *Essay towards a Description of Bath*, Wood outlined his original proposals. The whole building area would have measured 75 feet by 128 feet in the middle of which would have been situated 'a circular court of forty-two feet in diameter, with an arcade round it of twelve feet broad'. There would have been a spacious schoolroom, dining room and accommodation for the Master's family, two under Masters and a hundred boarders. Standing in a 'high unconfined place', it would have been 'as healthy a School as any in the Kingdom'. Unfortunately, this splendid scheme, which aimed at putting the school 'upon a footing equal to its possessions', was shelved.

The Corporation did, however, continue its search for a suitable site. Eventually, in December 1644, they decided to purchase 'the Black Swan in Broad Street as a place to build a free School' paying Mrs. Deborah Chambers £556 17s. 6d. for the surrender of her lease. In choosing what was clearly an inferior site to the one originally selected, the Corporation missed a glorious opportunity of setting the school in open ground away from tightly grouped buildings. Better sites, however, were already being ear-marked for property speculators. Daniel Milsom was shortly to acquire The Town Acre and the garden land behind Broad Street for building development.

Further delays followed the purchase of the Broad Street site. Not until 5 March, 1752 did the Council resolve that 'Thomas Jelly's plans be used for building the free school provided he bring an estimate for expense'. A month later they formed a Committee 'for employing proper workmen for building the Free School according to Jelly's improved plan'. Then, on 29 May, 1752, the Mayor, Mr. Francis Hales, accompanied in a colourful procession by the Corporation,

King Edward's School, Broad Street. (Opened in 1754).

School Archives

several bands and nine City Companies, laid the Foundation Stone.

During the next two years a total of £3,933 13s. 9d. was paid for the new building, mostly to 'Brown, Jelly, Sainsbury and Smith' (presumably the main architects and contractors). Joseph Plura, a famous local sculptor and son of an Italian artist, was paid £26 5s. 0d. 'for engraving the City Arms at the School'. He was later to receive, in January 1755, a further sixteen guineas for '5 bustos', presumably the five classical busts set on the parapet. In final preparation for the arrival of Masters and pupils, the Corporation paid 'Evans the Collier' thirteen shillings for '12 Horse Loads of Coal for the new school'; four shillings and sixpence 'for a Pail, Mop and Brush for the School'; and one shilling and sixpence 'for Candles for the School'.

When the School was finally opened in 1754, it was unquestionably an imposing building. Built in the classical style, which characterised the whole development of eighteenth century Bath, it owed much to the inspiration and original design of John Wood. Boys arriving at the School in those days would have seen the beautiful lines and proportions of the building from *all* sides. Across the garden and meadows behind the school even the well -designed rear could have been admired. Uncluttered by later schemes and encroachments which hemmed it into a cramped site, the free Grammar School of King Edward VI now had a fitting setting for its scholarship growing reputation.

Controversy Over the Mastership

An extraordinary situation arose in 1754 when the new buildings were opened. The Grammar School under Mr. Walter Robbins, continued to function as a School in its old premises of St. Mary's, Northgate. Indeed, shortly prior to the official opening of the new School in Broad Street, Mr. Robbins inserted a remarkable advertisement in The Bath Journal of 11 February, 1754:

> The GRAMMAR-SCHOOL in the Market-Place is, and will be, (notwithstanding any malicious Insinuations to the Contrary) continued; where Classical Learning, with whatever is essential to Grammar, shall be carefully and expeditiously taught by Mr. Robbins, Professor of Languages, from Cambridge.

He was, in addition, quite prepared to teach French, Italian and Hebrew in the evenings. But he was not, apparently, prepared to move his Grammar School into the new buildings or to have anything to do with the new school. He and his pupils had been noticeably absent from the celebrations that attended the laying of the Foundation Stone in 1752.

Until his death in 1762, therefore, two schools existed side by side—The Grammar School and the 'New School'. Mr. Robbins continued to be paid his salary of £20 per annum by the Corporation and to enjoy the revenues of the Charlcombe Rectory. What caused this split is difficult to ascertain. It is possible that Mr. Robbins felt too old to undertake such a major upheaval; it is possible that he disagreed with the Corporation's plans to concentrate on the education of the sons of freemen for the ridiculously low fee of twenty shillings a year; it is possible that the Corporation themselves found Mr. Robbins unacceptable.

It is certainly true that they began to regard the school as their own creation, quite separate from that founded in 1552. The 'New School' was more than just a new building. It was to be dedicated 'to the Sons of the Freemen'; the City Arms, not those of King Edward VI, were carved over the portal; nor was any mention made of the original Founder on the Foundation Stone itself. This attitude partly reflected natural civic pride. But there is some evidence to suggest that Walter Robbins was the real stumbling block and that an amalgamation of the two schools was always envisaged on his death. A partially-obliterated entry in the Council Minutes dated 25 January, 1754 raised the question: 'What stipend shall the Master of the new School have yearly during the life of the Reverend Mr. Robbins?' The timing of his death was a matter of apparent concern.

The Corporation, in the meantime, proceeded to elect a Master for The New School at a salary of £60 per annum. Significantly, he was initially elected for a period of one year only—an election which was repeated annually until the death of Mr. Robbins. This would seem to offer further evidence that the Corporation was merely playing for time. The man chosen on 22 March, 1754 was Rev. Arthur Hele, a native of Salisbury and a graduate of St. John's College, Cambridge, who was then currently Master of the Grammar School in Basingstoke. He was forty-two, married and a man of private means. His Latin oration at the Opening Ceremony of the New School, which was warmly applauded by the Mayor, clergy and other dignitaries present, expounded on 'the dignity and utility of learning' and 'the generosity of the Corporation'. Shortly after his approval in Bath he was given the livings of Corston (1755) and Porlock (1763) and was appointed a Prebendary of Wells (1764). The new Master was clearly a man of ability, who had quickly established a fine reputation in the area.

Mr. Hele soon settled into the life and organisation of The New School. Boarders were taken in from the start, judging from the payment made by the City Chamberlain for '12 oaken bedsteads to be put up at the New School at the expense of the Corporation'. Shortly afterwards, presumably following an increase in the number of boarders, they resolved: 'The Bed Chambers at The New School to be divided'. The School yard was also prepared for the constant use it was to receive over the coming years when £4 8s. 0d. was spent on 'Halling gravel to the School', when £1 12s. 0d. was paid to a gardener for laying it and when, some time later, a man was employed to improve playground drainage.

On 10 August, 1762 the expected moment finally arrived. Mr. Walter Robbins died at the age of 70 and was buried at Widcombe. Just over a month later, on 27 September, the Corporation met to vote on the question: "Who shall be Master of the Grammar School in the Room of Mr. Walter Robbins, Clerk, deceased?" In the absence of any other candidate, Mr. Hele was elected unanimously. Then came the other critical vote: 'What House shall the Master of the Grammar School have to reside in as a Schoolhouse?' The reply was again unanimous: 'The house where he now lives in Broad Street'. By these two votes The Grammar School and the New School were now united, under the old name of The Grammar School or The Free School. The Corporation, too, seemed to abandon its original stipulation about low-cost education for the sons of Freemen. Free education for 'foundation' scholars still remained a thing of the future. The Master was now appointed on new terms. His official salary dropped from £60 to £30, but he received in addition the revenues of the Charlcombe Rectory (estimated to be worth £140 per annum). These, together with those of Corston and Porlock would have enabled him to live comfortably enough—even after he had paid Curates to look after his three parish Churches and Assistant Masters to help in the School.

Although detailed records are missing for the period of Mr. Hele's Mastership (1754–1778), it is evident that he contributed richly to the School's growing academic reputation. During his term of office an impressive flow of boys found their way to the Universities of Oxford and Cambridge, and to some of the great Public Schools of the day. The strong links which had been forged between King Edward's School and Winchester continued—as did its connections with Oriel College and Corpus Christi College, Oxford. Local people had good cause to be grateful to the School. Indeed, several families owed their rise in social position almost entirely to the educational opportunities provided by King Edward's School and Oxford. The Chapmans, the Sparrows and the Phillpotts, in particular, were mainly innkeepers, clothmakers, tradesmen and millowners in the sixteenth and seventeenth centuries. But their sons were sent, generation after generation, first to the Grammar School and then to Oxford. By the eighteenth and nineteenth centuries, these families had largely ceased to be traders. Instead, they served the local community as clergy, scholars, doctors, bankers and gentry.

Mr. Hele's Mastership also produced its share of distinguished former pupils, who contributed in a broader sphere to the life of the nation at large. French Laurence, the son of a watchmaker, eventually became Regius Professor of Civil Law at Oxford (1796–1809), Member of Parliament for Peterborough (1796–1809) and a close friend of Burke, Fox and Sheridan. His brother, Richard Laurence, became Regius Professor of Hebrew at Oxford before accepting the appointment of Archbishop of Cashel in Ireland (1822–1838). Samuel Lysons, Keeper of the Records in the Tower of London, became an emininent antiquary. Together with his brother, Daniel Lysons, he wrote *Magna Britannica*, a description of the Counties of England illustrated by famous artists of the day. Prince Hoare, a dramatist, was elected Foreign Secretary to the Royal Academy in 1799.

In October 1772, at the age of sixty, Mr. Hele effectively retired from work at the School, although continuing to retain the nominal title of Master until his death. He suggested to the Corporation that he should surrender his salary of £30 (plus the additional £5 they were paying him to cover the cost of taxes on the School House). In return they would appoint and pay the Rev. Nathanael Morgan as his Assistant Master to run the School. Mr. Hele, however, was to continue to enjoy the profits of Charlcombe Rectory as a sort of retirement pension. The Corporation agreed. Mr. Morgan, who had probably been helping Mr. Hele at the School previously, was appointed as Assistant Master on 24 June, 1773 at a salary of £60 (plus the £5 to cover taxes). Arthur Hele retired to Corston, where he died in 1778.

Samuel Lysons (Old Edwardian): Keeper of the Records in the Tower of London.

National Portrait Gallery

The Golden Age of Nathanael Morgan

When the City Council met on 29 June 1778 the confirmation of Mr. Morgan as Master of the School in succession to Mr. Hele was something of a formality. He had already been effectively in charge for five years and was now to remain at the helm for a further thirty-three, until his death in 1811.

During this period the school was to reach its pinnacle of prosperity and fame—a reputation confirmed by the acclamation of a long line of distinguished pupils. This was in no small measure due to the leadership given by Mr. Morgan, who was to prove himself a dynamic force and an outstanding headmaster, probably the greatest in the long history of the School.

He was appointed at a salary of £30, but was to enjoy, in addition, the lucrative profits of the Charlcombe Rectory. As taxation increased, his salary was also increased to compensate—first to £42 in 1781 and later to 80 guineas in 1802. In view of what had happened on Mr. Hele's retirement, however, Mr. Morgan was forced to accept an undertaking that he would surrender the Charlcombe Rectory on resignation as Master.

Teaching ran through the life blood of the Morgan family. His father, the Rev. John Morgan, was Master of the Queen Elizabeth Grammar School in Fotheringhay, Northants, for forty-six years. Coming from an affluent home, Nathanael had been sent to Eton, before eventually becoming a Scholar and Fellow of King's College, Cambridge. From there he followed very much in his father's footsteps, being first ordained into the Church of England. His marriage to Miss Mary Webster in April 1773 brought him a beautiful wife and, indirectly, a rich benefactor. Mary's father was agent to the Duke of Montagu, who subsequently arranged for the wealthy Rectories of Glooston-on-Seir, Corby and Deene, to be showered on Nathanael. The profits of the Rectory of Deene, for example, were worth well over £600 a year. These, together with the Rectory of Charlcombe, were to ensure that the Morgans were more than comfortably placed. He was certainly wealthy enough to buy a house in Pulteney Street and to give each of his two daughters a dowry of £10,000 on marriage. Mr. Morgan was quite clearly a man of independent means. When he became Master of King Edward's therefore, his motivation was not that of money but, quite simply, his love of scholarship and teaching.

The Morgans lived primarily in the School House in Broad Street, but escaped from time to time to the peace and quiet of the Charlcombe Rectory. Of their seven children, only four

The Rev. Nathanael Morgan, Headmaster 1778–1811; portrait in possession of the School.

Photo by Miss S. Wood

survived infancy—Mary, Edward, Nathanael and Louisa.
Both boys were educated at King Edward's and Eton, before
Edward finally went on to Oxford and Nathanael to Cambridge. At the peak of his Mastership, however, tragedy struck
the happiness and unity of the Morgan household. On 23
November, 1794, Mary Morgan died, according to the local
paper, 'after a few hours' illness, universally regretted'. This

was undoubtedly a shattering blow to Mr. Morgan, who was now faced with the task of running the boarding house single-handed. But then a remarkable thing happened. Within a few weeks, Rev. Thomas Wilkins, the young Assistant Master at the School (who was later to succeed Mr. Morgan as Master), had married Mary Webster's sister. It seems likely, of course, that Charlotte Webster had been staying with the Morgans. Whatever the circumstances, however, the new Mrs. Wilkins was able to take over the task of looking after the boarders. She and her husband lived in the School, while Mr. Morgan moved with his family to Charlcombe Rectory.

Under Mr. Morgan, the School became famous both locally and nationally. It acquired a quality far in excess of the ordinary Grammar School, catering for the needs of professional and business families over a wide area. According to former pupil, George Monkland, writing in his book *The Literature and Literati of Bath*, 'The boarders mostly consisted of the sons of the neighbouring county families, and some came from Cornwall and other distant parts'. The expansion and development of the City as an eighteenth century fashion and health resort was more than matched by the growing stature and excellence of the School. Indeed, it became one of the City's chief attractions. People actually settled in Bath just to ensure a good education for their sons. The reputation of King Edward's was acclaimed in local publications, such as *The Bath Guide* of 1810:

> Under the Rev. Mr. Morgan this school has been most eminently useful to the City, and to the Kingdom at large; several of its pupils having filled essential offices in Church and State, and others distinguished themselves highly in the service of their Country. Such a public school, where youth are so finely grounded in a pure classical education, and where the domestic arrangements are of the first order, will be ever considered an honour to the City.

Certainly if the merit of a school is to be judged by the distinction of its former pupils, then the Grammar School at Bath was almost without equal by the end of the eighteenth century. Locally the School produced, during the Mastership of Mr. Morgan, a number of scholars who were later to hold office as Mayors of Bath—Richard Shuttleworth Cruttwell, publisher and proprietor of *The Bath Chronicle*; William Clark, a Bath Solicitor; George Norman, a prominent surgeon; William Hunt, who was Mayor on five occasions; and Joseph Hume Spry, a leading doctor. Other men of considerable achievement in the County included local government officials like Thomas Cruttwell, who became High Constable and Sheriff; surgeons like Clement Cruttwell, who founded the Bath Eye Infirmary in 1811; and financiers like Francis Falkner, who became Director of the Somersetshire Bank.

It was, however, on the national level that pupils of King Edward's made their most dramatic impact. The academic world was well served by Lord Clinton, a Fellow of All Saints College, Oxford, and by the Rev. William Dalby, Fellow, Dean and Tutor of Exeter College, Oxford. The world of politics was represented by William Peter, M.P. for Bodmin (1832–1835), and later British Consul in Philadelphia. The world of medicine benefited greatly from the efforts of Alderman George Norman, a Governor of the Royal United Hospital in Bath, who helped to found the Provincial Association, a forerunner of the British Medical Association. The world of literature was deeply enriched by one of the School's most famous Old Boys—Thomas De Quincey, who was a pupil between 1796 and 1799. A friend of Wordsworth, Coleridge, Lamb and Hazlit, he wrote *Confessions of an English Opium Eater*, *On the Knocking at the Gate in Macbeth* and *The English Mail Coach*.

But, curiously enough, it was in the world of action that Mr. Morgan's scholars made their mark most distinctly. Rear-Admiral Sir Edward Parry had left School in 1803 at the age of thirteen to join the Royal Navy. He became a famous Arctic navigator and explorer, leading three expeditions in search of the North West Passage (1819–1820, 1821–1823, 1824–1825). His unsuccessful expedition to the North Pole in 1827 nevertheless achieved the highest latitude ever reached at that time. He also had the honour of having an island—Parry Island–named after him.

The French Revolutionary and Napoleonic Wars, which were raging during Parry's early years in the navy, brought

Rear-Admiral Sir Edward Parry (Old Edwardian): Arctic Explorer.
National Portrait Gallery

honour to three more Edwardians. Lieutenant John Western was quickly into action at the start of the war, serving under the Duke of York in the ill-fated Netherlands campaign. At the age of twenty-one, he commanded a force of three gunboats and forty-eight men which relieved the Dutch garrison of Williamstadt, then under seige from no fewer than five thousand French troops. Although, regrettably, he was killed in action a few days later, the Dutch Government awarded him a gold medal for bravery (which was later sent to his mother). Such was the impact of his heroism that The Duke of York personally ordered a monument to be erected in his honour in Dart Cathedral.

Admiral Sir Sidney Smith had left school in 1777 slightly earlier than Western, but he, too, had taken part in the preliminary skirmishes of the war. He accompanied Admiral Hood on the unsuccessful raid on Toulon in 1793, which had attempted to bring relief to royalist opponents of the Revolution. Captured by the French in 1796, he eventually escaped from prison in Paris before taking part in his most famous exploit in 1799. Napoleon Bonaparte had successfully landed an army in Egypt with the aim of marching into Palestine and then on to India. This serious threat to Britain's trade with the Levant and the Far East was thwarted by Smith's decisive action. Hurrying along the coast with his squadron of ships, he first captured French supply boats and then brought much-needed relief to the walled city of Acre. This he proceeded to garrison and defend against determined enemy siege. So successful was his resistance that the French army, seriously frustrated and riddled with disease, eventually retreated in disarray back to Egypt. He was promoted to Vice-Admiral in 1810 and knighted in 1815 by the Duke of Wellington in Paris after the Battle of Waterloo. It was, apparently, Mr. Morgan's favourite boast that he 'had thrashed the man who thrashed the French!'

One of Sidney Smith's close friends and contemporaries at School was Major-General John Gaspard Le Marchant. Although Mr. Morgan once referred to him at school as 'the greatest dunce he had ever met', Le Marchant was to realise his full potential in the Army. He, too, served under the Duke of York in the Netherlands Campaign and witnessed the total mismanagement caused by lack of officer training. On the evidence of this, he later established a Staff College at High Wycombe and, in 1802, the Royal Military College, Sandhurst, for the training of cadets. He remained as Governor of the College until 1811, when he was promoted to Major-General and sent to Spain as commander of a cavalry brigade

Admiral Sir Sidney Smith (Old Edwardian): Victor at the Siege Acre.
National Portrait Gallery

to fight under Wellington in the Peninsular Campaign. His moment of triumph came in the Battle of Salamanca when, with eight hundred cavalry, he defeated a force of five thousand French and took 1,500 prisoners in the process. On witnessing the event, Wellington apparently uttered the words! 'By God! Cotton, I never saw anything more beautiful in my life!' Le Marchant was killed moments later. Parliament recognised his bravery by passing a vote of thanks, granting a pension of £1,200 a year to his children and spending 1500 guineas on a monument in St. Paul's Cathedral to his memory.

If a school is judged on the character and calibre of the pupils it produces, then by the early nineteenth century Dr. Morgan's Grammar School had acquired a national reputation or an 'extensive celebrity', as the *Bath Chronicle* called it in 1811. Thomas De Quincey rated it more highly than Eton, where his mother was threatening to send him. He wrote to her in these words: 'If, then, you let me go to *any* public school, what can be better than the Bath one? The plan pursued there everyone allows to be incomparable. It is a very great improvement, I think, on the Eton method. If I had room, I would compare them together from what I have heard and observed at both places, and I am sure you would allow it . . . Everything you desire me I will do, and only ask for that one thing, to go to the Grammar School.'

In seeking an answer as to why the school was so outstandingly successful during this period, contemporaries bring us back time and time again to Mr. Morgan himself. A tribute to him in the *Bath Chronicle*, on the announcement of his death in 1811, highlighted his 'reputation for classical learning, for unblemished morals and unimpeachable integrity'. These human qualities, so rare in combination but so essential to the work of any Headmaster, provided the foundation on which the School's achievements were based. He led the young by the example of his own life. Profound scholarship, personal morality and perfect integrity earned him the undying respect and devotion of both staff and pupils.

We have already seen how his Assistant Master, Mr. Wilkins, and his own sister-in-law jumped to his rescue on the death of his wife. In his autobiography, De Quincey wrote of

Mr. Morgan: 'He . . . was a scholar, and a ripe and good one: and of all my tutors, was the only one whom I loved or reverenced.' Dr. George Norman, who was Mayor of Bath on three occasions, told his daughter of his unfailing devotion to his old schoolmaster. When, in 1853, Dr. Norman spoke at the Tercentenary Festival of the School, he paid this tribute:

> The School at that time stood on very high ground, which I attribute to the talents of the Master, The Rev. Mr. Morgan . . . Mr. Morgan as a Schoolmaster possessed high talents, true religious principles, honourable and gentlemanly feeling. He was kind, attentive, zealous and dignified. As a man Mr. Morgan possessed integrity and every principle of a right-minded man. As a Scholar he possessed profound learning and patrician elegance.

His kindliness, enthusiasm, dignity and helpfulness were, as always, irresistible to the ordinary schoolboy. Combined with his excellence as a teacher, these qualities enabled him to motivate even boys of average ability (like Sidney Smith and John Le Marchant) to accomplish great things. Pupils actually enjoyed his lessons. De Quincey spoke of his disappointment when he was initially placed under the care of Mr. Williams, the second master out of four, and not under Dr. Morgan himself! The Master so dominated the life and work of the School by his total involvement and commitment, that his own qualities gradually pervaded the whole atmosphere. Not without significance did contemporaries begin to refer to the school, no longer as The Grammar School or The Free School, but as 'Mr. Morgan's School'.

The spirit engendered by Mr. Morgan brought about a remarkable event on 6 January, 1795. The White Hart Inn was the setting for the first-ever Old Boys' gathering, when pupils taught by Mr. Morgan over his twenty-two years as Master of the School met to reminisce. This spontaneous outburst of affection for the School, unusual for the time, was in reality a heart-felt tribute to him. A special song was written for the occasion and sung heartily to the tune 'Down Derry'. Here is an extract:

'Tis acknowledged that one of life's favourite ends
Is the bliss, after absence, of meeting our friends,
To repeat the adventures we jointly have borne,
And the joys, pranks, and pastimes of life's early morn.

Though Homer and Virgil might often sore vex us,
And verses or themes in their order perplex us;
Yet our tasks being finish'd, what gambols went round!
Whilst the walls of old Broad Street re-echoed the sound.

Dispersed o'er the schoolroom, or spread o'er the yard,
The warrior in embryo, the lawyer, the bard,
Sow'd juvenile plans, which the hot-bed of time
Has matured into action, oration, or rhyme.

'Twas there gallant Western presages first gave
Of courage, that gain'd him a glorious grave;
'Twas there dauntless Sidney, famed herbes among,
First dreamed of the laurels he gain'd at Toulon.

How sweet the reflection, how pleasing the thought,
That those we so valued such honours have bought!
And may the same mansion still flourish, and boast
Of worthies, wits, heroes, a numerous host!

Then let us on this day henceforward ordain
To live o'er the days of our boyhood again,
And with hearts full of gratitude, thoughts not sinister,
Drink health, wealth, and bliss to our worthy Magister.

Quite apart from his work in the classroom, Mr. Morgan's scholarly mind had turned him into an outstanding preacher and an author of a best-selling Latin Grammar. He remained at the helm of the School until his death at the age of seventy-one on 16 February, 1811. *The Bath Herald* reported with sadness: 'A few days' indisposition finished the earthly career of this most able scholar and much respected man'. A thorough gentleman, a sincere Christian and a truly great Headmaster, his contribution to the history of King Edward's School had been immeasurable.

Life at King Edward's in the Eighteenth Century

Mr. Morgan's success, though largely due to his own out-standing ability, was in part the result of a long period of stability in education. Grammar Schools, such as King Edward's, free from the interference of both local Corporation and central government, were able to pursue a single purpose without being subject to the sort of pressures which were to characterise later periods. That single purpose had remained the same since its foundation in 1552. Thomas De Quincey expressed it in these words in his Autobiography:

> Men suppose a grammar school to mean a school where they teach grammar. But this is not the true meaning . . . *Grammatica* does certainly mean sometimes grammar. But it is also the best Latin word for literature . . . The school which professes to teach *grammatica* professes, therefore, the culture of literature in the widest and most liberal extent, and is opposed *generically* to schools teaching mechanical arts; and, within its own *sub-genus* of schools dedicated to liberal objects, is opposed to schools for teaching mathematics, or, more widely, to schools for teaching science.

Teaching in the eighteenth century, therefore, was still very much restricted to Latin and, increasingly, Greek. There was no place, as yet, for mathematics, science, history or the practical subjects. French, however, was taught as an extra on a private basis. Methods of instruction also remained basically the same, with the emphasis very much on repetition and memorising during the early years. Later, however, boys were expected to compose and converse in both Latin and Greek. De Quincey, for example, claimed: 'At thirteen I wrote Greek with ease, and at fifteen my command of that language was so great that I not only composed Greek verses in lyric metres, but could converse in Greek fluently and without embarrassment'. John Farington, recalling his school days in his *Diary*, stressed the Master's method in developing a boy's style: 'Mr. Morgan is accustomed to order his pupils to translate a certain part of a Latin Author into English, then putting aside the original to direct the pupils to render the English back into Latin, adopting the peculiar style of the original as far as he was able.'

Mr. Morgan's School had settled down comfortably into its fine new premises in Broad Street. According to Dr. George Norman in his speech at the Tercentenary Festival, there were at that time 'more than a hundred boys, comprising the sons of the principal inhabitants of Bath, and the sons of the gentry of the neighbouring counties'. These boys were all taught in the one large schoolroom by the Master, the Usher and two Assistant Masters. Occasionally, a senior boy would stay on at school to assist with teaching until a place at university became available. This was certainly the case with Francis Kilvert, who was Head Boy in 1807 and remained as a junior assistant until his entrance to Oxford in 1811.

Payment of the Assistant Masters' salaries was entirely the responsibility of the Master, as was the provision of books and stationery and the internal repairs of the building. He was, however, free to charge what fees he liked to both boarders and day boys. We know, from one of Mr. Morgan's prospectuses, the actual charges that were made:

Terms of Admission into the Grammar School, Bath kept by the Rev. Nathl. Morgan, late fellow of King's College, Cambridge:

Entrance to the Master	... ...	£2	2 0
Ditto to the Usher	... ...	0	5 0
Boarding per Ann	... ...	18	18 0
Tuition	... ...	4	4 0
Seat in Church 1s. per Qu	... ...	0	4 0
Cleaning Shoes and mending Stockings ...		0	8 0

Masters in every Science attend the School on reasonable Terms. Writing and Accompts 10s. 6d. French, Dancing, Fencing, Drawing, £1 1s. 0d. per Quarter, if required.

Boarders were accommodated in dormitories upstairs and fed in the dining room. If, however, they fell ill with an infectious disease, they were 'to be removed and a proper Lodging taken for them at the Expense of their Parents'. There were two terms in the year with a month's holiday at Christmas and six weeks in June and July.

For the ordinary schoolboy, life outside the classroom was similar in the eighteenth century to that of any other period. The playground at Broad Street in Mr. Morgan's time contained its fair proportion of bullies and tyrants who fed on the timid and weak. John Le Marchant's son wrote about his father's own such experiences at the School. 'He had little to recollect of this part of his life except the distinction he acquired by a successful fight with a boy of very superior strength, the tyrant and terror of the School, in which only one schoolfellow had the courage to stand by him—that schoolfellow was the late Sir Sidney Smith!' Thomas De Quincey, as a rather sensitive, scholarly boy, had his own problems to face at the hands of older boys as a result of his brilliance at Latin. He vividly described the ordeal in his Autobiography:

But, unhappily, Dr. Morgan was at that time dissatisfied with some points in the progress of his head class; and as it soon appeared, was continually throwing in their teeth the brilliancy of my verse at eleven or twelve, by comparison with theirs at seventeen, eighteen and even nineteen. I had observed him sometimes pointing to myself, and was perplexed at seeing this gesture followed by gloomy looks, and which French reporters call 'sensation', in these young men, whom naturally I viewed with awe as my leaders—boys that were called young men, men that were reading Sophocles (a name that carried with it the sound of something seraphic to my ears), and who never had vouchsafed to waste a word on such a child as myself. The day was to come, however, when all that would be changed. One of these leaders strode up to me in the public playground; and, delivering a blow on my shoulder, which was not intended to hurt me, but as a mere formula of introduction, asked me, "What the devil I meant by bolting out of course, and annoying other people in that manner? Were 'other people' to have no rest for me and my verses, which, after all, were horribly bad?" There might have been some difficulty in returning an answer to this address, but none was required. I was briefly admonished to see that I wrote worse for the future, or else—At this *aposiopesis* I looked inquiringly at the speaker, and he filled up the chasm by saying that he would "annihilate" me. Could any person fail to be aghast at such a demand? I was to write worse than my own standard, which, by his account of my verses, must be difficult; and I was to write worse than himself, which might be impossible. My feelings revolted against so arrogant a demand, unless it had been far otherwise expressed; if death on the spot had awaited me, I could not have controlled myself;

Thomas De Quincey (Old Edwardian): Author.
National Portrait Gallery

and, on the next occasion for sending up verses to the headmaster, so far from attending to the orders issued, I double-shotted
my guns; double applause descended on myself; but I remarked
with some awe, though not repenting of what I had done, that
double confusion seemed to agitate the ranks of my enemies.
Amongst them, loomed out in the distance "my annihilating"

friend, who shook his huge fist at me, but with something like a grim smile about his eyes. He took an early opportunity of paying his respects to me again, saying, "You little devil, do you call this writing your worst?"—"No", I replied; "I call it writing my best." The annihilator, as it turned out, was really a good-natured young man; but he was on the wing for Cambridge; and with the rest, or some of them, I continued to wage war for more than a year.

This 'warfare' was, nevertheless, disturbing to De Quincey who longed for 'peace and freedom from strife' at school. He remained, however a great advocate of the virtues of the Grammar School.

But at nine or ten the masculine energies of the character are beginning to develop themselves; or, if not, no discipline will better aid in their development than the bracing intercourse of a great English classical school. Even the selfish are *there* forced into accommodating themselves to a public standard of manliness. . . . Nowhere is the sublimity of public justice so broadly exemplified as in an English public school on the old Edward the Sixth or Elizabethan foundation. There is not in the universe such an Areopagus for fair play, and abhorrence of all crooked ways, as an English mob, or one of the time-honoured English "foundation" schools.

This 'fair play' was later to reveal itself to him when he was recovering from a serious illness as a result of an accident at school. During his year's convalescence, he was greatly touched by the kindness of the older boys who visited him and invited him to their homes. Indeed, he admitted that 'several among my public enemies had become my private friends'. George Monkland also found this sympathy and helpfulness with some of the senior scholars: 'When I entered the Grammar School I was only seven years old, and the youngest boy Mr. Morgan had ever received . . . Gratitude compels me to name one, Francis Skurray, who was then Captain of the School; I was a perfect stranger to him, but he most generously took me under his protection, and in that too faithful epitome of the world—a public school–sheltered me from many of those acts of petty tyranny experienced by the weak from the strong'. Such is the tradition of leadership and responsibility which, over the centuries, has developed in the office of Head Boy.

The young Edward Parry was another who willingly championed the cause of the oppressed at school. In later life his sister related that:

> . . . On one occasion, he came to his father, as was always his custom under any difficulty, and said, "Father, I want your advice; I can't bear to see that big boy G— beating and ill-treating little H—. I have rescued him once or twice, and this morning G— turned upon me, and we fought, and I think I should have beaten him if the school-bell had not rung. He challenged me on Saturday on Lansdowne, and all the big boys are to be present. Do you think I should meet him?" His father, after a few moments' reflection, asked him the age of his antagonist. "Fifteen", was the reply. "And you are not yet twelve? Try all you can to avoid a battle, and by expostulation to prevent him tormenting your little friend; but, if nothing else will do, you must fight; but be cool, and do not give way to anger." He went, and returned victorious, but with a dislocated finger; for this, however, he cared little, "for now", said he, "little H— will be safe!"

Schoolboy life had other characteristics then, which are equally familiar now. Clever boys, like De Quincey, were always under pressure to loan out their homework to their less able or more idle colleagues. De Quincey actually complained that the quality of his own writing had deteriorated for this reason: 'Several persons of my own class had formed the practice of asking me to write verses for *them*. I could not refuse. But, as the subjects given out were the same for the entire class it was not possible to take so many crops off the ground, without starving the quality of all'.

Mischievous and unruly elements, held in check by the natural authority and discipline of Mr. Morgan, were quick to seize their opportunity whenever he left the schoolroom under the control of his weaker Assistants. On one occasion, when Mr. Morgan was called out of the room, the Usher, Mr. Collins, 'jumped into the desk' to hold sway. In order to assert his immediate command, he struck a heavy blow with his cane at a trouble-maker called Wilbraham who was being cheeky. The boy ducked and the cane hit De Quincey on the head, causing him a serious illness which lasted a year. His mother subsequently withdrew him from the School, much to her son's distress and in spite of a pleading visit made by Mr. Morgan to their home.

One of the highlights of the School year was undoubtedly the Mayor-making ceremony. The whole School, led by Mr. Morgan in a Sedan-chair, took part in the procession to the Abbey where, first of all, a service was held. *The Bath Herald* describes the splendour of the occasion in 1792:

> Bath, Oct. 19th. This morning the Body Corporate of this City, accompanied by the Lord Viscounts Brayham and Weymouth, our two Members, preceded by a Band of Music, the children of the Charity School and the Young Gentlemen of the Grammar School with another Band, went in procession from the Guild-hall to the Abbey Church, where an excellent Sermon was delivered by the Rev. Dr. Phillott from Romans xiii.5. The procession returned to the Hall, when the oaths were administered to the New Mayor, Abel Moysey, Esq. . . . and to the two Justices, Chamberlain and Constables. A Latin Oration was spoken by Master Harington in a style of classic eloquence that showed he inherited those seeds of genius which have been so long nourished in, and have characterised his respectable family. An elegant entertainment is prepared at the Bear Inn.

Although the boys of the School were not invited to the splendid dinner held at The Bear, they nevertheless played a major part in the actual ceremony. Continuing a tradition started as early as 1600 (see above), the Head Boy made a Latin oration to the Mayor, for which he was rewarded by the gift of one guinea. From 1715, this Latin speech was followed by one in English given by a boy from the Blue Coat Charity School (established 1711). His reward was a mere half guinea! Although the Grammar School speech was written by the Master, the Head Boy was expected to learn it by heart and to deliver it faultlessly without the aid of notes. After the usual loyal tributes, the speeches of this period normally offered comment on current events, deploring the activities of the French Revolution and Napoleon, or praising the exploits of Sidney Smith and Nelson. The local press were just as quick to praise one orator for 'such a style of elocution as no less astonished than charmed the audience', as they were to criticise another 'whose voice though sweet was rather weak'.

Although records are scant, the dramatic tradition of the School was certainly kept alive during this period. Edward Parry, for instance, took part in a play which was 'performed by the members of Dr. Morgan's school in aid of some charitable object'. According to his son, 'Edward had always shown considerable talent in this line . . . On this occasion his services were called into requisition by his schoolfellows, who were well aware of his skill in acting; and, in the course of the evening, he sustained three different characters, each with great applause from the spectators'. Little did they realise that this was Parry's last appearance at school. Originally destined to a career in medicine, he had suddenly changed his mind. On the morning after the play (in June, 1803) he left Bath, accompanied by an old family servant, and travelled to Plymouth, where he joined the ship *Ville de Paris* as a volunteer of the first class. Before long he was to find himself caught up in the action of the Napoleonic Wars.

CHAPTER THREE

Broad Street—Years of Turmoil, 1811–1870

'I think it right to remind you that we are not in a condition to compete with Grammar Schools. Just at present ours is rather a middle school to which boys come who wish for a cheap commercial education,' (Rrev. H. S. Fagan's letter to the Trustees, 12 May, 1862.)
'. . . . even I have been startled of late to hear the School spoken of by persons connected with it as "not a mixed school, but something lower," a place full of young ragamuffins.' (Rev. H. S. Fagan's letter to the Trustees, 6 January, 1863.)

City, State and Education, 1811–1870

By 1831 Bath was a town of impressive size. Its population of 50,802, which was one of the largest in the West, was still expanding. Even the old original city parishes of St. James, St. Michael's, St. Peter and St. Paul, and Walcot now housed over 38,000 people—a far cry from the two thousand or so who had lived there in the seventeenth century. Yet, unlike most cities, Bath had escaped the Industrial Revolution virtually unscathed. Its prosperity and fame had been based, not on coal seams and cotton machines, but on an unquenchable supply of hot, bubbling mineral water.

In the eighteenth century the city had been a health resort of the rich. By 1821 the buildings which had housed them remained, but Beau Nash had gone—and the upper classes now preferred Brighton. Bath lost its social vigour; it became middle-aged and middle-class. Men of lower birth and newly-acquired wealth moved in to fill the vacuum and keep the health industry alive. Yet in spite of its social decline, Bath found a new role as a centre for radical thought. 'A place which has the reproach of being *a hot-bed for revolution*', complained a Tory poster in 1837. Quiet, respectable Bath not only returned two radical M.P.s after the Great Reform Bill in 1832, but also became a meeting place for Chartists from 1837. The City Council adopted a most progressive outlook during the 1830's and 1840's when the demand for reform was in the air. Bath was one of the first cities, for instance, to set up a new Poor Law System and a new Police Force in 1836.

During this period the city still catered largely for the quality market of a wealthy consumer society. Even by 1841, over 87 per cent of the working population living in the old city parishes devoted their time and energy to providing

Bath Guildhall and High Street in the mid-19th century.

services and luxuries. Many of these were engaged in domestic service (as housekeepers, grooms, cooks, footmen, etc.), whilst others made clothes for fashion-conscious residents and visitors. A further large group were involved in skilled crafts which helped to bring elegance to their homes—cabinet makers, chair makers, goldsmiths, basketmakers, pipemakers, etc. As many as four per cent worked in the entertainment sector (innkeepers, musicians, chairmen, writers, coachmen, comedians, etc.). Only 1·4 per cent were engaged in major industry, working in the Twerton textile factory, the iron and brass foundries, the pin factory, the breweries or on the road and railway construction.

Nationally the country was, by 1821, just beginning to recover from the exhausting wars against France, which had ended in 1815 with the overthrow of Napoleon. But chronic unemployment in the post-war slump combined with the human misery of the Industrial Revolution to bring just a hint of revolution to the scene. Disease-ridden slums, long working hours, cramped factories, low wages, corrupt local governments and an archaic electoral system all cried out for reform. Lord Liverpool's tough Tory Government temporarily silenced protest and put the rabble firmly in its place. But reform could only be delayed, not averted.

The period now under review is, therefore, often referred to as The Age of Reform. Faced with a growing volume of popular discontent, successive governments reluctantly gave their minds to a gradual improvement in the state of affairs. Mass meetings, marches and riots underlined what social reformers like Wilberforce, Shaftesbury and Fry had been saying for years. The Great Reform Bill of 1832 was followed slowly but surely over the next half century by the reform of local government, factories and mines, public health and housing, poor law and education.

This internal re-examination was accompanied by bold, aggressive policies abroad. The age was, after all, dominated by Lord Palmerston with his 'gunboat diplomacy'. British interests were to be vigorously protected without fear of consequences. This mounting confidence stemmed largely from the country's lead in industrial development and the growth of overseas trade. Consequently Britain became far less interested in European wars and far more involved in the idea of Empire. It was to preserve the richest part of that Empire that troops were sent to crush the Indian Mutiny in 1857.

Not surprisingly, the Age of Reform also made its mark on the field of education. In a period when the country's greatness was being built up on the twin foundations of industry and trade, old educational values were being increasingly questioned. A newspaper leader in 1861 expressed public feeling in these words:

'No Latin or Greek may make Master Jacky a dull boy; but Latin and Greek without anything else go far towards making Master Jacky a very dullard. Parents are beginning to feel this, and to ask whether a skinful of classical knowledge, with a little birching thrown in for nothing, be an equivalent for the two hundred a year they pay for the education of a boy at Eton.' Apart from this critical approach from parents and boys, which was certainly evident (as we shall see) at King Edward's, there was also a growing awareness of the educational needs of the poor, ordinary citizens. In State Education this was, of course, to find expression in the Education Act of 1870, which attempted to establish a national network of elementary schools.

More immediately, however, it showed itself with the appointment of the Charity Commissioners in 1818. These were empowered to investigate all Endowment Trusts, including Grammar Schools, to ensure that resources were being properly applied. The Reports of their enquiries (including that on King Edward's in 1820) led to dramatic changes in the character and composition of these schools. Their insistence that Endowment Funds were intended for the free education of boys from poor homes led to the admission of a deluge of youngsters who were ignorant, unmotivated and totally unsuited to classical education (see below). The Municipal Corporations Act of 1835 transferred control of King Edward's from Bath Corporation (which had been totally responsible for the school since its foundation) to the Bath Charity Trustees (a committee of local worthies who rather relished the opportunity to become far more involved than the Corporation had ever been.) The seeds of conflict had been sown.

Meanwhile, some of the leading Public Schools had been meeting the criticism by introducing reforms of their own. Two great headmasters, Samuel Butler of Shrewsbury and Thomas Arnold of Rugby, had revised teaching methods, examinations and curricula to meet the changing needs. There was, too, a great improvement in the tone of these schools as life there became less harsh and spartan. The roasting of small boys before an open fire was not completely unknown at Rugby even in the days of Dr. Arnold, but his prefectorial system helped to counter these undesirable happenings. He wrote that his aim in giving this power to Sixth Formers was 'for the sake of securing a regular government amongst the boys themselves, and avoiding the evils of anarchy; in other words, of the lawless tyranny of physical strength.' The independent Grammar Schools certainly benefited from the improved reputation of large Public Schools during this period. Their most successful experiments were quickly copied.

In 1861 a Royal Commission under Lord Clarendon was set up to investigate nine of the country's leading Public Schools. This led almost immediately to the Schools Inquiry Commision in 1864 under Lord Taunton, whose brief covered the visitation of Endowed Grammar Schools (including King Edward's School at Bath). Its Report, published in 1868, resulted in the Endowed Schools Act of 1869. This appointed three Endowed School Commissioners to draw up new schemes for the management and working of the schools in question. The one provided for King Edward's in 1872 was to have considerable impact on its future development. (See Chapter Four).

Gathering Clouds: The Charity Commissioners

On 6 March, 1811 the City Council elected the Rev. Thomas Wilkins to succeed his brother-in-law, Mr. Morgan, as Master of the Free Grammar School. There were no other candidates. Mr. Wilkins had, of course, already been largely responsible for the daily running of the School in his capacity of Second Master. After the death of Mrs. Morgan in 1794, he and Mrs. Wilkins had lived in the School house to enable Mr. Morgan to move with his family to the larger space of Charlcombe Rectory.

Thomas Wilkins had been educated at Worcester College, Oxford. A man of considerable means, he had been appointed to the living of Weston in 1808 while he was still Second Master of the School. To this was added the rectory of Charlcombe, which was by now linked with the Mastership of the School (see Chapter Two). Three houses were, therefore, at the disposal of the Wilkins family, which consisted of two· sons and a daughter. His eldest son, Edward, was sent to Eton where he was elected a King's Scholar. His youngest son, Nathanael, remained at King Edward's where he eventually became Head Boy in 1817.

In 1811 it must have seemed as though Mr. Wilkins was set to enjoy a long period of calm and prosperity. He had inherited a school with a reputation for excellence which was attracting able boys from far and wide. Highly regarded as its Usher and fully experienced in its traditions, he was already part of that reputation himself. Although competition to King Edward's was increasing slightly through the establishment of a number of private boarding schools in the vicinity, Thomas Wilkins had little reason to fear the future. And yet, by 1823, he had resigned amid bitterness and controversy, and the School had been given a jolt the effects of which were to damage its reputation until the end of the century.

In 1818 the government had appointed commissioners to investigate various charities, including all endowment trusts. This meant that King Edward's, and every other endowed school in the land, duly received a visit from the charity Commissioners. Their main report, published in 1820, gives a clear description of the School:

> The Rev. Thomas Wilkins . . . has a house with a school-room, and conveniences for boarders, and a yard or playground attached to it. The building is large, handsome, substantial and convenient, situate in Broad Street, Bath, the exterior of which the Corporation keep in complete repair; the repairs of the interior fall upon the master who also pays all taxes whatsoever. The master receives the salary of £84 a year from the Corporation, which was raised about 15 years ago in consequence of an application by his predecessor, who, on account of the rise in taxes, applied to the Corporation for an increase of the salary; it had previously been £50 a year. No gratuity whatever is paid to him, nor any allowance made to him for stationery or books. Mr. Wilkins has never had any boys upon the foundation, nor has he ever had any application made to him for the admission of any such boys; but we understand from him, that he has been ready at all times to receive and instruct the sons of freemen, gratuitously, if properly nominated, on application being made.

It appears that there are many other schools in Bath which may appear to be better calculated to give the instruction which tradesmen may require for their sons; and there are no emoluments at the university belonging to the grammar school. No public notice, however, is given of nominations to be made to the school, nor does it appear that the Corporation of Bath have ever, in fact, appointed any boys to the school. The master takes boarders and day-scholars; his whole number at the time of our visiting the school, being between 70 and 80; these boarders pay him £55 a year, which includes the charge for teaching French. The day-boys pay £8 8s. 0d. a year each. The corporation are doubtless well acquainted with this use of the school premises for private tuition, the same having been customary with the predecessors of the present master. The education given to the boys of the school is in classical and general literature; and we understand from the master, that if any free boys should be offered to him, their education would be confined to the Latin and Greek classics, being the only instruction which he conceived himself bound to give by the charter. It appears from the Rev. Mr. Wilkins, that he has been at a heavy expense in keeping the internal parts of the premises in repair, which, with the addition of taxes, has far exceeded the amount of his salary.

Controversy was to be centred not on the cost of repairs or the size of the fees, but on the admission of 'foundationers' into the school. It will be seen from the above report that the commissioners discovered that Mr. Wilkins had 'never had any boys upon the foundation' and that the Corporation of Bath had never 'appointed any boys to the school'. In other words, over 268 years of the school's existence, the Corporation had never used money from the endowment funds to educate poorer children free of charge. As we have already seen, Grammar Schools believed that they had been founded with the specific purpose of advancing learning through the study of Latin and Greek. Although some such schools *did* admit a certain number of boys from more humble homes without charge, they always insisted on proof of academic ability. No compromise was ever made on the *type* of education offered.

All this was to change. The Charity Commissioners based their investigation on the assumption that schools had been endowed 'for the education of the poor'. As a result of their reports, trustees were instructed to set aside some of their funds for the assistance of poorer parents. Consequently, in a great rush of blood to the head, free scholars were elected to most of the country's Grammar Schools with out any educational test at all. This was nothing short of disastrous. Schools were compelled to take in poorly-grounded boys, most of whom were totally unsuited to the type of teaching being offered. Premises were frequently inadequate—as were existing staff for the new demands made upon them. Some schools faced up to the problem by constructing a 'pen' in the big schoolroom for these Free Foundationers. There, segregated from the regular scholars, they were instructed in elementary subjects by an assistant. Other schools merely threw the Foundationers in at the deep end by forcing them to join the classes in Latin and Greek (much to their distress).

This was certainly the attitude taken by Mr. Wilkins at King Edward's. He had already warned the commissioners that if any free boys should be admitted 'their education would be confined to the Latin and Greek classes, being the only instruction which he conceived himself bound to give by the charter! When, therefore, the Corporation elected ten Foundationers on 11 July, he duly proceeded to implement his threat. The Corporation had earlier decided, on reading the commissioners' report, that they would elect ten boys each year 'provided candidates properly qualified should offer themselves'. By that, however, they did not imply academic qualifications. Boys to be considered for election were first to be nominated 'by twenty of the chiefest and most substantial inhabitants of the said city.'

The first Foundationers so elected were Benedictus Cuff (son of a druggist), Frederick Jones (son of a saddler), John Stamp (son of a baker), Charles Simms (son of a bookseller), James Hulbert (son of an upholsterer), Thomas Austen (son of a haberdasher), James Willis (son of a coachmaster), George Kirkham (son of a lodging-house keeper), George Lansdown (son of a lodging-house keeper) and Henry Harford (son of a saddler). Mr. Wilkins was ordered in a writ of execution dated 14 October, 1822, which outlines his duties, to instruct these boys 'gratis'—i.e. without any financial recognition of the extra demands involved. He was, amongst other things, required to take 'his schollars, on every Sunday morning and evening, and on every holy day, Wednesday and Friday morning' to the Abbey Church. On other days prayers were to be read in the morning and evening at school.

But Mr. Wilkins had had enough. A few days later he submitted his resignation. After some discussion, he agreed to continue until mid-summer in 1823—although he hung on to the rectory of Charlcombe until later in the year (much to the distress of his successor). He retired to his vicarage at Weston where, shortly afterwards at the age of sixty-one, he died a saddened and disappointed man (24 April, 1824).

As a footnote to the visit of the Charity Commissioners, it should be added that they also pressurised the Corporation into fulfilling some of their obligations set out in the Chancery Decree of 1735 (see Chapter Two). They agreed in future to keep separate the identifiable property granted by King Edward for the benefit of the School and to maintain independent accounts for that fund. The Commissioners had managed to pin-point five properties which belonged to the school—Fountain Buildings (which stood on the site of the former St. Werburgh's Church), New Westgate Buildings (near the site of Westgate House, pulled down with the Gate in 1776), part of The White Hart Inn (in Stall Street), Monk's Mill (just outside the East Gate) and The Horse and Jockey Inn (formerly The Bell Inn on the corner of Stall Street and Beau Street). They concluded, however, that the remaining ninety per cent or so of the School's endowment was now completely unidentifiable.

The Arrival of James Pears, 1823

Late in 1822 the Corporation advertised for a new Master in the local papers of Bath, Oxford and Cambridge. They appointed the only candidate to receive full consideration in Council—the Rev. James Pears. Educated at Winchester and Oxford, Mr. Pears had been ordained before joining the Staff of the Royal Military College, Sandhurst as a teacher of classics and history. He had later established his own private school, Woodcote House near Bagshot, where boys had been

The Rev. James Pears, Headmaster 1822–1853.

School Archives

prepared for entry to both the Royal Military College and the Colleges of the East India Company at Haileybury and Addiscombe. Chaplain to William IV, he had previously been responsible for the education of several members of aristocratic families.

The Corporation had, therefore, received the services of an outstanding character of proven quality and experience. He came with excellent references from friends, university dons, parents and employers. One carried the signature of Colonel Le Marchant, Governor of the Royal Military College and himself, of course, an Old Edwardian. Le Marchant's successor there, Colonel Butler, wrote that he was 'a Gentleman of attainments which must do honour to any Establishment for education, and of the most exemplary private character in every respect.' There is no doubt that Mr. Pears had been attracted to the job partly by the excellent reputation which the School had built up under Mr. Morgan, and partly by the generous amount of family accommodation available at both Charlcombe and Broad Street. Aged forty-six, he had a family of eight sons and three daughters. Although, by 1823, four of the boys were at college, the financial burden on him was still very considerable.

His sons were all to follow interesting careers. James Robert, the eldest, had been educated at Winchester and Oxford. He was eventually ordained and returned to Bath as his father's Second Master at the School. William studied at the East India Company's College at Addiscombe before joining the Madras Engineers. He died, unfortunately, shortly after reaching India. Charles, his third son, also died young at sea, having entered the Navy from Portsmouth College. Thomas studied at Addiscombe, served with the Madras Engineers and ended a most distinguished military career as Major-General Sir Thomas Pears, Military Secretary at the India Office. Arnold went on from King Edward's to Addiscombe, reached the rank of Lieut.-Colonel in the Madras Artillery and finally became Inspector of Schools for the Madras Government. Stuart, who was educated at King Edward's and Oxford, taught at Harrow before becoming Headmaster of Repton. There he transformed a modest, country grammar school into a nationally famous establishment. The youngest son, Alfred, became a solicitor.

Meanwhile, the high expectations held by Mr. Pears of his new school had already been shattered. He arrived to find not a prosperous, thriving centre of learning, but a school that was virtually empty. Between his appointment in March 1823 and his arrival in July, the eighty boys mentioned by the Charity commissioners had completely vanished! Only one remained—plus the ten free Foundationers. Most had probably moved to other private schools in the area in an attempt to avoid the controversy caused by the resignation of Mr. Wilkins.

Nor was Mr. Pears at all impressed with the state of the accommodation, which he had originally seen as one of the main attractions to his new job. Because he was unable to obtain immediate possession of the Charlcombe rectory (thanks to the reluctance of Mr. Wilkins to resign from it), he and his family crowded into the available rooms at Broad Street. He was horrified by what he saw. Penning a hurried letter to the Mayor and Corporation, he pointed out that 'the premises appear to want various repairs'. Speed was vital 'as I have but a short time to put my furniture into the house and prepare for the reception of pupils'. Pupils were, in fact, slowly attracted back. Some of his scholars from Woodcote House undoubtedly came with him as boarders. Even so, such was the crisis and pupil-shortage that the tradition of providing a Grammar School boy to deliver the Latin speech at the annual Mayor-making was suspended for two years. By 1826 standards and numbers had recovered sufficiently for the custom to be revived.

During the first seven years of his Mastership Mr. Pears tried desperately, but with limited success, to goad the Council into improving the somewhat spartan conditions he found at the school. The problem of heating such a large school room was uppermost in his mind when he wrote to the Council in January 1825. Bath was apparently in the middle of a sharp winter with freezing conditions making teaching difficult:

> . . . the extreme coldness of the School-Room has been, as I understand, always complained of, and I feel it very much myself. Being so large and having two doors opening into the external air, it cannot be regularly or properly warmed even by two large fires, and nothing will do it but a Bristol warm air stove underneath. This would cost between 30 and 40 pounds, which sum I cannot well afford, and as it is a complete fixture, and of little value to be removed, I take the liberty of requesting the Corporation to affix one to the House. It will be a great permanent benefit to the School.

The Council declined to support this request, presumably

because they felt that *internal* repairs and alterations were the responsibility of the Master. Five years later, in January 1830, when requesting on this occasion a new water closet, he pointed out that he had already 'put up a warm air stove' at his own personal cost for £80. An indoor water-closet, he wrote, was now essential but outside the scope of his pocket. 'We have been greatly inconvenienced from the want of it, having but one place in the open court for this huge house.' This application, at least, was supported. A new closet was installed on the first floor for the sum of £42 9s. 8d.

Gradually he managed to rectify the neglect of many years. Furniture in the schoolroom was replaced or renovated by the Corporation in 1830. Four new desks and three new forms were purchased 'for the centre of the School Room'; one new desk and 'sundry repairs' for the north side; two new desks and 'sundry repairs' for the south side; two new desks and 'sundry repairs' on the west side. The desks of the assistant masters were also patched up. The rough estimate for £48. 18s. 9d. submitted by the contractor provides a fleeting glimpse into the lay-out and organisation of the big School Room. Five classes were clearly in operation. No longer did boys sit with books on their knees. Desks were now the order of the day.

Mr. Pears next gave his attention to the exterior fabric. He persuaded the Corporation to obtain an estimate for repairs to the roof, removal of moss from the main walls, replacement of window sills and repaving the large yard at the back. However, when it was discovered that this work was to cost a staggering total of £239, they had the audacity to suggest that the Master himself should foot the bill for all 'dilapidations' to the exterior. Mr. Pears immediately submitted an indignant protest (September 1830), pointing out that their demand was quite contrary to his written agreement. It was, he said, unjust that he 'should be subject to the accumulated dilapidations of 50 years', especially when it was quite obvious that nothing had been done by the Corporation during that time, 'not even a little paint applied'. Under this pressure, the Council eventually gave way.

Thus, by 1830, the School had not only recovered to a large extent from the disaster of 1823, it had also been given a

The front of the School in 1842.

School Archives

much-needed face-lift. The way now seemed open at long last for the professional talents of the new Master to be given full play.

The Parents' Complaint, 1830

But outward appearances were to prove deceptive. Simmering discontent, which lay hidden beneath the surface, was shortly to break out in a most unexpected manner. In November 1830, some of the parents staged a forthright protest. The ensuing controversy, prolonged and bitter, was to undermine the aspirations of Mr. Pears and, ultimately, to rock the very foundations of the School.

Although many difficulties had been overcome during the settling-in period of the new Master, the *real* problem still remained. Mr. Wilkins had resigned in 1823 over the matter of the admission of free Foundationers. Questions of both principle and practice raised by this issue had not been solved merely by the appointment of Mr. Pears.

It is true that the Council now accepted that it was unreasonable to expect the Master to teach Foundationers without any extra financial recognition. They had, therefore, agreed to pay him an additional £40 annually for the special instruction in 'English, Writing, Arithmetic and Mathematics' that these new boys so badly needed. No longer were they to be flung indiscriminately into classes in Latin and Greek and expected to fend for themselves. Their lack of basic grounding in the 'three R's' was now at least accepted as an established fact. The boys were consequently taught at a separate table 'at the lower end of the schoolroom' until they were ready to join other classes. It was a slow process, but some free Foundationers *did* eventually make good (see below). According to the later reminiscences of Dr. Julian Hunter (at School 1820–1825), the free boys in his day 'had to sit apart from the others in a wooden pen or enclosure in the large schoolroom near the door leading into the playground. They were not allowed to mix in any way with the boys whose parents paid a fee.'

Mr. Pears accepted, with some obvious reluctance, the new role he was expected to play. He assured the Council, in a letter dated 30 November, 1830, that it was both his duty and his desire 'to give particular care to those boys, for whose benefit the School was founded'. There was, however, to be no compromise on the *type* of education being offered. Once the boys had polished up on the basic elements, they were still expected to follow a course of classical studies. He pleaded with the Council, therefore, to be more selective and to maintain 'the character of the foundation' by 'the appointment of boys, to whom a learned education would be useful in their future lives'.

His experience of the free Foundationers over his first seven years at the School had clearly been a great disappointment. Although his ambition was to 'bring forward promising youths, whose talents without such an opportunity would be lost to the world', circumstances had conspired against him. Lack of initial grounding, distractions at home which hindered serious studies and their early removal to apprenticeships had thwarted their progress as classical scholars. His greatest regret was that he had never had 'one sufficiently advanced to be able to make the speech on the Mayor's day'.

Mr. Pears had clearly made a real attempt to face up to the *educational* difficulties raised by the introduction of Foundationers. But a problem far more sinister and insidious was beginning to destroy the unity and morale of the School from within. The bombshell was finally dropped in the November of 1830. A letter of protest, signed by the parents of seven Foundationers, was sent to the Mayor and Corporation. It demanded an inquiry into the methods and attitudes of the Master.

The main complaint against Mr. Pears, which was elaborated in more detail when a Chancery suit was instituted in 1832 (see below), was that he deliberately treated the Foundationers as second-class citizens. It was alleged that the free scholars were forbidden to speak to his private pupils, that they were banned from playing in the school yard and that they were made to walk separately at the tail of the procession to the Abbey at the Mayor's inauguration. This treatment had resulted in the most deplorable consequences. The Foundationers had been made to feel that they were 'of an inferior grade' and had therefore lost heart. On the other hand, 'a strong feeling of arrogance' had been created in the private pupils. They were now openly abusive to the free boys, using insulting language and calling them 'Paupers and Charity Boys'.

There is no doubt that social problems had become acute in a school which had previously confined its entry to the sons of wealthy parents. Class distinctions, after all, still played a predominant part in the England of 1830. Even the Great Reform Bill two years later failed to produce anything like the democratic society which is a feature of modern life. Mr. Pears, a man of property and social standing himself, had absolutely no intention of encouraging or permitting the sort of integration which nowadays is thought desirable. There was to be no classless society at King Edward's. He would do his duty by educating the Foundationers, as best he could, in accordance with the wishes of their parents. But he would also do his duty to the parents of his private pupils by protecting them from influences which had been thrust into their midst and which he secretly resented.

In his letter of reply to the Corporation, Mr. Pears first of all dismissed the charges raised against him by the parents as being either 'frivolous' or 'false'. He absolutely denied that he had ever forbidden the Foundationers to speak to the other pupils—except on one occasion. 'Three or four of the free boys were in the habit of persecuting a very little boy as he went home, upon which I charged them not to speak to him again, and I remember telling them that they had no right to speak to any young gentleman in the street unless they were personally acquainted with him'. Nor did he have the slightest knowledge of any Foundationer being insulted—except by other Foundationers. 'Hobson, a foundation boy, came to me in tears, and said he was afraid to go home because two or three boys, also on the foundation, threatened to beat him. Upon enquiry it appeared that he had been calling them names with contemptuous reference to their parents' occupations'. Mr. Pears did admit that Foundationers had walked separately to the Abbey service, but this was in keeping with the tradition in all public schools. In future they would walk at the head of the procession. After all, he added, 'my private pupils . . . merely attend voluntarily in compliment to the Mayor and because it is an old custom.'

Although he pleaded innocence to the accusations, there can be little doubt that Mr. Pears deliberately kept his prize pupils, the boarders, at arm's length from the other boys. Once out of class, there was absolutely no social contact between the two groups. Day boys of any kind (whether Foundationers or not) were forbidden to play in the school yard, which was regarded as part of the Master's private residence. Nor were they permitted to stray from the school-room itself into other rooms of the house. This was very much in keeping with the system which Mr. Pears had operated within the School from his arrival. He explained the principles of his plan to the Corporation:

> I know from long experience that all the evils of large schools arise from the unrestrained intercourse of boys of all ages and dispositions . . . To restrain natural corruption in boys *apart* is not easy, but if numbers indiscriminately associate it becomes

impracticable. Pride and Tyranny are in continual action in
those of superior Rank, Fortune or Strength; Servility, False-
hood and Malice in the others . . . Most men who have been at
a Public School will know this to be true: and, it is *my*
conviction, these evils are *so great*, that no advantage in learning
can compensate for them. Acting upon this conviction, I unite
with parents in endeavouring that boys may go straight home
after school-hours, and I charge them to make *no acquaintancy*,
but such as their families know and approve.

There was, therefore, to be no communal life or social mix
in the School as a whole. The Foundationer was to be thankful
for educational opportunity alone, because 'whilst at School
he has the great incitement and assistance of competing with
boys of talents or attainments superior to his own.' That was
benefit enough. Friendship and moral habits were best formed
'in the bosom of his own family'—not at School. But for the
private boarder, the situation was completely different. Removed from the bosom of his own real family, he looked to the
Master of the School for direction in friendship and moral
habits. Mr. Pears, therefore, felt it his duty to prevent any
'natural corruption' by forbidding, as far as possible, the
association of boarders and day boys of a lower class. Whatever his denials to the contrary, this duty was seemingly
carried out with more vigour as the number of free Foundationers increased. It is easy to condemn this attitude. But
Mr. Pears, a product of his own time, could see his school
slowly being ruined by the pressures placed upon it from
without.
A sub-committee was appointed by the Corporation to
investigate the complaint. The conclusion of its report, presented on 16 December, 1830, stated: 'although it appears
that there is no intimacy between the free boys and the other
pupils, Mr. Pears is no party to any such restrictions, but that
it arises from the private feeling of his pupils which he cannot
control and with which he considers he cannot interfere'.
Furthermore, it commended him for providing the Foundationers with equal advantages in education. Mr. Henry
Nelson and the other complaining parents were furious.
Two years later in 1832, others took up their cause and
instituted an action in the Court of Chancery. At a time when

the country as a whole was ravaged with demonstrations in favour of Parliamentary Reform, Samuel Jameson, cabinet maker, Edmund Davis, tailor, and Ralph Walker, iron founder, brought forward two charges against Bath Corporation. First, that in spite of the Chancery Decree of 1735, the Corporation had failed to hand over to other trustees the property granted by Edward VI for the maintenance of the School. Secondly 'that the School was utterly ineffectual as a free school for the City of Bath' in view of the attitude of Mr. Pears towards his free scholars and the inexcusable restriction in the number of free scholars to ten per annum.

The suit was to drag on for fourteen years, much to the anxiety of those who had brought it in the first place. Alarmed at the fear of mounting costs, both they and the Corporation tried in vain to end the proceedings. But Chancery thought otherwise. By January 1836, a Master in Chancery had been instructed to investigate 'of what the charity and estates do now consist, and to make a proper scheme for future application'. The ultimate results of this investigation were threefold. First, an additional part of King Edward's original endowment was identified in 1846 and handed over by the Corporation for the School's use. This consisted of some houses in Bladud Buildings and Paragon Buildings. Secondly, the costs of the suit (amounting to well over £2,000) were charged to the Corporation. Thirdly, a new scheme for the management of the School was established by the Court of Chancery in 1849. The consequences of this were to ensure that the last remaining traces of the School's excellent reputation, which had been gained under Mr. Morgan in the eighteenth century, vanished from sight. (See below). Meanwhile, in August 1836, as a result of a re-organisation of local government, the management of the School had been transferred from Bath Corporation into the hands of Bath Charity Trustees.

King Edward's School and the Indian Mutiny

The flagging fortunes and reputation of the School were somewhat revived by the personal connections and influence of Mr. Pears. In his previous Preparatory School, he had been responsible for preparing boys for entry into the East India College at Haileybury and its military branch at Addiscombe. These institutions were run by the East India Company as training grounds for admission into the Indian Civil Service and the Indian Army. Through regular contact, Mr. Pears had cultivated a close relationship with many members of the Company's Court of Directors. Several became his life-long friends.

It was not surprising, therefore, that they should place their sons' education entirely in his hands on his arrival in Bath. His most distinguished patrons, all of whom sent their boys as boarders to King Edward's, included R. D. Mangles (M.P. for Guildford), Lieut.-Colonel J. Oliphant (a member of the Court of Directors), Sir George Lawrence, Sir John D'Oyly and J. Lewis (a member of the Supreme Council of India). It is interesting to notice from the Census Returns of 1851 that, of the thirty-five boarders then resident at Broad Street, no fewer than thirteen had been born in the East Indies. Mr. Pears had, therefore, partly managed to fill the empty school he had inherited in 1823 by drawing on the goodwill of his personal friends.

Many of these boys went on from King Edward's to Haileybury or Addiscombe before seeing distinguished service in India. Most of them contributed richly either as soldiers or as administrators during the critical years of the Indian Mutiny (1857–1859). Sir Bartle Frere, Commissioner of Scind, managed through force of personality to maintain peace in his own province. The troops and supplies he was therefore able to spare helped to save the Punjab from anarchy. 'It is certain that there is no man to whom India owes a deeper debt of gratitude' was the accolade bestowed on him in the House of Lords. He later became Governor of Bombay.

Amongst others to serve in the Civil Service section in Bengal were two Lawrence brothers, three Lewis brothers and three Mangles brothers. Warren Hastings D'Oyly went out to serve in the Calcutta Volunteer Rifles at the end of the Mutiny. Outside Government House in Calcutta he heard the proclamation that Queen Victoria had taken over the government of India from the East India Company (1858). He was

Sir Henry Bartle Frere (Old Edwardian): Governor of Bombay.
National Portrait Gallery

later appointed Inspector General of Gaols in Bengal. Of
other Old Edwardians, Colonel Lord Mark Kerr commanded
the 13th Light Infantry throughout the Mutiny, E. J. McNair
was decorated for his part in the Siege of Delhi and Colonel
Thomas Pears (son of the Master) continued his work of

constructing railways with the Madras Engineers. But perhaps the most famous of all was Ross Lewis Mangles, who became the first civilian to win the Victoria Cross. An extract from Hart's Army Lists tells the story:

> Ross Lewis Mangles, Esq., Bengal Civil Service, Assistant Magistrate at Patna . . . volunteered and served with the force despatched to the relief of Arrah, in June 1857 . . . The force fell into an ambuscade on the night of the 29th July, and during the retreat on the next morning, Mr. Mangles, with singular gallantry and generous self-devotion, and notwithstanding that he had himself been previously wounded, carried for several miles, out of action, a wounded soldier of her Majesty's 37th Regiment, after binding up his wounds under a murderous fire which killed or wounded almost the whole detachment: and he bore him in safety to the boats.

Some years later (in 1875) he was presented to the Prince of Wales (subsequently King Edward VII)—and immediately ticked off for wearing his V.C. in the wrong position! Earlier, another hero had emerged—Robert Fitzgerald, one of five brothers who lived in St. James's Square. Nicknamed 'Fitzgerald of the Stormy Hand', he was rated the finest swordsman in Western India. By personal valour he saved the life of Sir Charles Napier at the Battle of Meanee in Scind, where he commanded the 5th Punjab Cavalry. After his death at sea at the age of thirty-six, his fellow officers erected a marble pulpit to his memory in St. Paul's Cathedral.

Although these former pupils undoubtedly stole the limelight in the middle of the nineteenth century, some of their contemporaries were at the same time continuing to add to the School's reputation in other spheres. The world of education gained J. W. Richards (left in 1827—High Master of Manchester Grammar School), S. A. Pears (left in 1832—Headmaster of Repton) and H. S. Crook (left in 1825)—Government Inspector of Schools, 1860–1870). The church benefited from the services of the Rev. Canon James Fleming (left 1849—Chaplain to Queen Victoria), the Very Rev. Philip Eliot (left 1852—Canon and Dean of Windsor, Domestic Chaplain to Queen Victoria and King Edward VII) and the Rev. Canon Wright Phillpott (left 1834—Canon of Hereford).

Perhaps the variety and richness of the School's contribution to the public life of the nation is best illustrated by mentioning just five more Old Edwardians—J. W. East (left 1848—Rear Admiral of the Navy 1888), E. L. Fox (left 1849—President of the British Medical Association, 1894), W. B. Odgers (left 1859—Recorder of Bristol and Director of Legal Studies at the Inns of Court), Sir Joseph Rickett (left 1860—Postmaster General) and Cedric Chivers (left in 1867 because he 'did not like learning Latin'—six times Mayor of Bath and a world-famous book-binder).

Life at King Edward's in the Mid-Nineteenth Century

The Masterships of Mr. Pears, Mr. Macleane and Mr. Fagan were to witness a gradual change in the life and atmosphere of the School. Outwardly things seemed much the same as ever. The new Scheme of 1849 at least paid lip-service to the past. Classical instruction, it pledged, was 'at all times to be regarded and treated as the principal object of the foundation'. A glance at the timetable for a top class in the 1850's rather seemed to confirm that impression:

All the old ingredients were present—endless learning by heart, repetition and testing of Latin, Greek and Scripture. But, at the same time too, there was the merest hint of change—Mr. Cogan's lecture on Monday afternoons. J. D. Cogan, later styled a 'science master', brought a most welcome breath of fresh air into the School. A former pupil, writing in the Edwardian on the announcement of Cogan's death in 1912, recalled with pleasure the enormous range of his lectures on practical subjects—physics, chemistry, astronomy, photography, acoustics, pottery, glass blowing, the vibrations of a monochord and cooking. Vivid memories were cherished of the occasion when, at the end of a lecture 'some tinned meat, cooked and potted by him several years before' was handed round for tasting. No wonder the boys loved him! By 1868 Mr. Fagan had persuaded the Trustees to grant £5 to help in forming a 'chemical class' and a further £5 for the purchase of 'chemical apparatus'.

Change was also, of course, being forced on the School by the needs of the uneducated Foundationers from within and

	9 to 10	10 to 11	11 to 12	2 to 3	3 to 4	4 to 5
MON-DAY	Scripture History	Eton Grammar & Cornelius Nepos	Prepare Greek Grammar & Delectus	Say Greek Grammar & Delectus	Writing	Mr. Cogan's Lecture
TUES-DAY	Read Bible	Say Key's Grammar and Ovid	ditto	ditto	Latin Verse	Read History
WEDNES-DAY	Read Bible	Eton Grammar & Cornelius Nepos	Prepare Thursday's Lesson	Holiday		
THURS-DAY	Scripture History	Say Key's Grammar and ovid	Prepare Greek Grammar & Delectus	Say Greek Grammar & Delectus	Latin Verse	Read History
FRI-DAY	Read Bible	Eton Grammar & Cornelius Nepos	ditto	ditto	English into Latin	Read History
SATUR-DAY	Read Bible	Repeti-tion	Prepare Monday's Lessons	Holiday		

by the pressures of an industrial world from without. The new Scheme gave a growing prominence to mathematics, history, English language, literature, foreign languages, the practical arts and the elements of science. Gradually these found their way into the timetables of the lower classes. A prospectus issued by Mr. Pears in about 1850 boasted two 'Mathematical Masters' and offered, as extras, instruction in French, German, Drawing, Drilling and Hindustani. The School's connection with the East India Company was clear for all to see.

The broadening of the curriculum was further developed

under Mr. Fagan, who also encouraged self-expression in a number of out-of-school activities. Writing in 1911, J. C. Odgers recalled:

> Hitherto very few boys had learnt French; now the study of both French and German became quite popular under Monsieur Florian. Mr. Fagan offered prizes for the best collections of ferns, flowers, and shells, and for the construction of simple machines. Not one of us knew how to use a lathe, but we attempted the manufacture of pumps and windmills with our pocket knives only.

The playground had, in fact, at last been thrown open to day boys as well as boarders. After a row with the Trustees in 1856, Mr. Macleane had finally agreed to permit day boys to

The Playground at Broad Street in 1842.

School Archives

play there for half-an-hour before both morning and afternoon school. He greatly feared, however, that by allowing so many boys at once into the yard 'there would be great collisions amongst them'. Experience, of course, was to prove him right! Nevertheless, all restrictions on the use of the playground were removed on Mr. Fagan's appointment in 1858.

That small, confined area was put to considerable use, as J. C. Odgers later remembered:

> The games most in vogue in my time were racquets and fives, and to this hour I recall the sharp ring that was heard when the racquet-ball struck a beam of wood which divided the courts in the high wall on the north side of the playground. But the number of boys who played racquets was never large . . . As for fives, I found you could knock your hands into a pulp in five minutes, and I desisted. We never thought of playing in leather gloves, as I believe is now done at the great public schools. In 1854, if I remember rightly, some kind Alderman of Bath, who was a trustee of the school, presented us with a giant's stride, parallel bars, and some more apparatus for athletic training; but we had no instructor, and the parallel bars, etc. were allowed to rot in the rain unused. We all took kindly to the giant's stride, but two or three bad accidents resulted from our ignorance of its proper use.

The Trustees had already responded favourably to a petition sent to them by twenty-six boys requesting 'a new net for the Racquet Court, as the present net is entirely rotted in so much that the balls go through and frequently break the windows on the opposite side'. Instead of a new net (which had been fixed on top of the wall), they agreed to increase the height of the wall.

Although physical education was not yet taught, the optional 'drilling' lessons advertised in the prospectus of Mr. Pears were, in fact, a reality. An Old Boy writing in *The Edwardian* of 1913 remembered with amusement those occasions 'when we attempted evolutions that were too difficult for us, to form up in fours, and eights, and dozens, to make hollow squares, etc., and we turned in wrong directions and looked in each other's faces when we should all have been gazing similarly and demurely at distant chimney-pots. The old sergeant who had us for his pupils must have had a very bad time, for we had no heart for such a thing.'

Organised sport, as such, was still a thing of the future. There were, however, clear signs that its introduction could not be long delayed. Rev. Edward Bartrum, appointed Second Master in 1858, attempted to stir up some interest in physical activities. According to Odgers, he 'once tried to incite us to take up an active interest in athletic sports, and arranged a contest in running, leaping, and throwing the cricket ball in a field to the north of Pulteney Street, but as nobody had undergone any sort of training we certainly did not distinguish ourselves . . . Some of the older boys got up a sort of Boating Club, which was fairly successfully carried on for two summers (1861–1862). It was but a frail institution, however, depending on our ability to contribute from our rather small supplies of pocket money, but it afforded us a delightful method of spending our summer afternoons on the Avon. At one time we had an eight-oar boat, but we generally went out in two or three boats having seats for four rowers only. These we hired at a boat-house about a quarter of a mile beyond the Sydney Gardens'.

Mr. T. S. Gandy, speaking at an Old Edwardians' Supper in 1914, recalled attempts made by boys in the 1860's to play a primitive form of soccer on their afternoons off school. 'He could not help thinking of the old times when he used to play football at school. In those days they had no apparatus, no poles, no nets, no jerseys, no studs or bars for their boots. Even their ball used to get flabby sometimes; its inside was a pig's bladder. When one boy had blown as much into it as he could—they had no pump—he would hand it to another. They used to play in what is now the Bath Cricket Ground, but in those days there were great ridges for the sake of drainage, and they had to kick the football over them. Still, in spite of everything, they had some good games.'

Cricket seems to have first made its appearance at School in 1862, entirely due to the initiative of the boys themselves. They had clubbed together to hire a field only to end the season in debt. Their appeal for the Trustees to bail them out was rejected on that occasion. From 1864, however, £10 a year was provided from Endowment Funds for the hire of a cricket ground. When, in 1866, Mr. Topping (the Second Master) obtained use of a ground near North Parade Bridge for £7 per season, he was permitted to spend the remaining £3 on the purchase of bats.

Schoolboy crazes were as much in evidence then as now. Marbles, tops, hopping-toys and stamps all had their turn—

but the favourite of all was the dreaded pea-shooter. J. C. Odgers wrote:

> In my time, for a half-year or more, pea-shooters became a positive scourge and perpetual nuisance. A triple-shooter was a deadly thing. The ordinary shooter was about twelve inches long, and could be carried out of sight in the sleeve of your coat; but three such shooters could be rapidly fitted together, and as easily detached and hidden. With a triple shooter one could take a sure and deadly aim. I remember what happened one afternoon in 1859 or 1860, when the large schoolroom was occupied by a drawing class. A number of boys occupied the desks, which lined the north and south walls, as well as those which then, as now, filled the centre of the room. We all had drawing-books, and were set to copy a model placed at the end of the room. For some twenty minutes all the masters happened to be absent except the drawing-master from the School of Art, who was quite unable to keep order. Pea-shooters from each side of the room poured volleys of peas into the centre, where they passed like showers of hail-stones across the surface of each drawing-board, carrying off the point of your pencil, and stinging your fingers until you could use them no longer. The hurricane lasted until every available pea had been fired, and then everyone was upon the floor gathering up pocket fulls of ammunition for future use! Suddenly, the head-master entered, and peace fell upon that bear-garden. Many and severe were the impositions imposed that day.

Discipline, indeed, was still extremely strict. Serious offenders were subjected to a public flogging 'upon the bare person' in front of the whole school. In 1856 Mr. Macleane successfully resisted attempts by the Trustees to make him abandon flogging as a form of punishment (see below). However, in J. C. Odger's time, it was not Mr. Macleane but Mr. Bartrum 'who administered the most terrible thrashing I ever saw given in the School or elsewhere, not with the birch but with a long stout cane. A lad had purloined another boy's *Student's Hume* and sold it to a second-hand bookseller, who within a few hours sold it again to a boy in the same class. The original owner who could point to his own signature written on a certain page in the middle of the book brought the matter under Mr. Bartrum's notice, who asked the bookseller to come and identify the lad who was guilty of the theft. The thrashing took place before the whole school in front of the head-master's rostrum. Mr. Bartrum was a very muscular Christian; and the strokes fell with alarming rapidity upon the back of the sinner, who spun round and round the execution-er. It was a terrible performance but was richly deserved'.

During this period the School gradually changed from a two-term year (with holidays at Christmas and Midsummer only) to a three-term year. The new Scheme of 1849 stipulated holidays of one week at Easter, six weeks at midsummer and five weeks at Christmas. Although School uniform had not yet been introduced, the parents of the free Foundationers were reminded that they were responsible for sending their son to school 'clean and neat in his person and apparel.' Mr. Macleane abandoned his attempt to make them wear 'caps and gowns' after a protest to the Trustees from a group of parents.

One colourful tradition came to an end in 1834, just before control of the School passed from the Corporation to the Charity Trustees. The Municipal Corporations Act of 1835 not only severed the School's official links with the Mayor but also abolished the ceremonial of mayor-making itself. Head Boys of King Edward's were no longer obliged to suffer the prospect of making speeches in Latin in front of a disting-uished gathering in the Guildhall. But during the final years of a tradition, which had first begun in 1600, these young scholars had been better treated than ever before. From 1826 the Speech Maker had been rewarded with a valuable prize of books, had been invited to join guests at the civic dinner—and had been required to compose the speech himself!

The School itself varied enormously in size during the sixty years at present under review. Its high point, numerically, was reached in 1860 under Mr. Fagan with 103 boys on the School roll. Its lowest ebb occurred in 1823 with 11 boys on the arrival of Mr. Pears. On the whole, numbers fluctuated between 60 and 80. Fees remained fairly constant, as reflected by a prospectus issued in the time of Mr. Pears. Day Scholars were charged 16 guineas a year, Day-Boarders (who had lunch at School) 30 guineas and Boarders 60 guineas. Parents were, however, re-assured that 'the additional expense of a Boarder, including the bills of the stationer, tailor and shoemaker for repairs, pocket money etc. does not usually amount to five pounds in each half year'. Private boarders who required a separate bedroom and a separate study were charged 120 guineas a year.

One physical change of note took place in the 1850's when the Headmaster lost his private drawing room (now, of course, the Headmaster's Study in the Junior School). It was taken over by the Trustees as a Board Room for their meetings, equipped with table, chairs, carpet and an iron safe. By 1859 a portrait of Edward VI, presented by Mrs. Street, graced its walls. Urged on by a growing sense of historical heritage, the Trustees also bought a tin box in 1865 for the purpose of protecting the Charter.

The 1849 Scheme and the Ruin of the School

The new Scheme for the management of the School was finally issued by the Court of Chancery on 9 June, 1849, although its terms were not really implemented until 1852. Its basic objective was to bring about three main reforms—the introduction of a greater number of free Foundationers, the widening of the syllabus in order to cater for that type of boy and the imposition of restrictions on the running of the School by the Master.

The exact number of boys to be admitted as free scholars was to depend 'upon the state of the revenues of the said charity . . . but, as a general rule, the number of scholars to be admitted shall be in the ratio of one scholar for every £4 paid to the headmaster'. When, therefore, the Trustees finally decided that the initial salary offered was to be £200 (although the Scheme had actually suggested £400), the maximum number of Foundationers permissible was fifty. The scheme furthermore stipulated that before the number (or the Headmaster's salary) could be increased, the Trustees were first to establish up to four leaving Exhibitions for use by able Foundationers at University. Few qualifications were required for entry into the School. Candidates for election by the Trustees were to be at least seven years of age, to be nominated by twenty ratepayers and to be able to read English 'with tolerable facility'.

The range of subjects offered was to be considerably increased. Gone were the days when Foundationers could be thrust at will into Latin classes before they could even write properly in English. Clause 8 stipulated:

> That the scheme of education for the free scholars of the School shall comprise instruction in the Greek and Latin languages, and all subjects requisite for a good classical education; and, also, instruction in mathematics, arithmetic, writing, reading, general English literature, geography, English composition, and sacred and profane history; but all such extended instruction shall be given simultaneously with, and in no case independently of, classical instruction, which shall at all times be regarded and treated as the principal object of the foundation. Instruction shall also be provided for such free scholars as require it in French and German, with the elements of the practical arts and sciences of instruction as shall be fixed by the headmaster, with the approbation of the Trustees.

In order to effect this varied plan of teaching, the Scheme envisaged the appointment of two assistant masters—the Second or Under Master, who would share the teaching of the older boys with the Headmaster, and the Third Master or Usher, who would concentrate on the 3 R's with the younger boys. They would be paid by the Trustees.

Perhaps the most revolutionary change, however, was the Master's loss of independent control over the affairs of the School. For over two hundred and eighty years the Corporation had allowed the Master to enjoy total freedom from any form of interference. The impending change was perhaps best symbolised by the alteration in his title. No longer was he to be styled the *Master*, which implied full supremacy. In future he would be called the *Headmaster* which would not even hint at any possible diminution in the power of the Trustees.

They—and not the Headmaster—were to elect the Foundationers. For his part, he was required to submit half-yearly reports to the Trustees on the progress of the free scholars. In other ways, too, he was hampered by restrictions. A limit was placed on the number of private boarders (30) and day boys (50) he was permitted to take for his own profit. Hours of work and length of holidays were all laid down in advance. Although in disciplinary matters he had the right to expel or suspend any free scholar, the Trustees were empowered to overrule his decision after an appeal from the parents. Appointment and dismissal of the Second and Third Masters, tasks which had previously been undertaken by the Master himself, were now made the responsibility of the Trustees. Finally, in spite of his continued tenancy of the Charlcombe Rectory, he was required to live in the School House.

All this proved quite too much for Mr. Pears and his family. He was already an old and disillusioned man. For some time he had left the running of the School in the hands of his son James (who had, of course, been his Second Master). Towards the end he only paid occasional visits to the schoolroom, where he was known affectionately as 'The Old Man'. In fact, although still nominally Master of the School, he left Bath for good two years before his death. By that time he was broken in health and depressed in spirit at the impending ruin of the School. He died, at the age of seventy-six, on 21 January, 1853 at his daughter's home in Wilcot.

Meanwhile, a dramatic twist to the course of events had already taken place. James Pears, described later by one of his former pupils as 'a sarcastic, irritable man with stupid lads', had decided that he would not wait to endure the agony of a further influx of Foundationers. Consequently, in June 1851, he left the School—and took with him thirty-three boarders (out of a boarding house of thirty-five and a total School of seventy-seven). Amongst those who left were most of the boys with prominent connections with the East India Company. With them went some of the Assistant Masters to re-establish his father's old school at Woodcote House, renaming it Windlesham School.

King Edward's was temporarily left in the hands of a younger brother, Edmund Pears, who battled on until the middle of 1853. A year earlier the dreaded deluge had occurred. In May, 1852, the Trustees had decided on an immediate election of forty additional Foundationers without the slightest test of ability. There was no thought of increasing the numbers gradually to enable the school to adjust and adapt by stages. Instead, Broad Street was suddenly flooded with boys of little ability, poor grounding and slight motivation. The limited resources of the Trustees were squandered in one quick move with little held in reserve for improvement of facilities, payment of staff or provision of leaving Exhibitions. Although their ideals were worthy, their actions were both impetuous and irresponsible. The character of a famous school with a long academic tradition had been changed overnight. Headmasters would in future find it increasingly difficult to attract private pupils of ability and promise, either as boarders or even as dayboys, into an atmosphere that was hardly conducive to the highest scholarship. When Edmund Pears handed over in the summer of 1853, the reputation of the School lay in ruins.

The Total Despair of Mr. Macleane (1853–1858)

The man who first experienced the full consequences of the new scheme of 1849 was the Rev. Arthur John Macleane, elected from a list of thirty-five candidates on 3 May, 1853. Educated at Winchester and Cambridge, he came to King Edward's from Brighton College where he had established a fine reputation as Principal. A man of renowned scholarship, he had produced editions of Horace, Juvenal and Persius, as well as editing a series of classical authors for schools.

What clearly attracted him to the new post was the challenge of re-establishing the School's academic reputation, added to the financial advantages which appeared to be real. For although the Trustees had negotiated a comparatively low starting salary (£200) with the new Headmaster, Mr. Macleane could still look forward to enjoying the revenue from both the Charlcombe Rectory and his own private pupils. The thirty fee-paying boarders and fifty dayboys permitted under the Scheme would, in theory, produce an income of £2,500 a year. Prospects, therefore, looked good in the summer of 1853 for the School and for the Headmaster. Indeed, before the year was out, Dr. George Norman (a distinguished Old Boy) was to say: 'I feel a thorough conviction that under this government, the Bath Grammar School will rise like a Phoenix from her ashes.'

This was not to be. Mr. Macleane's driving ambitions to raise the standard of scholarship among the free Foundationers were frustrated at every turn both by the Trustees and by

The Rev. Arthur Macleane, Headmaster 1853–1858.

School Archives

the parents themselves. His initial hopes and high expectations were concisely expressed in a letter to the Trustees just two days after his appointment: 'I am anxious to secure such assistance as shall be the first and a certain step towards raising the character of the School.' The Trustees rejected his plea for additional staff to cope with the mass influx of Foundationers. Funds were simply not available.

By the beginning of his first term as Headmaster, the harsh reality of the situation had already struck him. As early as 12 September, 1853, Mr. Macleane wrote a gloomy, eight-page letter to the Trustees outlining his dreadful predicament. He made two main points. First, he stressed that his 'desire to raise the position of the School in the estimation of the country' was dependent chiefly on the recruitment of a large number of private pupils. These scholars were vital, at a time when funds were low, to subsidise the appointment of quality staff. Bath, a city with a world-wide reputation, was an ideal location for making 'the school one of the most important in England'. In reality, however, the private pupils had virtually disappeared. The boarders had been taken *en bloc* by Mr. James Pears to his new school. All attempts to recruit new ones from among Mr. Macleane's own friends had been frustrated. Many dayboys had drifted away to other schools. Only twelve remained. The truth of the matter was, he argued, that they had all been frightened away by the prospect of mixing with such large numbers of low-class Foundationers:

> But the election of the sons of small tradesmen, unless it be in exceptional cases, has the effect of preventing persons in a different grade of life from sending their sons. They argue naturally that the distinction of such boys is widely different from that of their own children; that their habits and associations are different, and that much practical inconvenience must arise from the mixing during the period of education of classes which cannot meet on equal terms when that age is past.

The result of this shortage of private pupils was a financial crisis for the Headmaster. In order to recruit suitable staff, he had paid the Second Master and an extra Assistant completely out of his own pocket. The whole of the sum allocated by the Trustees for the remuneration of staff (£150) had been given by him to a highly-qualified Third Master.

His second point was that 'on the character of the Foundation must in a great measure depend the character of the entire School.' It was essential to elect the right *type* of boy if the academic reputation of the School was to be salvaged. Mr. Macleane (unlike Mr. Pears) was not personally a social snob. 'I have no sympathy', he wrote, 'with the man who would consider his son contaminated by sitting on the same form with the well behaved son of a humble tradesman, merely on account of his birth'—especially if that boy were one of 'ambition and promise' who intended to continue his studies seriously. But few boys of 'ambition and promise' had been elected by the Trustees. Most of the recent influx were 'still very ignorant'. Furthermore, the School was now bottom-heavy, with four classes composed entirely of Foundationers 'of which the highest are scarcely able to scan a latin verse, and the lowest can hardly spell their own language.' The education for which the school was designed was scarcely suitable for 'boys destined for the lower departments of commerce.'

During the ensuing months, Mr. Macleane repeatedly urged the Trustees to improve the *quality* of boys elected to free places. The pages of the *Minute Books of the Charity Trustees* describe his vain attempts to raise academic standards which had fallen to an appallingly low level. He succeeded at least in persuading the Trustees to agree that future candidates for vacancies should be subjected to tests in writing by dictation, Latin, scripture, geography, and arithmetic. These examinations, however, did little to improve the situation. They merely exposed the abysmal ignorance of the type of boy seeking entry. In his report on the examination of forty-one applicants for two vacancies in September 1853, Mr. Macleane classed eighteen as 'ignorant' or 'very ignorant', thirteen as 'backward' or 'very backward', and only five as at all promising.

In March 1854, he was only able to recommend four candidates for six vacancies out of the thirty-seven who had applied. The others on the list, he suggested, would be 'a positive disadvantage to the School' if elected, 'as well as a departure from the principle of merit involved in the Examination'. The boys had been given 'a printed paper of questions than which easier could hardly have been given without reducing the Examination to an absurdity'. In December 1854 he reported almost in a state of despair. 'It has never been my misfortune to examine so many boys of their age who were all so ignorant.' Even this was not quite so bad as the situation in August 1855 when he submitted 'the worst report' he had yet made.

Although the Trustees paid some lip-service to his wishes, they frequently elected boys of marginal ability to make up the numbers. One candidate, for instance, was elected in March 1855 after being assessed with three 'bad', one 'moderate' and two 'nothing to show' grades in the six tests taken. Furthermore, within the body of Trustees, an increasingly vociferous lobby led by Thomas Jolly opposed not only the principle of examinations, but also the Headmaster's reluctance to fill up numbers with inferior material.

Mr. Macleane was equally depressed at the lack of progress shown by the majority of free Foundationers once they had joined the school. In his quarterly reports to the Trustees on the conduct and performance of these boys he lamented 'that the lower part of the school is still encumbered with a number of boys who make no progress' (March 1854); 'several of the boys who have been two years or more in the school have made no progress at all . . . the advantages of the foundation must not be wasted upon those who are neither willing nor capable of benefiting by them' (June 1854). It was certainly true that many of the boys in the lower classes consistently received 'bad' or 'very bad' assessments for their industry and achievement. This type of boy frequently left early to go into business, discouraged either by the strict approach to discipline or by the compulsion to learn Latin. His parents saw in King Edwards an opportunity for cheap basic education rather than a pathway to academic excellence. The Headmaster had no power to stop this incessant drift from the School.

He tried as best he could to upgrade the status of the free boys. He renamed them the 'King's Scholars' and even attempted to provide them with a distinctive uniform of mortar board and gown. The parents, however, would have none of it. A group of them petitioned the Trustees against such a scheme as being 'injurious to the prosperity of the School'.

Mr. Macleane was nevertheless encouraged in 1854 when the Trustees offered £10 a year to be spent on prizes for Foundationers in Classics, Mathematics, History and Geography. A further boost was given in the same year when a Prize Fund was established out of public subscriptions raised in the memory of the Hon. W. J. Brodrick (Rector of Bath, 1839–1854). Out of this were granted the Brodrick Medals, awarded by the Trustees for academic excellence. Some Foundationers did actually go out to win these Medals before gaining considerable distinction in later life. Of these, one of the best known was Charles Crowden. According to the examiner, his performance in the Sixth form examination of 1854 'would have done credit to any school in the Kingdom'. He was awarded a Brodrick Medal, and £10 worth of books by the Trustees in 1855 as a tribute to his outstanding success on being elected a Scholar of Lincoln College, Oxford. He went on eventually to become Headmaster of Eastbourne College.

Similar achievement could be claimed by Edwin William Watts, who was elected a Foundation Scholar in 1854, gained an Exhibition to Lincoln College, Oxford and later became Headmaster of Newport Grammar School (Isle of Wight). James Edwin Odgers, on the other hand, won a Scholarship at University College, London before finally establishing himself as Principal of Manchester College, Oxford. His brother, William Blake Odgers, was perhaps even more successful. Awarded a Brodrick Medal and a School Leaving Exhibition in 1865, he went first to Trinity Hall, Cambridge before being called to the Bar. He later served as Recorder of Winchester and then of Bristol before taking up an appointment as Professor of Law at Gresham College.

It was this vision of the possibility of academic attainment by bright boys from humble backgrounds that had sustained Mr. Macleane during the early months of his Headmastership. Wishing to boost the morale and the reputation of the School from the outset, he set about organising a Tercentenary Festival of its foundation. This was held on 28 December, 1853 and attended by six other Headmasters from King Edward VI Schools. A group of famous Old Boys was recruited to serve as Stewards of the Festival, including The Lord Clinton, Rear-Admiral Sir Edward Parry, Thomas De Quincey, George Monkland, George Norman and R. Stothert. After a procession to the abbey of Trustees, Stewards, Bath Clergy, visiting Headmasters, Mayor and Corporation, Headmaster and boys, a service was held at which Dr. Kennedy (Headmaster of Shrewsbury School) preached the sermon. After lunch, a public meeting in the Guildhall was followed in the evening by a celebration Dinner at York House. In his speech, Mr. Macleane emphasised his own attitude towards the recruitment of Foundationers from poor families for places at the School:

> These institutions were intended for those who were *apt* at learning . . . We should not , through any false liberalism, drag the poor man out of his natural position, while we should not keep him out of that which the providence of God has designed for him, by giving him ability and aptitude for learning.

This concentration on the able poor did not, as we have seen, meet with the unqualified approval of the Trustees.

By 1856, relationships between the Headmaster and the Trustees had become decidedly strained. Quite apart from differing attitudes over the basic question of the quality and progress of free Foundationers, there now arose three other controversial matters which heightened the conflict. First of all, the Trustees received a letter from a group of parents of Foundationers urging the abolition of flogging. They argued 'that the punishment of birching particularly before the whole School, as practised by the Headmaster of the Bath Grammar School, has a demoralising and brutalising tendency.' Mr. Macleane vigorously defended his right to flog. 'I believe', he stated, 'that if applied with judgment and fairness the mode of punishment referred to is well suited for the correction of moral evil and habitual idleness in young boys. It is resorted to in every public school in the country . . . I cannot, with proper regard for my own efficiency, abandon the course of discipline I have hitherto pursued, with the best effects upon the moral tone of the School'.

Mr. Macleane won immediate support from a rival group of twenty-three parents (also of Foundationers) who wrote to the

Trustees advising them to leave discipline entirely in the hands of the Headmaster. Birching, they argued, 'should be done before the *whole* School in order to deter his schoolmates from following his evil example, particularly in cases of breach of trust or theft.' The Trustees, however, did not agree. After a heated debate, they carried a resolution—passed on the Chairman's casting vote—which stipulated that 'the mode of punishment by birching or flogging on the bare skin is not necessary to the discipline of the school, is very degrading to the individual punished and injurious in its influence on the school at large, and that the Headmaster be requested in future to substitute some other method of enforcing discipline.' The Headmaster refused to co-operate. Consequently, the Trustees decided to appeal to the Charity Commissioners in support of their right to intervene in the management and discipline of the School. By June, 1856 the matter had been settled. The Commissioners ruled that 'the propriety of continuing the practice of corporal punishment should be left by the Trustees (with other matters of internal discipline) to the determination of the Headmaster.

But although Mr. Macleane had won that particular battle, he was becoming increasingly worried by the growing interference of the Trustees in the organisation of the School. The same group of parents had also protested about the playground rules, which reserved that area for the exclusive use of boarders. This, they argued, was unjust. In answer to subsequent pressure brought to bear on him, the Headmaster reluctantly agreed to a compromise. 'In answer to your request'. he wrote, 'I have given the King's Scholars leave to come into the playground behind my house for half-an-hour before morning and afternoon School. I have also given the boys in the head class permission to come in whenever they please'. But he reserved his rights to that area (which traditionally had been part of the Headmaster's house) and would request the Trustees to hire a separate playground for Foundationers if the arrangement became troublesome. The Trustees were furious at this stance.

Relationships were to deteriorate even further in the May of 1856, when they refused Mr. Macleane's request to recommend a successor for the vacant post of Second Master. They insisted that it was their exclusive right to select and appoint both the Second and the Third Masters of the school. By now Mr. Macleane had suffered enough. There was more than a note of resignation in his reply: 'I believe the course hitherto pursued has worked well for the good of the school, but if it be not fully assented to by the Trustees, I think it had better be discontinued . . . What I most desire is harmony, without which the School cannot prosper.' His spirit, as well as his health, was broken. He could battle on no longer for the principles that once had fired his enthusiasm. These had now been permanently stifled by the growing faction in the Trustees, led by Mr. Hunt and Mr. Jolly, who opposed his every move. It is not, therefore, without significance that the Minute Books for the latter part of 1856 and the whole of 1857 are strangely silent about the School's affairs. The Headmaster had completely lost heart.

Frustration had by this time been turned into gloom and despair. Disappointed, disillusioned and completely dispirited, he finally broke down in health, leaving the running of the school during his latter days in the hands of a substitute (Rev. John Bright McCellan). He died at Charlcombe on 14 May, 1858. His family were left in an impoverished state, most of his private resources having been squandered in a futile attempt to improve the internal fabric of the school. An Old Edwardian, writing in 1911, remembered him 'as an awe-inspiring personality, pale, thin, gaunt, who was never known to smile, and had a far-away look in his steel-grey eyes. I suppose the cold shadow of illness was upon him during the last two years before his death. His funeral at Charlcombe Churchyard was attended by all the boys.'

'A Place Full of Young Ragamuffins'

The new Headmaster, elected in 1858, was the Rev. Henry Stuart Fagan. Educated at Pembroke College, Oxford, where he had studied Classics, Mathematics and Physics, he had been ordained into the Anglican Church before starting his teaching career at King Edward's School, Birmingham. He came to Bath as an experienced Headmaster, having served

The Rev. Henry Fagan, Headmaster 1858–1870.

School Archives

for four years in that capacity at Market Bosworth Grammar School.

Although he tried hard at first to recover from the depressing legacy of Mr. Macleane, insuperable difficulties were eventually to combine with weaknesses in his own temperament to cause further tension and unhappiness before he finally left in 1870. In spite of a new restriction of the number of boarders (limited now to a total of four), Mr. Fagan quickly increased the size of the school. Inheriting a mere 65 in August 1858, of whom 50 were free Foundationers, he had boosted the figure to an impressive 103 by February 1860. There was, at the same time, a most noticeable upsurge in the popularity of the 'new' subjects. No fewer than 86 boys were studying French, 76 Drawing and 42 German. Accommodation previously used for boarding purposes (including the Dining Room) was being speedily absorbed for class teaching.

Mr. Fagan, however, was not at all impressed by these apparent signs of recovery. As early as May 1862, he wrote to the Trustees deploring the lack of *quality* in the School and questioning the aims of the education they were providing.

> Our present numbers are ninety-five; of these only twenty-three learn Greek, two, at most, are going in for the Oxford middle class examination. I have been told of a letter in one of the Bath papers contrasting the success of Ipswich School in these examinations with our want of candidates. It is not my wish to give a public answer to this; but I think it right to remind you that we are not in a condition to compete with Grammar Schools. Just at present ours is rather a middle school to which boys come who wish for a cheap commercial education, and who leave us before they have been here long enough to receive that thorough grounding in a few subjects which is needful for success in these examinations. You will excuse my pressing on your consideration the question whether you are satisfied with this, as the purpose of the Grammar School, or *whether you do not think it desirable to try to maintain its character as a school, founded for the advancement of sound learning, and intended not so much to be a place for teaching reading and arithmetic as for training up children of professional men and others in the elements of a high class education.*

This, of course, was no more than Mr. Pears and Mr. Macleane had been saying for years. The traditional quality of the education provided by the School had been totally debased by the influx of unsuitable material. 'Cheap commercial education', far removed from the original intentions of the Founder, had mockingly been seized by unworthy boys who distinguished themselves only by the frequency of their absenteeism and the shortness of their stay.

Rather surprisingly, the Trustees at long last took notice. They set up a sub-committee to discuss with Mr. Fagan 'the future success of the School.' Its report, presented in January 1863, recommended that standards in the entrance examination should be raised, that only boys who attained the required standard should be elected as free scholars, that a university don should be appointed annually to examine the progress of boys currently in the School, that attendances should be regularly recorded by the Headmaster and that boys who neglected their studies were liable to expulsion by the Trustees. New-style entrance examinations were immediately put into operation. Boys under ten were given tests in reading, the rudiments of grammar, writing, arithmetic, scripture and geography. To these were added, for candidates over ten, two papers in either Latin or French.

Mr. Fagan wrote to the Board welcoming these proposals which, in the long term, would undoubtedly bring improvement. In the short term, however, he pleaded with the Trustees to start raising morale and confidence by saying good things about the School in public. It was necessary 'to cry up the School as much and as systematically as by many persons it has hitherto been cried down. I hear perhaps less of what goes on than any one else in Bath, but even I have been startled of late to hear the school spoken of by the persons connected with it as "not a mixed school but something lower", a place full of young ragamuffins. It will need an effort on the part of well-wishers to persuade parents in professions that this is not so.'

The Trustees, at least for a time, gave support to the Headmaster's aspirations. Parents of Foundationers were reminded forcibly of the rules on regular attendance. Two boys were even sent official letters threatening expulsion if their record did not improve. But undoubtedly the most encouraging development was the establishment in 1861 of the first university leaving Scholarship. Provided jointly by the Mayor, the M.P. for Bath and two Trustees, it was worth £40 a year for four years to 'the best scholar in the school', selected by examination. All boys, whether Foundationers or fee-payers, were eligible. Able pupils were, therefore, given a much-needed incentive to stay on and complete their course in the top class.

Mr. Fagan would, nevertheless, have preferred a more drastic solution to his current problems. In May 1862 he advocated a revolutionary plan aimed at giving the School a completely fresh chance to restore its former character and excellence. The scheme was to transfer King Edward's to a site on Lansdown, which was shortly to become vacant.

'One argument, to my mind, for removing the School to Lansdown and cutting it off from its present associations, is just this—that we should then get a class of candidates who would appreciate such an education as a grammar school ought to give. I think the main arguments for that removal are: *1st.* the greater healthiness of the situation (specially important for those who will in after life have to work down in the City); *2nd,* the playground and cricket field close at hand; here it is all but impossible to hold boys together for any general games; we have been playing football with fields of 7 and now got 12 or so down for cricket. The boys disperse and cannot be got together for any common purpose. Thus one of the most valuable elements in school life, the feeling which grows up from joining in common sports, is lost, and the boys wander in twos and threes about the streets, a practice for many reasons very undesirable. The only valid objection urged against this removal is distance—surely not greater than that which most schoolboys throughout England have to walk. Dinner for a number could be provided at so cheap a rate as to do away with the need of coming down in the middle of the day. Wishing to get some notion of the parents' feelings on the subject, I had the enclosed paper taken round by one of the boys. The result gives twenty-six *foundationers* for, seven against. Total for 34, against 12.'

The Headmaster clearly hoped that the 'ragamuffins' at present in the School would find the journey to Lansdown too exacting. He was also beginning to feel, as others were to feel later, that the Broad Street site was far too confined for either health or development. He was certainly starting to reflect a growing belief in nineteenth century public schools that team games held the key to community spirit and achievement. Unfortunately, his forward-looking plans, which even envisaged school dinners and parental questionnaires, were quickly dashed to the ground. The Trustees simply ruled that 'it was not desirable to remove the School' to Lansdown.

Mr. Fagan had good reasons for wishing to escape from the reputation that King Edward's had acquired in Broad Street. It is true that his 'ragamuffins' cared little for learning and less for the reputation of the School. But it is also true that Mr. Fagan was not suited to the task of controlling them. Consequently, there was, during his term of office, a serious crisis in discipline.

A letter of complaint to the Trustees from the Rector of St. Michael's in December 1861 underlined how far behaviour had deteriorated since Mr. Fagan's arrival at the School. —'The windows of my Parochial School Rooms have sustained, (especially during the last two years) considerable damage from balls and stones, thrown from the playground of the Grammar School. In former years (as my Schoolmaster tells me) panes of glass, from time to time, were broken by balls, *never* by stones.' The Rector delivered a bill to Mr. Fagan in person 'together with 27 stones, which had been picked up in the School Rooms.' Mr. Fagan declined to pay, and recommended that the Rector should lay his case before the Trustees, 'as during play hours', he claimed, 'the boys are not under my charge'. 'I can only say', observed the Rector, 'that in my humble judgment they *ought* to be.' The Trustees inclined to agree with the judgment, but not with the claim. When, however, eighteen months later a similar complaint was made, they felt obliged to pay St. Michael's £3 in compensation.

Meanwhile, the boys had clearly developed something of a taste for breaking windows. In April 1865, after an inspection of School premises, the Trustees drew to the attention of the Headmaster the inordinately large number of broken and cracked windows which were to be found within the School itself. He was instructed to ascertain the names of boys who wilfully damaged school property in that way. Even as late as

1869, a neighbour, Mr. Broad, was still complaining of 'a window having been broken by stones flung from the School playground.'

Playground behaviour certainly left a lot to be desired. The gift in 1860 by Mr. Dowding, a Trustee, of 'swings and gymnastic poles' had quickly been vandalised. Six years later the swings and ropes were removed, by order of the Trustees, as being 'dangerous and out of order'. A threat to remove the remainder of the gymnastic equipment was made in 1869 after a complaint from another neighbour, Mr. Webster, about the bad conduct of the boys in the playground. Their disgraceful pranks, which included trespassing on adjoining property, resulted, in the opinion of the Board, 'from want of proper supervision'. Mr. Fagan promised the Trustees that he would establish 'better discipline' in that area and consequently appointed a 'Playground Monitor'.

These periodic complaints were but an outward sign of a serious situation which was developing within the School. The crisis really broke in September 1864, when the Second Master, Rev. O. H. L. Packman, made an official complaint to the Trustees about the discipline and management of the School. They felt that the accusations raised against the Headmaster of laxity in control and neglect in teaching were sufficiently grave as to warrant a full investigation. Their findings expressed deep regret at 'the state of feeling which appears to exist between the Head Master and the Second master, which feeling is most painful to the Trustees and most detrimental to the working of the School'. They went on to 'express to the Headmaster the urgent need there is that additional order, punctuality and discipline should be exercised throughout the School; that the scriptures should be read daily in the school and that the attention of the Head Master should be *wholly given during the hours of the school to the studies of the boys*, and the Trustees would call the earnest attention of the Head Master to the only chance of future success for the school being a union of feeling and a union of work between the Head Master and the Second and Third Masters'.

The scathing criticism of Mr. Fagan implied by this verdict was more than justified. Although he was undoubtedly a fine preacher at Charlcombe Church, he lacked the basic qualities essential in a Headmaster. Good on paper when drafting plans for developments on Lansdown or writing persuasive reports for the Trustees, he was pathetically weak when dealing with human relationships. Choosing to communicate with his small staff by means of the written memo, he frequently failed to support them in the hour of need (see below). Hesitant and indecisive in the face of difficulty, he lacked the moral courage to take unpopular decisions over truculent boys. He longed to escape from the confines of living on the premises to the freedom of Charlcombe Rectory, far away from the pressures of boys.

Endowed by nature with an imposing figure and an impressive long red beard, he nevertheless failed to command the respect of boys and staff, so essential for the well-being of any School. He chose, instead, to adopt the pose of an eccentric who was totally lacking in dignity. A cartoon of him appeared in *Punch*, showing him riding to School from Charlcombe on a small pony with a string of vegetables slung round his neck. Needing at all costs to be liked, his search for cheap popularity was at the root of the playground indiscipline, so bitterly complained about by Broad Street residents. Even one of his former pupils, writing later, found his approach surprising and his impact disturbing.

'Mr. Fagan even countenanced by his presence our crude attempts at making election speeches (in times of political excitement) from the top of the lavatories in the playground, a coign of vantage from which we were usually driven with ignominy by the cruel squirts of the boarders, who bombarded us from their dormitory windows. During Mr. Fagan's time it must be confessed that the relations between the masters were occasionally (to say the least) very strained. When I was head boy I was once sent to fetch a policeman to take up . . . but perhaps I had better draw a veil over an incident which was painful and unprecedented, and yet had its comical side. It was more in line with the adventures of "Midshipman Easy" than with the academic decorum of so distinguished an institution as the Bath Grammar School.'

The smouldering dispute between the Headmaster and Second Master was again referred to the Trustees in November 1864. Their earnest plea that the discipline of the school should be maintained went largely unheeded. A month later they were forced to deal with another serious outbreak of the same problem. There had, apparently, been a most unprofessional and distasteful confrontation between the two men in front of the whole School. Mr. Packman had excluded a boy called Oxley from his class for gross insubordination and failure to produce an imposition. On seeing this, the Headmaster (who had previously expressed his dislike of this type of punishment) ordered the boy back to join the lesson. Mr. Packman refused to accept him. 'I reminded him', he explained to the Trustees 'that I could not have the boys in my class after he had refused to do my work and had stood at that door and hissed while I was going out'. Poor old Oxley was thrust backwards and forwards between the two men as they shouted angrily at each other across the Schoolroom. Finally, Mr. Packman abandoned his teaching for the day, setting his pupils work to do on their own.

In his own defence, Mr. Fagan tried to persuade the Trustees of the Second Master's brutal approach to discipline, reminding them of a previous occasion when Mr. Packman was seen 'rushing at a boy in the middle of class and savagely boxing his ears.' 'His whole idea of discipline,' he continued, 'is *punish, punish*. Only a few days ago he wished me to cane a boy for hissing him as he was leaving School'. He could scarcely have damned himself more thoroughly if he had tried. By those words he demonstrated to the Trustees his pathetic ignorance of the nature of boys and his unforgivable blindness to the feelings of staff. The Trustees, quite rightly, ordered Mr. Packman in future 'to obey the instructions of the Headmaster who has supreme authority in the School'. Their most severe censure, however, was reserved for Mr. Fagan. He was informed 'that they consider he does not maintain the discipline of the School and that in relation to the Second Master he had not afforded him that support which the Trustees consider he had a right to expect'. They clearly hoped that this would settle the issue. The wounds already inflicted, however, could not be healed. Within a month Mr. Packman had resigned after yet another unsavoury incident in the Schoolroom.

Mr. Fagan's years at King Edward's ensured that the

downward trend, already set in motion, continued unchecked. As Headmaster, at this particular point in the history of the School, he was an unmitigated disaster. It was appropriate, therefore, that he should be the one to preside over its official relegation in 1870 to Second Grade Status (see below).

By the Spring of 1867 he was already finding the strain far too great. He pleaded with the Trustees to let him live in 'a more healthy locality' than that of Broad Street. They agreed to allow him to have a 'change of air' for a few weeks on the grounds of ill-health, as they did again in 1869 when he spent three months at Charlcombe. Finally, he faced up to reality. He concluded, what had been apparent to others for years, that he was in the wrong job. When, therefore, he proposed to exchange his living at Charlcombe with that of the Rev. J. R. McDowell, Vicar of St. Just-in-Penwith in Cornwall, the Trustees joyfully agreed. And so, in one of the most curious appointments ever made, Mr. McDowell came to King Edward's in 1870 as the new Headmaster. Mr. Fagan, restored to his true calling as a parish priest, lived on happily for another twenty years.

CHAPTER FOUR

Broad Street—Years of Reorganisation, 1870–1921

'In spite of the unfavourable conditions as to buildings and equipment under which the School is conducted, it is doing in many respects sound and useful work on somewhat old-fashioned lines, and in the main essentials is in a healthy condition.' (Report of the Board of Education Inspectors, 1920.)

City, State and Education, 1870–1921

Bath during this period is vividly remembered by N. V. H. Symons, the youngest son of the Headmaster appointed in 1896. He arrived at the School, when he was just under two years of age, to live with his parents in the front part of the Broad Street building.

'In the entrance hall the room opposite the Headmaster's Study was the Dining Room, above which was my parents' bedroom, while over the Study was the Drawing Room. The other bedrooms were at the top of the school. I remember that there were often on winter mornings wonderful frost patterns on the inside of the nursery windows which I do not remember to have seen anywhere since, which suggests that those days were colder . . .

In those days Bath's streets were lit mainly by gas lamps but there was an electric standard just outside the school. Every day a man came with a satchel full of sticks of carbon about the size of candles. He would wind down the lamp, which was on a long electric cable, and remove the two burnt-out candles and put in new ones. He would throw the stumps of the old candles into the gutter and we often used to seize them to use as crayons. What happened with this kind of electric light was that the two candles just, or almost, touched and the electric current passing between them produced a brilliant whitey-blue flame accompanied by exciting humming and spitting noises.

The streets in Bath had a great dignity with the stately progress of fine carriages drawn by beautiful horses with the coachman and footman in cockaded top hats and fawn liveries with shining brass buttons. Crossing sweepers kept places free of horse droppings for pedestrians and got an occasional copper from kind-hearted citizens. The Bath Chair took ladies up Milsom Street from the Pump Room. They were often greeted by retired Colonels in tussore silk suits. It was said that Milsom Street at mid-day smelt strongly of curry. The only tram in Bath ran between Bathford and the Guildhall and was drawn by horses. When electric trams made their appearance they went much greater distances, right up Combe Down and out to Newton, but they never ran up Lansdown.

The streets were also much livelier and more fun. There were German bands, performing bears, monkeys, and guinea-pigs, barrel-organs and hurdy-gurdies, individual musicians of all kinds as well as singers. There were a number of itinerant sellers—every evening a man with a tray of oysters on his head went through the streets. He used to rather frighten me. Much better, at tea-time, were sellers of muffins and crumpets announcing their progress by ringing a hand-bell which brought the maid servants out. One of the sounds I remember most vividly is that of men sharpening their scythes as they cut the long grass in the Victoria Park.'

Nationally, the country was literally riding the crest of a wave—for this was the golden age of overseas trade and Empire. The Industrial Revolution at home had put Britain ahead of the world in the production of manufactured goods. Her Navy commanded the seas. Politicians, like Disraeli and Chamberlain, whipped up a frenzy of Imperialism, which made Queen Victoria Empress of India and encouraged Cecil Rhodes to tap the wealthy resources of South Africa. Patriotic fervour followed the troops as they set sail to fight in the Boer War at the turn of the century. Thereafter, the smell of war hung rather heavily in the air as Germany mounted its industrial, naval and imperial challenge under the Kaiser's ambitious leadership. Against this background, the School—like many others of its kind—founded its Cadet Force. The First World War (1914–1918) made serious demands on the youth of the country, as Old Edwardians and Masters alike found to their cost. Heavy inflation, which accompanied the war and the post-war years, was to add further pressure to the School's unhealthy financial state. These were also the years of social reform, largely inspired by· Lloyd George and the Liberal Government (1905–1914). National insurance, old age pensions and fair wage settlements were some of the policies implemented at Westminster, which had surprising repercussions at Broad Street. (See below.)

Successive governments made great strides during the period to set up a national system of education. The Education Act of 1870 established School Boards in each district to try and plug gaps by building Elementary Schools in areas where Church Schools did not exist. School attendance, which in 1880 had been made compulsory between the ages of five and thirteen, was made free of charge at all Board Schools in 1891. The Education Act of 1902 (Balfour's Act) abolished the School Boards and established Local Education Authorities, which were responsible for co-ordinating all elementary and secondary education in their areas. They were, furthermore, given the power to build and control grammar schools of their own.

Old Endowed Grammar Schools, like King Edward's, were gradually invited to play a part in the new system. It was hoped that their long tradition of scholarship, greatly valued at the time, could be made more freely available on the new educational ladder. Hence the Endowed Schools Act of 1869 attempted to introduce some modernisation and reform into these establishments by drawing up a new scheme of management for each school after a thorough inspection. The Schools retained their independence and, from 1872, were managed by Boards of Governors, who were answerable to the Charity Commissioners in London. Each School was, however, carefully graded and given a specific objective (see below). After the Report of the Royal Commission on Secondary Schools (1895), an Act of 1899 set up a central Board of Education to take general responsibility for all aspects of education. Endowed Schools, therefore, passed from the control of the Charity Commissioners to the control of the Board. They became subject to official Inspections, (which were held at King Edward's School, for instance, in 1904, 1912 and 1920). These Inspectors' Reports were purely advisory in nature, but substantial benefits in the form of grant aid awaited those old Grammar Schools which applied for 'Recognised' status.

Although such a step did not mean surrendering their independent status, it did involve the modernisation of both buildings and teaching methods, together with the acceptance of 'free place' boys from the Local Education Authority. The Governors of King Edward's resisted such a move as long as they could.

A Second Grade School

The Endowed Schools Act of 1869 echoed a general feeling that changes needed to be made in the organisation and attitude of the country's ancient Grammar Schools. Based on detailed investigations made by the Schools Inquiry Commission (the Taunton Commission), the Act authorised the drawing up of new schemes of management for the schools in question. The Trustees of King Edward's School had, from early in 1867, been in close communication with the Commissioners as they set about their work of inspecting and assessing the worth of each establishment. Their Report on King Edward's, issued in 1869, complained: 'The standards of education and discipline are below average. The condition of the school is unsatisfactory.' Mr. Fitch, the Assistant Commissioner, conducted a number of personal meetings with the Trustees in 1870 before details of the new scheme for the school were finally agreed. Reluctantly, the Trustees were obliged to accept what in reality was now inevitable. King Edward's School was officially classed as a 'School of Second Grade'.

The down-grading of a school which had achieved national fame and academic distinction under Mr. Morgan in the eighteenth century, was the bitter climax of thirty disastrous years. Charity Commissioners and Charity Trustees had together combined to destroy the School's foundations of academic excellence, to ruin its local reputation for disciplined, cultured pupils and to undermine the confidence of a succession of talented Headmasters. In classifying schools, the Commissioners had decided that 'the grade of the School depends on the head form, and the character of the head form depends on the age up to which the majority of pupils stay at the school . . . First Grade Schools are those whose special function is the formation of a learned or literary, and a professional or cultured class. This is the class whose school life continues till 18 or 19, and would naturally end in the universities'. With the prolonged influx of poorly-qualified Foundationers, King Edward's School was no longer in any position to fulfil these conditions.

As a Second Grade School, with a leaving age of about sixteen, it would now be expected to cater for boys whose parents were less well off, or who wished to enter careers requiring early special training, (e.g. business, the Army, etc.). Latin would be retained, but would be supplemented by 'a certain amount of thorough knowledge of those subjects which can be turned to practical use in business'. The Trustees tried in vain to persuade the Endowed Schools Commission to establish *two* Schools under the King Edward's endowment in Bath—a First Grade School (with a Classical curriculum) and a Second Grade School (with a Modern curriculum), each with its own Headmaster.

The New Scheme came into force on 25 June, 1872. Management of the School and its endowment property passed from the Charity Trustees to a new Board of Governors, consisting of three ex-officio Governors (the Mayor of Bath, the Chairman of the Bath Royal Literary and Scientific Institution and the Chairman of the Bath School Board), four representative Governors (to be elected by the Bath City Council) and eight co-optative Governors. The Governors were required to pay £280 per annum out of endowment funds towards the support of St. Catherine's Hospital, (which remained under the control of the Charity Trustees). This sum continues to be paid by the Governors to this day.

Under the terms of the Scheme, all rights to the revenues from the Charlcombe Rectory were sold for the benefit of the School. They were bought in 1874 for £1,900 by an outsider and were thus no longer available to supplement the salary of the Headmaster. In future the Headmaster was to receive a fixed stipend of £150 a year plus a capitation fee for each boy in the School. Assistant Masters and teaching apparatus were to be paid for out of a sum granted to the Headmaster for that purpose. The Scheme certainly went a long way to restoring the authority of the Headmaster within the School. Although the Governors retained final jurisdiction over curriculum, fees, holidays and buildings, full consultation in these matters would always take place with the Headmaster. He was, furthermore, given complete control over the internal organisation, management and discipline of the School, including the right to expel a boy, and the sole power of appointing and dismissing all Assistant Masters.

The most significant change brought about by the New Scheme was undoubtedly the abolition of that notorious system for the recruitment of Free Foundationers. No longer would boys of low educational standards be able to qualify for free Places at King Edward's simply by gaining the nomination of a few worthy citizens and by passing a pathetically easy entrance test. All boys in future were required to pay fees ranging from £6 per annum for Juniors and £9 for Seniors. Exemption from these fees could only be gained on the basis of academic merit. Foundation Scholarships were granted either to new boys on the result of the annual Entrance Examination or to boys already in attendance on the basis of their performance in the internal Examination. A 'Senior' Scholarship entitled the holder to full remission of fees, whereas a 'Junior' Scholarship covered just half the cost and was normally granted to boys in the Junior Department. Foundation Scholars, limited to a maximum of twenty per cent of the total number in the School, were liable to forfeit their awards for bad conduct or poor work. Thus a new impetus was given to the restoration of the School's academic reputation. No longer would it be called locally 'The Free School'. The Scheme specified that its official name henceforth was to be King Edward's School, Bath.

It was to be divided into two sections—a Junior Department (taking boys from the ages of seven to fourteen) and a Senior Department (taking boys from the ages of ten to seventeen). Subjects for study in the Senior Department were to consist of English, Latin, French, German, Arithmetic, Mathematics, Geography, Natural Science, Ancient and Modern History, Political Economy, Drawing, Vocal Music and Drilling. Greek became an optional extra. All boys were to be examined annually by an external Examiner who would report to the Governors on the standards and discipline of the

School. The Headmaster himself was also required to make an annual report to the Governors and to keep a Register of Applications. The Scheme did not rule out the possibility of Boarders, either as lodgers in the homes of the Masters or as residents in a proper boarding house. As funds became available, the Governors were instructed to consider the education of girls, the establishment of a Preparatory School and the setting up of a pension fund for the Headmaster. Meanwhile, the School year was firmly divided into three terms with holidays at Christmas (four weeks), Easter (two weeks) and Summer (six weeks).

When the School re-opened under the New Scheme on 20 August, 1872, only 41 boys were present (21 in the Senior Department and 20 in the Junior). Parents of the old Free Foundationers had been warned in advance that only those elected *before* the passing of the Endowed Schools Act of 1869 could continue to receive free education after the Summer of 1872. Only fourteen boys qualified on this basis. The remaining thirty-one Foundationers were faced with the choice of either leaving or paying the full school fees. Many of them left.

The Rev. John McDowell, 1870–1874

Mr. McDowell became Headmaster of King Edward's School in a most extraordinary manner. In 1870 the Trustees of the School, anxious no doubt to rid themselves of Mr. Fagan, sanctioned an exchange of livings between Mr. McDowell (as Vicar of St. Just-in-Penwith) and Mr. Fagan (as Rector of Charlcombe). Although they had carefully examined Mr. McDowell's testimonials before appointing him Headmaster, they found it unnecessary—for reasons best known to themselves—to subject him to any kind of interview. This, as events were to prove later, was a disastrous decision. For in spite of sound academic qualifications as a graduate of Trinity College, Dublin, he was both sickly in health and completely devoid of any teaching experience. It is almost unbelievable that the Charity Trustees could take their duties so lightly at a time when a vigorous and enterprising Headmaster was clearly needed to implement the demands of the New Scheme. Their action is yet another example of the ruinous effect they had had on the school over a period of thirty years. Its gradual recovery dates from that moment in 1872 when the Trustees handed over their control of the School to the new Board of Governors. The ghost of Mr. Morgan must have breathed a big sigh of relief!

The Governors, meanwhile, were having their patience stretched to breaking point in dealing with that unfortunate legacy bequeathed to them by the Trustees—Mr. McDowell.

School Group, 1872; The Rev. J. R. McDowell (Headmaster, 1870–1874) seen standing on extreme left.

In October 1873, for instance, they were absolutely horrified to read in the press that the County Court had ordered their Headmaster to be committed to prison for eighteen days. He had failed to re-pay a debt, for which judgment had already been issued by the Court. The Governors met hurriedly to discuss the situation and warned McDowell that any repetition of this behaviour would be 'so injurious to the School as to warrant their most serious action'. In the immediate future, because it was 'essential to the prosperity of the School' that the debts be paid off, they demanded that he should submit to them a complete account of his liabilities and assets.

Their main concern with the Headmaster, however, was over the extent of his involvement with the School. He was

frequently absent and often late without ever making arrangements for the discharge of his duties. In June 1873, the
Governors insisted that 'in future he should attend school at
its opening each day and should not absent himself from it
without communicating with the Governors through the
Clerk'. This warning seems to have had little effect. Six
months later, the Board of Governors received two letters
from parents complaining of his 'gross neglect' of the School,
his unpunctuality and his irregularity of attendance. On
detailed investigation, the Governors found that these complaints were well-founded. They therefore invited the Headmaster 'to consider if, in the uncertain state of health to which
he attributes his irregularities, he will place his resignation in
their hands'. Mr. McDowell refused to resign, asking instead
to be allowed six months grace in which to prove himself.

After lengthy discussion at their meeting in January, 1874,
the Governors decided to sack him. He was to be given six
months notice to leave at the end of the Summer Term. But
when they met again shortly afterwards to confirm their
decision, they agreed to modify their original proposal. After
reading various letters sent by Mr. McDowell, they accepted a
written undertaking from him that he would reside at the
School House (or within a quarter of a mile from it), arrive at
School by 9.00 a.m. daily, give his whole attention to the work
of the School and resign in the Summer of 1875.

Events, however, were soon to overtake them all. Whatever
his personal faults, there can be no doubt that Mr. McDowell
was a sick man. By March 1874, he was again confined to bed
with a serious illness. On 18 May, he died at the age of
forty-nine. The Governors wrote a letter of sympathy to his
wife, in which they chose to praise 'his domestic virtues'
rather than his talents as a schoolmaster.

The Rev. Henry Sanderson, 1874–1896

The Rev. H. E. Sanderson, selected as the new Headmaster
from a short-list of three, was a Scholar of Sidney Sussex
College, Cambridge. An accomplished student of Classics, he
had previously held the position of Second Master at Dedham
Grammar School in Essex. Later described by a former pupil

The Rev. Henry Sanderson, Headmaster 1874–1896.

School Archives

as 'ardent and clever', Mr. Sanderson immediately brought much-needed vigour and enthusiasm onto the scene, which greatly impressed the Governors. Indeed, from the outset, relationships between the Board and the Headmaster were noticeably harmonious. Entries in the Minute Books reveal a depth of trust and co-operation which stand in stark contrast to the bitter conflicts aroused by the unwise meddling of the Charity Trustees.

The new Governing Body was a well-balanced unit, drawing on the experience and wisdom of a wide range of distinguished local people. Apart from the Mayor of Bath (an ex-officio member), the original Board appointed in 1872 included Sir Jerom Murch (Chairman of the Royal Literary and Scientific Institution), the Rev. Charles Kemble (Rector of Bath and Chairman of the Bath School Board), Richard King (draper), Benjamin Bartrum (auctioneer), Randel Falconer (doctor), Robert Commons (chemist), Thomas Jolly (businessman), Edmund Bagshawe (surgeon), George Moger (banker), and William Titley (provision dealers)—the last five of whom had also seen long service as Charity Trustees. These men, and others who later replaced them, threw themselves into the work with energy, pride and understanding. Intensely ambitious for the reputation of the School, they endeavoured by various means to improve both the quantity and quality of the annual intake. Ever conscious of the long-standing tradition built up by King Edward's over the centuries, they were nevertheless flexible in adapting to the changing outlook of the world around them. In 1882, for example, they opened their ranks to the first female Governors (Mrs. E. S. J. Pakenham and Miss P. H. Bridges). Naturally expert in business affairs, the Board handled the property and financial interests of the school with great efficiency and skill, gaining a good price (£4169) for the sale of their Town Mills site on the river in 1884.

The new Headmaster responded well to their encouragement. One of his top priorities was clearly to build up the size of the school—and not simply because the size of his salary depended in part upon it. On his appointment in 1874, he had inherited from Mr. McDowell a paltry total of 23 pupils. By 1876 Mr. Sanderson had increased this figure quite dramatically to 105. Although it had temporarily slumped to 71 by 1881, a new peak was reached just ten years later when 125 boys had been entered on the register. This was undoubtedly one of Mr. Sanderson's major achievements during his term of office. Even so, both he and the Governors remained disappointed at the lack of response from the citizens of Bath. As the chief guest at the Prize Giving of 1883 remarked: 'The smallness of the number of scholars in the School was a disgrace to the city.'

There were, of course, good reasons for this situation which were not easy to correct in the short term. The School, for instance, faced keen competition from an increasing number of private schools in the area, including The Bath College which opened in 1879. Furthermore, the regulations of the New Scheme had imposed a maximum age limit on pupils of seventeen, which was totally inadequate for boys whose ambition and ability led them to think in terms of University Scholarships. Although it was possible for promising youngsters to apply later for special exemption from this clause, its very existence was a discouragement in itself. Most boys who entered King Edward's tended to leave school early for jobs in local business—a constant drain on the overall numbers which Mr. Sanderson was striving to build up.

The ultimate solution to the problem, of course, depended on the School's ability to raise its academic standards with the limited means at its disposal and then on its persuasive attempts to gain reclassification as a First Grade School. An impressive start was made on this uphill struggle by the joint efforts of the Governors and the Headmaster during the twenty-two years of Mr. Sanderson's regime. He immediately tightened up the discipline, which had become notoriously lax under Mr. Fagan and Mr. McDowell. A distinguished former pupil, J. B. Eames, later described 'the awesome precincts of the big schoolroom' where the Headmaster, 'a strict disciplinarian', presided. He was, nevertheless, highly successful in raising the standard of behaviour to an impressive level—a fact commented on by a succession of visiting examiners. In spite of his desire to increase numbers, he did not hesitate to expel a boy in 1877 who, after being punished for an offence, angrily raced out of School without permission. Few of the complaints from outsiders, which littered the pages of the Trustees' Minute Books in the time of Mr. Fagan, disturbed the deliberations of the new Governing Board. It is true that some scholars were guilty of 'disorderly conduct' in 1880 as they let off steam in Broad Street after the Science Examinations. It is also true that Mr. Sanderson himself was rebuked in 1884 for using 'expressions unbecoming to his position' when he disciplined a boy for using a catapult. Otherwise, however, the citizens of Bath seemed delighted with the improved manners and attitude of the young gentlemen from King Edward's.

In a sustained attempt to raise the standard of work, the

Headmaster introduced two new ideas in 1874—opening the Schoolroom in the evenings to enable boys to do their homework under supervised conditions, and sending monthly reports to parents in the hope that he could gain their active involvement. The Governors, meanwhile, gave their minds to the task of encouragement and motivation. A whole series of new prizes were awarded through the generosity of individual Governors or friends of the School—the Mayor offered a silver gilt medal in 1875 to be competed for at Christmas; J. S. Turner inaugurated an annual prize for French and German after the standard in foreign languages had been seriously criticised by the Examiner in 1891; two Governors' Prizes for Mathematics were granted in 1893; Edmund White established a Prize and Exhibition Fund of £4,000 in 1894; the Silver Brodrick Medals were revived in 1890 (after the original die had been found!) for outstanding academic achievement; and a specially designed die was made so that all prize-winners' books could be suitably stamped.

Full use was also made by the Governors of the power granted to them by the New Scheme to award Exhibitions for merit. By 1876 they were advertising for such Exhibitions to be competed for annually by examination—two for use in the Senior Department and two for use in the Junior Department of the School. Of these, two were reserved for new entrants and two for successful boys already in the School. Interest in these was sufficiently keen for the standard to be maintained. Only on rare occasions was an Exhibition withheld through lack of suitable candidates. In 1889 an attempt was made to extend the area of recruitment even further in the search for able boys. Two additional Exhibitions were offered for boys from the public elementary schools in the city. This experiment, however, was withdrawn in 1892 after misgivings within the Governing Body itself and complaints expressed by the Bath and District Teachers' Association—although boys from elementary schools (such as Bathforum School) were still eligible for the regular Exhibition. The Governors did, however, fulfil the expectations of the New Scheme over the education of girls when, in 1894, they set aside part of their funds to establish two Exhibitions of £16 per annum for the benefit of girls at Bath High School.

A decision of even greater importance was taken, however, in 1878 when it was agreed to award a maximum of four Leaving Exhibitions (one per year) for use at University. These Exhibitions worth £60 per annum and awarded on merit after competitive examination were tenable for a period of four years. The first of these was granted to Robert Herman, who won a Scholarship to Trinity College, Cambridge where he had the distinction of becoming a Senior Wrangler, before eventually being elected a Fellow of the College. Other talented boys who were encouraged by these Leaving Exhibitions to stay on at School to complete their studies included Arthur Withy, who also gained a Scholarship at Trinity College, Cambridge, and eventually became a Governor of the School; Philip Johnstone, who won an Exhibition at Keble College, Oxford; Hugh Cruttwell, who gained an Exhibition at Christ Church College, Oxford before going on to teach at Harrow; James Eames, who won an Exhibition at Worcester College, Oxford and was later appointed Recorder of Bath.

Eventually the Governors extended the original idea of the Leaving Exhibition when, in 1893, they established a Science Exhibition of £60 per annum to be tenable at any College or Polytechnic. This successful attempt to encourage young scientists, who wished to study away from Oxford and Cambridge, immediately bore fruit. Oswald Griffiths became the first holder, having won a Scholarship at the University of Wales College, Aberystwyth. Just before the resignation of Mr. Sanderson in 1896, the Governors created three further Leaving Scholarships of £40 per annum from the revenue of the Edmund White Fund. This enlightened policy helped to re-create a faint glimmer of the School's excellent academic record of former days. Needless to say the Governors lost no opportunity to advertise their proud successes at Prize Givings and even on the back of the School Prospectus. They discussed endlessly at Board Meetings the importance of setting up an Honours board in the School—without ever managing to achieve it!

The annual Prize Giving (or The Public Day as it was called) was an important public relations exercise. Chaired by the Mayor of Bath and held in the Guildhall during late

December or January, it was an occasion that attracted considerable public interest and critical press comment. The Governors seized the opportunity to parade a long line of distinguished former pupils as the Prize-Givers—Sir Bartle Frere, Dr. Blake Odgers, Dr. Bartrum, Canon Fleming, the Dean of Windsor and R. A. Herman. These obliged by offering encouragement, praise and stirring reminiscence. The most tense moment in the year, however, came when the Special Examiner (appointed by the University of Cambridge Syndicate) read his report on the Examination of the School conducted in December. These reports, detailed in content and critical in tone, spared no punches and were not given to flattery. Handwriting and spelling were frequently condemned, as was the cramped, dark and smoke-filled atmosphere of Broad Street. Individual forms and particular subjects were, on occasions, subjected to public rebuke—'In my opinion this subject (Geography) does not receive as much attention as it deserves'. 'In the upper classes the answers to the papers were very meagre and unsatisfactory, and betrayed surprising ignorance'. Nevertheless, the School, on the whole, came out of this searching scrutiny surprisingly well. Examiners regularly praised 'the demeanour and behaviour of the boys, which left nothing to be desired'. Mr. Payne, the Examiner in 1882, went even further: 'On the whole, the work of the School seems to be thoroughly satisfactory. Many of the papers sent in to me were really excellent, and several of the younger boys showed much promise.' A note of high optimism was struck in 1887 by Mr. Taylor, who, after examining the School, declared that 'the name of the School will again be heard in the Universities'.

The members of the Governing Board listened eagerly and attentively. They were quick to follow up with the Headmaster every trace of criticism or weakness—whether it be the lack of proper Games Field (1881), weakness in the teaching of Modern Languages (1890), the lack of technical education (1890) or the need for more 'teaching power' (1875). Mr. Sanderson was firmly, but politely kept up to the mark. The Governors, however, were equally quick to congratulate success and encourage initiative. This was particularly noticeable over the annual results of public examinations taken by boys from the school—namely, the Oxford Local Examinations and the examinations of the Art and Science Department at South Kensington.

In 1877 the Board had expressed their concern at the very small number of scholars who were being entered for the Oxford Locals—often no more than one a year. Mr. Sanderson responded to this pressure as best he could. By 1881 the number of entries had risen to eleven, all of whom had passed. Even so, on analysing detailed performances, the Governors were disturbed to notice the large number of failures in music. Gradually their active involvement reaped its rewards. In the Examinations of 1887, Tovey was placed first in Drawing in the whole of England. Four years later, Eames distinguished himself even more by being placed third in England in the overall assessment. When, in 1892, eight boys gained a total of seventeen distinctions, the Chairman of Governors made a personal visit to the School to congratulate the boys.

The same pattern was largely true with the Examinations of the Art and Science Department at South Kensington, which were actually invigilated at Broad Street by a team of Governors. Early attempts at these examinations (which tested drawing, geometry, inorganic chemistry, magnetism and electricity) were disastrous. In 1878, for instance, 20 out of the 25 boys who took the drawing examination failed, as did all 26 candidates in the inorganic chemistry paper. The Governors were furious. They were, however, quick to congratulate all concerned at the Prize Giving of 1882 when they received the much-improved results of that year with 'sincere pleasure, hoping that the gratifying results of the exertions of the Headmaster and his Assistant Masters will lead to the increase of the numbers of pupils availing themselves of the opportunities of King Edward's School'.

Nor were the Governors slow to provide additional staffing and accommodation, which increased numbers inevitably made necessary. A 'Mathematical Master' (Mr. W. E. Sadd) was appointed for the first time in 1876 when, in addition, a full-time Modern Languages and Drawing Master (Mr. E. Ehrke) replaced the part-time 'Professors' who had previously given instruction. Extra space for the influx of new boys was created partly by the equipping of 'a room under the small

continued on page 138

King Edward's School, Bath.

(An Endowed Grammar School, founded by King Edward VI., and subject to Regulations embodied in a Scheme approved by Her Majesty in Council on the 25th day of June, 1872.)

GOVERNORS.

THE MAYOR OF BATH.

Mr. R. D. COMMANS. J.P., *Chairman.*

Mr. J. S. BARTRUM, J.P., *Vice-Chairman.*

Mr. C. F. MARSHALL, J.P.	Miss BRIDGES.	Mr. WALTER PITT, M. Inst. C.E.
Mr. W. C. JOLLY, J.P.	Mr. R. H. MOORE.	Gen. R. Q. MAINWARING.
Mr. J. CHAFFIN, J.P.	Mr. J. W. MORRIS, F.L.S.	Mr. B. H. WATTS.
Mrs. PAKENHAM.	Mr. E. A. BAGSHAWE, J.P., M.A.	

Clerk : Mr. F. ERNEST SHUM.

Head Master :

Rev. H. E. SANDERSON, M.A., Late Senior Scholar of Sidney Sussex College, Cambridge.

Assistant Masters :

Mr. W. E. SADD, B.A , Late Scholar of S. Catherine's College, Cambridge.

Mr. R. S. CRUMP, M.A., late Exhibitioner of Queen's College, Oxford.

Mr. W. B. LANGRIDGE, London University.

Professor of Modern Languages : Herr EDWARD EHRKE.   **Teacher of Vocal Music :** Mr. F. WATTS.

Lecturer on Natural Science : Mr. GATEHOUSE.   **Drill Master :** Sergt. DARGAN.

King Edward's School, Bath,

Enjoys, from its ancient endowments and modern developments, the advantage of being able to afford an Education of high efficiency, qualifying either for a University career, or Commercial and Professional pursuits, at a cost to parents and guardians exceptionally moderate.

The Governors are impressed with the importance of boys being sent to the School at the earliest suitable age. The Junior School is open to Boys of the age of seven, and it is the experience of the Governors that those who have entered young have ever proved the most successful in the School and in after life.

School Charges.

The School is divided into Two Departments—Boys between the ages of 7 and 14 are eligible for the Junior Department, and between the ages of 14 and 17 for the Senior Department. The Tuition Fees are £6 per annum in the Junior, and £9 per annum in the Senior Department There are three terms in the year, and the Tuition Fees are paid in advance at the commencement of each term.

An Extra Fee of £1 per term is payable for tuition in Greek.

Subjects of Instruction.

In the Junior Department —Reading and Writing, English Language and Literature. Arithmetic, Elements of Geometry, English History, Geography, Rudiments of One Branch of Natural Science, Latin or some Modern Language, Drawing, Vocal Music, Drilling.

In the Senior Department—English, Latin, French and German Languages and Literatures, Arithmetic and Mathematics, Geography, at least One Branch of Natural Science, Ancient and Modern History, Political Economy, Drawing, Vocal Music, Drilling.

At the commencement of every Term a Special Class is formed for Boys intending to compete in the Oxford Local Examination, or preparing for the Universities or for appointments in any branch of the Civil Service.

University and College Exhibitions.

The Governors have from time to time granted Exhibitions tenable at the Universities of Oxford and Cambridge. The Governors being desirous of encouraging the study of Science in he School, and so extending the opportunities of its scholars in the choice of a calling in life, have determined to extend the Grant of Exhibitions to Students desiring to proceed to any College or Polytechnic selected by the Exhibitioners and approved by the Governors.

Entrance Exhibitions.

Two Entrance Exhibitions are granted each year, upon the result of an Examination held at the School in the month of December; and each Exhibition entitles the holder to exemption from payment of all Tuition Fees (except the extra Fee for Greek). In the case of Juniors, such Exhibitions are renewable upon the holders attaining the age of 14 years, provided that they have made satisfactory progress in the School, and have the recommendation of the Head Master. Particulars as to these Examinations may be obtained of the Clerk to the Governors.

Foundation Scholarships.

Foundation Scholarships of partial or total exemption from School Fees (except the extra fee for Greek) are granted from time to time by the Governors, to boys *in the School*, upon the recommendation of the Head Master and upon the Reports of the Examiners.

In the case of Juniors holding Foundation Scholarships, such Scholarships are renewable upon their holders attaining the age of 14, provided that they have made satisfactory progress in the School, and have the recommendation of the Head Master.

Examinations.

The School is examined annually by the Oxford University Local Examination Syndicate.

Boarders.

Terms for Boarders may be had on application to the Rev. The Head Master at the School House, or of Mr. W. E. Sadd, B.A., Mathematical Master, who receives Boarders at his residence.

Admission.

The Head Master attends at the School House on the Saturday previous to the commencement of each term at 11 a.m. to receive and register applications for the Admission of New Pupils, for which a fee of 1/- is payable.

An Examination of Candidates for Admission is held in the Schoolroom on the Saturday previous to the commencement of each term at 11.30 a.m. By the Scheme of Management it is provided that:—

> " 1.   The examination for admission to the Junior Department shall never fall below the
> "following standard, that is to say :—
> " Reading simple narrative ;
> "Writing text hand ;
> "Easy sums in the first two rules of Arithmetic.

" 2. The Examination for admission to the Senior Department shall be graduated "according to the age of the boy, but it shall never fall below the following standard, viz :—

" Proficiency in reading and writing ;

" Ability to write simple sentences from Dictation ;

" An elementary knowledge of Arithmetic ;

" Some knowledge of Geography and of the Outlines of English Grammar.

"The Governors may raise the minimum standard from time to time if they deem it "advantageous for the School.

A playing field and play ground are provided.

A Month's Notice is required before the Removal of a Pupil.

Entrance Forms and all particulars may be obtained on application to the Clerk, Mr. F. ERNEST SHUM, 3, Union Street, Bath.

Honours.

R. A. HERMAN—1st in London University Matriculation ;
　　　　　Senior Mathematical Scholar, Trinity College, Cambridge ;
　　　　　Senior Wrangler and First Smith's Prizeman ;
　　　　　Fellow and Lecturer of Trinity College, Cambridge.

F. L. TURNER—1st in Competitive Examination for Clerkships in Civil Service.

A. E. WITHY—Scholarship, Trinity College, Cambridge.

P. M. JOHNSTONE—Classical Exhibition, Keble College, Oxford.

H. M. VIZARD—52nd in Honours List, London University Matriculation ;
　　　　　6th Senior Optime ; Honours Mathematics, Cambridge (Tripos) ;
　　　　　2nd in Examination held by Peterhouse, Pembroke, Corpus Christi, Queen's
　　　　　　　and St. Catherine's Colleges for Senior Scholarships ;
　　　　　Professor Dewar's Prize for Organic Chemistry.

H. M. CRUTTWELL—Classical Exhibition, Christ Church, Oxford ;
　　　　　2nd Class Classical Moderations ; 3rd Final School, Modern History.

L. C. W. THRING—Scholarship, Trinity College, Cambridge, and Second-Class Classical Tripos.

J. B. EAMES— 3rd in First-Class Honours Oxford Local Examination (Senior) ;
　　　　　Non Collegiate Exhibition, Oxford ;
　　　　　Dyke Exhibition, Oxford ;
　　　　　Open Mathematical Exhibition, Worcester College, Oxford ;
　　　　　1st Class Mathematical Moderations ;
　　　　　1st Class Final School, Mathematics.

O. S. GRIFFITHS—9th in First-Class Honours Oxford Local Examination (Senior) ;
　　　　　Open Scholarship at University College of Wales, Aberystwyth ;
　　　　　9th in London University Matriculation, with Prize ;
　　　　　London Intermediate Arts ;
　　　　　London University B.A., First Division.

Schoolroom' (1876) and partly by the conversion of the large Dormitory into two classrooms with a spiral iron staircase for access (1877). Staff salaries were readily increased as a reward for merit. Mr Sadd, who was generously praised by the Examiner at the Prize Giving of 1887 for showing 'a great power of leading boys a long way into new subjects in a short time', received a £20 rise shortly afterwards—and a further £10 income in 1891, making a total of £180 per annum. By then the Headmaster was himself receiving £453 a year, which included capitation fees.

During the period of Mr. Sanderson's Headmastership, the School's curriculum fell broadly into line with the regulations of the New Scheme. A growing emphasis was placed on Mathematics, Science, Modern languages and Drawing. Mr. J. W. Gatehouse, the part-time Science Master, frequently took the most promising pupils for evening lectures or demonstrations into his own Analytical Laboratory in Broad Street. There was a strong feeling, too, that boys ought to be taught a practical subject like carpentry. When, therefore, two Headmasters (both Old Boys) wrote to the Governors suggesting that every self-respecting school now had a workshop, the Board ordered the setting up of an experimental class. The old dining room in the basement was hurriedly equipped with benches and a local craftsman persuaded to come in to give instruction. Shortly afterwards, the Headmaster proudly reported to the Governors: 'Sixteen people, including myself, joined the class. For the sum of fifteen shillings each a complete set of carpenter's tools was supplied to every member of the class'. The initial interest could not be sustained. Within a year the class had dwindled in size to two members. The experiment was consequently abandoned in failure.

Physical exercise, over the country as a whole, was fast gaining in popularity during the latter part of the nineteenth century. The New Scheme had listed 'Drilling' as one of the subjects to be taught. This was conducted by a uniformed sergeant at the end of morning school on Tuesdays for Seniors and on Fridays for juniors. The old 'gymnasium' in the playground, consisting of ropes, ladders and bars, had fallen into serious decay and was in a dangerous condition. It was removed in 1876 after an accident and was not replaced. A playing field was, however, rented at the Headmaster's request in 1876 for the purposes of cricket and football. Unfortunately, the field chosen (the Militia Drilling Ground) proved unsuitable because it was frequently needed for military purposes. It was eventually replaced, after considerable pressure from the 1881 Examiner, by a field 'near the River Avon, between Pulteney and North Parade Bridges'. When in 1894, this land was bought up by the Bath County Recreation Ground Co. Ltd., the School was eventually permitted, after lengthy negotiations, to continue its use at the increased rent of £40 per year.

The Governors had certainly spent a fair amount of money on draining, levelling, rolling and fencing the ground to make it suitable for sport. 'Proper posts for the game of football' were erected, as was a small pavilion which was soon 'carried away from its foundations by the late severe flood'. It was, however, questionable whether either the boys or the staff really appreciated what had been done for them. Although Mr. Sanderson claimed in 1883 that the field had greatly raised 'the moral tone of the School, developing greater energy, and a wider *esprit de corps* than previously existed', the evidence for this is far from certain. Indeed, two years earlier, the older boys had lobbied the Headmaster for 'the use of a boat on the river instead of continuing to rent a cricket field'. Nor was much enthusiasm for sport engendered by members of staff. The Governors actually went as far as interviewing Mr. Sadd in 1895 'with regard to the Cricket Club and the lack of interest which there appeared to be in the School as regards Cricket and other games'. They went on to express their hope 'that the Assistant Masters would arrange to be present on the Cricket Ground and encourage the sports as much as possible'. The Games Club was, apparently, run by a Committee consisting mostly of Old Boys, who also played in any teams raised.

Nevertheless, in spite of minor set-backs and failures, Mr. Sanderson seemed to be riding on the crest of a wave by the January of 1893 when the customary Prize Giving took place. Praise was heaped upon him from all directions. The Examiner reported: 'The Upper Forms did excellent work in all subjects. The work of the Junior Forms was most promising and gave unmistakable evidence of great pains taken to ground the boys thoroughly at the bottom of the School'. Mr. Commans, the Chairman of the Governors, warmly remarked that 'they had a most able Headmaster and one who was most sympathetic for the success of his pupils, whether it be in school hours or not'. Another Governor, Mr. Bagshawe, congratulated Mr. Sanderson and his staff on their success in winning 'the love of their scholars' and on the 'incessant pains and the affectionate interest' taken in every individual boy. To all outward appearances, the Headmaster had good reason to sit back in his chair on the platform and bask in the glow of success. Numbers had risen impressively; examination results were creditable; university scholarships were gaining good publicity for the School. Little did he realise that his position was already in jeopardy—or that three years later he would effectively be sacked.

The reasons for this swift change of fortune are not difficult to find. In spite of the seemingly cordial relationship which existed between the Headmaster and the Board of Governors, there had always been a deep difference of opinion over one matter. Mr. Sanderson, an able classicist and first-rate academic, yearned for a revival of the traditional Grammar School with Latin and Greek to the fore. The Governors, as men of the modern business world, saw things quite differently. As early as 1879, after lengthy consideration of the existing course of study, they came to the decision that 'inadequate provision is made by the present time-table for instruction in modern subjects, especially in French, History and Science'. From that moment on, they became determined to introduce a 'Modern Side' to the curriculum for the benefit of boys entering commerce. Indeed, the Charity Trustees (some of whom were now members of the Governing Board) had even suggested something similar in 1869 to the Schools Inquiry Commissioners. The Headmaster, who was requested to draw up definite proposals along those lines, was horrified. He duly replied that, after consulting with parents, he felt that the present curriculum was perfectly satisfactory and not in need of change. The Governors gave way—at least for the time being. But the feelings of both sides continued to fester just below the surface.

As Mr. Sanderson grew in confidence, he gradually seized the opportunity to expound in public his rather inflexible views on the type of education to be offered in the future at King Edward's. Speaking at the Prize Giving in 1883, he stated: 'Although I am fully alive to the obligation and even the absolute necessity of offering to the citizens special opportunities of acquiring for their sons a sound and thorough education adapted to business pursuits, yet I cannot help feeling very strongly that it would be a sad day for this ancient institution if it ever came to be looked upon as a mere seminary of commercial education'. His most forthright statement, however, was reserved for the Prize Giving of January, 1891. The guest of honour, Dr. Edward Bartrum (an Old Boy of the School and Headmaster of King Edward's, Berkhamsted), had rather lent force to the Governors' case by attacking the School's lack of provision for both carpentry and technical education. Nor had they any right 'to call it a good second rate school', he continued, 'unless there was a proper chemical laboratory'.

Stung into action, Mr. Sanderson lashed out furiously in defence of his own ideals. The *Bath Journal* summarised his reply: 'He believed that a Grammar school was a grammar school, and did not believe it was a technical school, he believed it was meant to develop the mental qualities of boys. Let them do what they liked elsewhere, but he had not time and the boys had not time to take up these things . . . The success of a school, he maintained, was shown by its results, and as an instance he referred to an ex-pupil named Pinch, who had just gained an entrance scholarship into the Bristol Infirmary. If he had wasted his time over carpentering he would not have done that. If they wanted technical education, let them bully the School Board to provide it. Last year the Governors decided to draft two boys from the Board schools into this school. Well, that was an experiment—he hoped it would succeed. But in his opinion the School was not meant for that, and he had systematically endeavoured to raise the tone instead of lowering it.'

The Governors now knew exactly where they stood. Even so, it is unlikely that they would have taken any decisive action had it not been for a remarkable combination of circumstances. In the summer of 1895, news reached the 'School Committee' of the Governing Body that the Bath School Board were considering the idea of setting up a new secondary school in Bath. The Governors were quick to realise that the type of teaching offered in such a school would be very attractive to boys intent on going into business. Competition of this sort would almost certainly have a damaging effect on the number of pupils applying for King Edward's. Then, almost immediately afterwards, the Report of the Royal Commission on Secondary Education (the Bryce Commission) was published. It strongly advocated the setting up of local authorities to make provision for secondary education in all areas.

By the January of 1896, the Governors were in a state of undisguised panic. They were determined to salvage the School at all costs. The 'School Committee' (which consisted of nine of the most influential Governors) put forward a two-point plan to rescue the situation—first, that the Headmaster should revive the tradition of taking boarders in a suitable rent-free house provided for the purpose and secondly, 'that in view of the educational demands of the present day' a definite 'Modern Side' to the School should be established. Boarding had almost totally been allowed to lapse, although Mr. Sadd had recently taken a few boarders into his own home under the terms of the New Scheme. As far as the curriculum was concerned, the Governors intended to create two 'sides' to the School—a 'Classical Side' (with Greek restored as an official subject) and a 'Modern Side', based on the pattern of Bradford Grammar School (with Shorthand and Book-keeping taught alongside Modern Languages, Mathematics, Sciences and Drawing.)

There is no doubt that the Governors, knowing full well the outspoken views of Mr. Sanderson on this subject, expected him to resign in immediate protest. He disappointed them. Indeed, much to their surprise, he readily agreed to co-operate on both points and quickly produced a timetable for the new system. As he was later to say to the School Committee, he was getting older and really wished to stay on at the School where he had spent the best years of his life. This clearly upset their plans for they were by now, determined to

appoint a new Headmaster who would implement the forthcoming changes with conviction and enthusiasm. Much to
their discredit, therefore, they began to build up a case against
him based on the flimsiest of evidence.

Mr. Jolly and Mr. Commans, two prominent Governors,
secretly interviewed a number of disgruntled parents and
boys. The following allegation were made—that Mr. Sadd's
manners, language, behaviour and 'state when in School' left
much to be desired; that Mr. Ehrke was hardly ever seen in
School and certainly taught no French; that on some occasions certain masters were incapable of teaching at all; that,
finally, there was no respect shown by the boys for the masters
or by the masters for the boys. When these matters were
reported to the May meeting of the Board, the Governors
reacted with righteous indignation. Mr. Morris considered the
matter 'hopeless' and felt that an absolute change was necessary. Mr. Moore 'spoke of the kindness his sons had received
at the hands of the Headmaster, but considered it useless to
spend a lot of money until the machinery of the School was
put into proper order'. He suggested that Mr. Sanderson
should be called upon to resign. Mr. Jolly felt that no new
schemes could be carried out 'unless the present management
be altered', adding that 'the reputation of the School was bad'.

And so, the hero of the 1893 Prize Giving, that 'most able
Headmaster', had suddenly become the incompetent villain of
1896; that talented Mathematics Master (Mr. Sadd), whose
'great power of leading boys a long way' had twice earned him
increases in salary, was now unfit to teach; that caring staff,
who had won 'the love of their Scholars' in 1893, had now lost
all their respect just three years later. The argument was not
convincing. It is true that the school had lost the services of
Mr. G. L. Topping, the Second Master, who had retired in
1891—a man of great experience and wisdom, whose contribution had been immense. It is true that the 1894 Examiner
had been much harsher in his criticism and that a few critical
letters had appeared in the local Press. But there is no real
evidence that the School was now in a state of anarchy.
Nevertheless, the Governors found Mr. Sanderson's reply to
the allegations unacceptable. Unanimously they called for his
resignation. But, in recognition of his twenty-two years'

service, they granted him a lump sum payment of £500 (the maximum that the Charity Commissioners would allow—a gift of £1500 had originally been intended). A further £250 was awarded in lieu of six months' notice, when he agreed to leave forthwith at the end of the Summer Term.

Their final letter to Mr. Sanderson was generous in tone, betraying perhaps a few slight pangs of conscience:

> The Governors desire to record their sense of obligation to you for the manner in which you raised the School from the low condition in which you found it, both as regards numbers and the successes attained by the pupils (the numbers having risen from 23 in 1874 to 125 in 1891) and especially for the unfailing and effectual help you have always shown yourself ready to give boys anxious to attain a higher standard of education.
>
> Having regard, however, to recent circumstances and the important changes which the Governors desire made in the School, I am desired to inform you that they accept your resignation. . . . The Governors desire to offer you their sincere thanks for past services and all good wishes for your future prosperity.

The Governors, of course, were right in their judgement. Mr. Sanderson was not the man to take King Edward's into the twentieth century. But his contribution in providing stability at a time of crisis must not be underestimated in the history of the School. He died in South Africa in 1910 at the age of sixty-six.

E. W. Symons (1896–1921): His Problems

The man appointed by the Governors to lead the School into the twentieth century was Mr. E. W. Symons, eventually selected from eighty-seven applicants and a short list of six. A former Scholar of University College, Oxford, he had gained a First Class degree in Mathematics before being appointed Fereday Fellow and Lecturer at St. John's College, Oxford. Thereafter he had taken up positions as Senior Master on the Modern Side at Bromsgrove School, Headmaster of Huddersfield College and Headmaster of Banbury Secondary School. He arrived at King Edward's School in September 1896 at the age of thirty-eight with an excellent reputation.

Mr. E. W. Symons, Headmaster 1896–1921.

School Archives

The Governors, after half a century of disappointments, were at last able to congratulate themselves on their judgment. Over the next twenty-five years they worked closely and amicably with their new Headmaster, inviting him from the start to attend their meetings whenever he wished. One of the most urgent tasks was to complete the total reshaping of the teaching staff. Mr. Sadd, Mr. Langridge, Mr. Ehrke and Mr. Gatehouse quickly discovered that their services were no longer required. The School was given a completely new outward image as men with fresh ideas and youthful vigour were drafted in. The plan worked. With dramatic suddenness, numbers started to rise as the new team established its reputation. From a base line of 88 boys when Mr. Symons arrived in 1896, the School roll had increased to 123 in 1897, 167 in 1898, 191 in 1900, 207 in 1903, 218 in 1910 and 225 in 1918. The years of stagnation were now at an end.

Success of this kind, however, created serious problems of its own. Overcrowding in buildings, which were already unsuitable for teaching purposes, became a perpetual nightmare. The Board of Education Inspectors, who visited the School in 1904, were forthright in their condemnation—'The site is cramped and confined . . . the school buildings are poor, and are nearly all badly lighted and ventilated'. It would be a waste of money, they concluded, to try and adapt the buildings. The 1920 Inspectors, however, were even more scathing about the premises and equipment—'The office and lavatory accommodation is antiquated and insufficient . . . The Staff Room is very dark and cramped . . . The equipment generally is old fashioned. New desks should gradually be substituted for the present long benches.' Furthermore, the permanent use of the large School Room for the simultaneous teaching of two classes was 'open to grave objection'.

In the face of this criticism and in the light of their own observation, the Governors repeatedly considered the possibility of selling the Broad Street premises and moving to another location. As early as 1899, for instance, they established a committee to consider suitable sites for building a new school. They even debated whether or not to purchase The Bath College (situated in North Road), which was shortly to come on the market. Most Governors, however, agreed with the view of Mr. Commans that 'the distance from the city was too great'! The 1904 Inspectors strongly recommended moving the School to 'a new and fairly central site'. Buildings occupied by the former Sydney College at the end of Pulteney

Street were suggested. But by this time, the Governors had already decided against a move on principle. Their reply to the Board of Education's Report outlined their arguments:

> 'Apart from the serious difficulty in finding a suitable site, and the lack of funds to provide a new building, no other site so central as the present one is available, and they are of the opinion that the removal of the School from the centre of the City would be prejudicial, and would probably result in a reduction in the number of scholars, bearing in mind the fact that King Edward's School is essentially a day school, and that the bulk of the boys in attendance are the sons of citizens engaged in trade in the City.'

Nevertheless, the Governors were not totally blind to the problem of overcrowding. Their instant reaction was to adapt existing buildings to provide additional teaching space. Immediate difficulties had been created by the rapid influx of very young boys. A Preparatory School had therefore been established in 1898 under two lady teachers in a room over the small School Room. Within a year, its numbers had rocketed to a total of 49 boys. Additional rooms were clearly essential. Under these circumstances the Governors decided to buy a new official residence for the Headmaster, thus freeing his accommodation at the front of the School for use as classrooms. Mr. Symons consequently moved into No. 20 Belmont (purchased for £1,000 in 1899), while the Preparatory School spread across into his former bedrooms under the watchful eye of Miss Neal and Miss Shum. This, at least, provided a temporary respite.

By 1905, however, the situation had again become critical. Ignoring the Inspectors' recommendations that the School should be moved, the Governors set about the task of making conditions more bearable by enlarging classrooms and raising ceilings in an attempt to create more light and air. At the same time, they began to consider the future possibility of accommodating the Preparatory School in a neighbouring house. It would, they considered, be advantageous anyway 'as at present the small boys must be to some extent subject to rough play on the part of the bigger boys'. Nothing, however, was done until after the publication of the Inspection Report of 1920, which insisted on the removal of the Preparatory School as a condition of recognition (see below). This was finally achieved on the retirement of Mr. Symons, when his official residence at No. 20 Belmont was taken over for that purpose.

Any ultimate solution to the problem of overcrowding inevitably rested to a large extent on the financial circumstances of the School. The period of Mr. Symons's Headmastership was to demonstrate in full measure just how impoverished the School really was. Income was derived mainly from house property (amounting to £2,001 in 1919–1920) and school fees (£2,830 in the same year). Repair bills, already high for the older buildings owned by the School outside Broad Street, suffered badly from rising costs both during and after the First World War. In 1904 the Inspectors concluded that 'the School is just paying its way'. By 1920, it had plunged into the red with an adverse balance of £345 for the last financial year. In a constant battle to remain solvent, the Governors had adopted a number of expedients. Four loans had been raised between 1900 and 1913, amounting to £3,923, to cover the cost of major repairs, alterations and the purchase

School Group, 1899.

School Archives

of the Headmaster's house. An Appeal for funds to the public in general and the Old Boys in particular had been considered. Exhibitions already established for the benefit of girls at the High School, had been suspended 'with great regret' in 1912 in an attempt to save money. Fees, which had remained constant for many years, were raised in 1912, 1918 and again in 1919. They then stood at £10 10s. per annum for the Preparatory School, £13 10s. for juniors and £15 for seniors.

Most regrettable of all, however, was the policy of economising on the pay and working conditions of the assistant masters. This was roundly condemned by the Board of Education Inspectors in 1920. Hopes expressed by their predecessors in 1904 that a scale of salaries should be instituted 'so that each member of the Assistant Staff may be assured of fixed increments at regular intervals' had simply not been fulfilled. Similar expectations of a new pension scheme had also been shattered. The Inspectors did not mince their words:

> The Salaries paid to the Assistant Staff are abnormally low, very far below the scales which are in force in other schools of the same character. If the services of an efficient staff are to be secured and retained, it is imperative that a very large increase should be effected immediately in the salaries offered. . . . Undoubtedly the Staff is numerically insufficient for the size of the School. The Masters are teaching almost continuously and have hardly any free periods . . . Though few hold any high academic qualifications and only four are graduates, they are, as a body, hardworking and conscientious, and accomplish much good and useful work under exceedingly difficult conditions.

Whereas the average salary of a certified teacher in 1914 was £129 a year, four members of Staff at King Edward's (Mr. Stuart, Mr. Dunn, the Rev. Hardy and Miss Neal) were only being paid £93. It is true that, from 1900, the sons of masters had been educated at the School free of charge. It is also true that, in the absence of a pension scheme, the Governors had sought to use their limited means to assist Staff who were in distress. In 1916, for instance, they gave a term's notice and a gratuity of £100 to Mr. Stuart, a teacher for nineteen years, who lay seriously ill suffering from 'advanced pulmonary tuberculosis'. But these small gestures far from satisfied a teaching Staff, who were becoming increasingly agitated as they struggled for mere survival.

From October, 1917 they submitted a series of written requests to the Governing Body, pleading for an annual 'War

Bonus' (or cost of living increase to meet the demands of inflation), the creation of a proper scale of salaries and the adoption of a new Government Pension Scheme. The Governors did what they could, granting the War Bonus and offering a small salary increase in 1919. Their resources, however, were already stretched to breaking point. The Staff, almost in despair, continued to lobby either by letter or by the personal approach of Captain Langley, the Second Master. In 1920 they demanded 'that something should be done immediately in connection with their inadequate salaries', requesting that staff should be placed on the Burnham Scale.

The Governors, now at the end of their financial tether, decided at last to seek help from outside. This possibility had already been considered in 1912 when a meeting had been held with His Majesty's Inspector of Schools to discuss a plan of Recognition by the Board of Education in return for financial aid. Although the Governors, jealous of their independence, had shelved the idea for the time being, by 1920 they were in no position to reject such comforting help. After joint talks with Bath Education Committee, it was agreed to apply for official Recognition and Aid. This would enable the School not only to participate in the Teachers' Pension Scheme, but also to receive a grant of £750 per annum from the Local Authority towards increases in salary. In return, the Governors were required to offer ten per cent of their places in School to the Bath Education Committee. Consequently, after an Inspection by the Board of Education in October 1920, the School was duly granted its 'recognised' status. The Inspectors' Report emphasised how urgent had become the need for financial assistance from public funds:

> 'The time has now come, however, when it can no longer maintain its present position, much less develop on modern lines, without substantial assistance from public funds. With the present numbers the School is seriously overcrowded and the Staff is inadequate . . . The School admittedly occupies a very important place in the educational scheme of the City, and it is essential that its progress should no longer be hampered by lack of the funds which are indispensable if it is to maintain its old traditions and at the same time worthily to fill the position which it ought to occupy in the provision of higher education in Bath.'

School Life, 1871–1921

The gradual revival in the fortunes of the School brought with it a growing sense of pride and corporate spirit. This was reflected partly in the creation of several outward symbols of the School's identity. As early as 1872, mortar-boards had been introduced as a compulsory item of clothing (seen clearly in the School Photograph of that year). Senior Foundation Scholars were granted the distinction of having gold tassles, instead of the standard black. Under Mr. Sanderson, however, mortar-boards quickly became optional and eventually fell into disuse. Nevertheless, in 1892, the Governors resolved that all boys attending the School should wear 'a distinguishing cap' and that no boys should be allowed on the Cricket Ground without one.

The original design for a cloth cap, bearing the letters B.G.S., proved unsatisfactory. It was badly shaped and could only be worn on the back of the head. An improved version, with the monogram K.E.S., was itself superseded in 1908 by the more familiar cap in maroon and blue. The Tudor Rose was now adopted as the School badge and registered under the Patents Act. In order to stop the illegal use of the new cap by other children in the City, the Governors encouraged parents to hand in disused caps by offering a sum of 3d. each. At the same time the Tudor Rose also became the basis of the Colours Badge, awarded in recognition of achievement in Games. Apart from the cap and the Eton collar, which both became compulsory, there were no additional requirements to School uniform at this time. The Staff, however, were expected to wear both gowns and mortar-boards.

The emergence of School spirit was also shown by the purchase in 1900 of a School Flag (bearing the Arms of Edward VI), by the adoption of a School Song in 1897 for use at Prize Giving (adapted from that used at King Edward's School, Birmingham), by the publication of the first *Edwardian* magazine in 1909 and by the creation of an Old Edwardians' Association in December, 1906 under its President, Dr. W. B. Odgers. This had first been suggested by the Mayor of Bath in 1902 after local Old Boys had rallied round to help finance the building of a new Cricket Pavilion in the previous year. The difficulty the Governors had had then in tracing the where-abouts of former pupils had emphasised the need for a well-organised association with carefully maintained membership lists. A highly successful Inaugural Dinner was held in the School Room in January, 1909. This was followed by a variety of activities in the early days—debates, smoking concerts and whist drives. The biennial dinner, held at Fortt's, normally concluded with speeches and a programme of songs and recitations. A London Association of Bath Old Edwardians was formed in 1921 and launched by a dinner at Gatti's Restaurant in the Strand.

Old Edwardians certainly began to look back on their School days with a degree of nostalgia. J. W. Gill, for example, writing later in *The Edwardian*, provided a vivid picture of life at Broad Street in 1876.

'Never shall I forget the first day or the first week, or weeks perhaps. By a process of what appeared, to my addled senses, a system of gentle driving and mysterious movements, we were drafted first to 'Taffy Morgan's' room, whence the black-boards, easels, chalk, dusters, caps, mortar-boards, slate-pencils seemed to abound in promiscuous and abandoned diffusion; books, ink and ink-pots seemed thick upon the desks: *those* desks, solid and secure in their oaken glory, beautifully designed for cribbing or hiding any forbidden thing; those magnificent locker-forms, too, (but I am afraid impossible to keep clean). This solid furniture, ink-stained, scratched, carved by the pocket-knives of generations of boys, impressed me much . . . It is probably forgotten that a holiday was given monthly to those boys who had obtained the requisite amount of marks, and the feature of that term to me was getting that holiday. The 'Mark Holiday' was abandoned a year or two after this, for I never won it again . . . On Tuesdays the seniors, and on Friday the juniors, were drilled after 12 noon. Friday afternoons we had our singing lessons; we descended to place known as the 'Black Hole', and were taught songlets by Mr. Watts, who either presided at the harpsichord or wielded a knotty walking stick. The Authorities were wise in smothering the noises evolved by relegating this class to the lower regions. 'Gems from afar' (the name of our songbook) might have been misnomered 'Yells from below' . . . The School hours were from 9 a.m. to 12 noon and from 2 p.m. to 5 p.m. For those who lived in the country or distant suburbs it can be guessed that their time was fully occupied . . .'

The long lunch break was, of course, necessary in the days before School meals were provided. Boys who were unable to get home had three choices—to eat a packed lunch in a classroom under the watchful eye of a monitor, to buy meals for £3 a term at Mr. Hardy's Boarding House (after its establishment in 1913) or to buy lunch for 4d. or 6d. at a restaurant in town. In other ways, too, little seemed to change—at least from a boy's point of view—between 1876 and 1910 when L. R. Bence was at school. He confirms that pupils who travelled in by train from Box and Chippenham had a long, hard day. To while away the time after school until his train left at 5.45 p.m., he frequently bought tea and cake at a cafe near the station. He also confirms that '*those* desks'—six desks joined together with a long bench—were still in existence. Indeed, they remained in all their glory until 1945, despite being roundly condemned by the Inspectors in 1920.

The covered playground under the big School Room (presumably the 'Black Hole' used for the singing lessons of Mr. Watts in 1876) was employed in various ways during the time of Mr. Symons. Its official purpose was undoubtedly to provide space for the drill and shooting practice of the Cadet Corps (see below). But Mr. Bence also recalls that it was used unofficially for the settlement of differences between boys. Masters, apparently, seldom ventured down there during breaks. Discipline, however, was good. The Inspection Report of 1904 praised the conduct and appearance of the boys and commended the disciplinary structure which operated under Mr. Symons: 'Corporal punishment is infrequent, and administered by the Head Master only. There are six monitors who take assemblies pending the Master's arrival, are responsible for the maintenance of good tone, and for the preservation of order at School out of School hours. They inflict no punishments, but are required to communicate with the Head Master.'

Communication of this kind with the Headmaster invariably led to a severe carpeting of the boy concerned. F. H. C. Mills recalls: 'All the boys quaked in their shoes if sent to

The Sixth Form, 1918. The five Monitors on the front row are (left to right):
Jackson, Hobbs, Bath, Spence, Hayward.

Photo by Dr. A. W. Spence

attend the Headmaster's study where one was called a
"booby" in no uncertain terms on occasions'. His power to
use effectively the spoken word is also attested by Dr. A. W.
Spence: 'I have the greatest admiration for the Headmaster,
Mr. E. W. Symons. He was indeed a most able teacher and a
disciplinarian. When one made a mistake one was termed a
"chucklehead", a greater mistake one had to stand up and a
greater still to stand on the form. One was also given so many
lines and to reduce the amount of time taken to produce these
lines I would put three nibs into the penholder, so that three
lines were produced in place of one. This invention of mine
was taken up by the rest of the form'. The 'Old Man', as he
was generally called, stamped his authority on the whole
school. L. R. Bence perhaps best puts his finger on the secret:
'Boys were not beaten, they were psychologically controlled'.
And when, in Prize Givings, the first line of the last verse of
the School Song ('Old Time is on our track boys') was, with
one voice, amended to 'Old Symie's on our track boys', it was

King Edward's School, Bath.

RULES.

Every boy must return to School punctually on the first day of term unless he is ill or has obtained permission to be absent.

Except on the ground of illness no boy is allowed to be absent from School *without previously obtaining the permission of the Head Master.*

When a boy returns to School after absence due to illness, a letter of explanation must be sent by the parent or guardian; and parents or guardians are required to give immediate notice of any infectious illness with which boys may have been brought into contact.

All boys are required to wear on week days in term time the uniform School Cap, which may be obtained only from Mr. F. G. Isaacs, 1 Cheap Street, on written order from the Head Master. Boys who wear straw hats must provide themselves with the School ribbon.

Boys must either destroy their old Caps or return them to the School Sergeant, who is authorised to make a payment of threepence for each Cap so returned. In no case must a Cap be given away to boys outside the School.

Boys are required to "Cap" Masters when they meet them in the street. Smoking is strictly forbidden.

Boys are not allowed to loiter in front of the School Buildings, to climb any walls, palings, or to do anything which may annoy a neighbour in any way.

Stone throwing, and the use of catapults, are strictly forbidden, and no boy must bring fireworks or gunpowder to School.

Boys are cautioned not to leave books, overcoats, or umbrellas at School after School hours.

A fine of one penny is inflicted for each article so left.

Every boy is expected to walk quietly in the streets and to conduct himself properly in public places at all times.

On the Recreation Ground boys are forbidden to climb on to the roof of the verandah or to enter the Pavilion through the window.

No boy is permitted to climb over the walls in search of Cricket balls without obtaining permission from a Master or the Captain.

All boys playing cricket must wear cricket boots or shoes, and boys must be provided with "knickers" and jerseys or football shirts when playing football.

The School Rules at the time of Mr. Symons.

School Archives

rather an expression of the genuine respect they felt for their Headmaster.

Sir George Beresford Stooke recalls one interesting interview he had with the Headmaster:

'I was preparing for the naval entrance exam, which I was to take in June 1914. But they changed the rules and I found I was eligible to sit for the December 1913 exam. The Headmaster and my Father thought that I had better have a shot at the December exam as it would be good experience. Neither they nor I expected me to pass. 85 candidates were nominated to compete for 15 vacancies. However, I sat and wrote the papers without any expectation of success. The results of the exam came out a few days after the school had broken up for Christmas. The first I heard was when a telegram arrived from Gieves, Matthews and Seagrove, the naval outfitters, offering congratulations, followed the next day by the official notification that I had taken 5th place. I could not believe it—and to this day I feel sure that there must have been some mistake.

I was, of course, cock-a-hoop and set off for Bath on my bicycle to convey the good news to Mr. Symons. I was ushered into his study where he was sitting at his desk—and I blurted out my message. He stared at me for a moment, then said "5th place, did you say?"—"Yes sir."—"I expect my boys to be first!" I have never been so deflated before or since.'

School sport, which had reached a low ebb under Mr. Sanderson and had been severely criticised by the Governors in 1895, revived a little under Mr. Symons. From 1898 physical training of boys took place in the YMCA Gymnasium in Broad Street at a cost to the School of £43 per annum. This was transferred in 1911 to a private Gym, which had been opened at 12 The Paragon by Mr. Cottle (the Gym Instructor from the YMCA). Although this arrangement was temporarily suspended in 1916, when Mr. Cottle was called up for war service, it was eventually to restart first under Major Chappel in Broad Street and then under Captain Olsen in The Paragon (1920). The Inspectors, who visited the School in that year, reported that 120 boys, who were not in the Cadet Force, attended the gym once a week in classes of twenty for a period of forty-five minutes. They wore ordinary clothes, with coats and collars removed, and rubber shoes (see

A Physical Training Class taken by Major Chappel at the Y.M.C.A.
Gymnasium, c.1918.

Photo by H. Creese

photograph). Normal gymnastic equipment—rings, bars,
horses—were used, as well as a series of gymnastic games.
Pupils in the Cadet Force were split into five squads under boy
N.C.O's for physical training in the playground under the eye
of a local Instructor.

Cricket and football continued to be played throughout this
period on the Recreation Ground—apart from one short spell
in 1918 when the field was taken over by the Army. A new
cricket pavilion had been built in 1901 to boost the interest of
boys. At least on the surface, School sport improved most
noticeably. Cricket results received special praise in the Prize
Givings of 1902 and 1904, which was claimed to be the best
season on record. A similar tribute was given in 1903 to the
Soccer team, which had recorded 10 wins and 3 losses before
Christmas. A. W. Spence recalls the interest taken in cricket
by the Headmaster, together with some of the notable
achievements of these years:

'Mr. Symons was very keen on cricket and every Monday
morning during the cricket season, after prayers at 9 a.m., he

1st XV Rugby Team, 1897. This was an 'unofficial' team (soccer was the official winter game) and was composed of a mixture of masters and boys. *Back row:* Mr. Stuart (referee), H. P. Quartley, C. E. Stevenson, Mr. Underwood, Mr. Barnes, Mr. Eden, E. B. Whitley, R. Harris, G. E. Peto. *Front row:* H. Edmunds, H. G. Barker, H. E. Lever, E. G. Barker, L. G. Edwards (Capt.), H. Tutton, A. P. H. Pond, A. W. Barker, J. Patterson.

would pass his comments on the behaviour of the 1st XI on the previous Saturday and woe betide the chucklehead who had dropped an easy catch—and greatly was lauded the boy who had made his 50. The cricketing hero was H. H. Simpkin, who in 1913 made his record score of 155 and the school was consequently granted a half holiday. His batting average was 40 and he was unrivalled in bowling and fielding. When he left in 1915 *The Edwardian* stated that he leaves a record unrivall- ed in our own cricket annals. In 1917, the 2nd XI, of which I was a member, put up three remarkable performances. They dismissed Bristol Cathedral School for 1 run, Bath City Secon- dary School for 2 runs and Bristol Cathedral School later in the season for 0 runs. Mr. Symons put this feat in Whittaker's Almanack.'

1st XI Cricket Team, 1910.
Back row: W. M. Huntley, C. V. Erwood, H. F. Baggs, A. G. Stevenson.
Middle row: A. W. Simpkin, P. B. Corbett, A. D. Symons (capt.), C. P.
Smith, H. H. Simpkin.
Front row: C. A. Symons, G. Tall, A. A. Cairns.

These stirring successes, however, tend to obscure the fact that sport in the School *as a whole* was still in an unhealthy state even by 1921. It is true that a start had been made to swimming in 1905 when fifty boys enrolled for a class in the Cleveland Baths. This activity flourished later under the Rev. F. Hardy, who provided regular instruction in swimming, life-saving and water-polo in the Royal Baths. By 1918 he had established an annual Swimming Sports, which even included a 'pyjama and umbrella' race! It is also true that the same master had encouraged some interest in boxing. Perhaps surprisingly, H. G. H. Long had been runner-up in the Light-Weight division of the Public Schools' Boxing Competition in 1920, only to be outdone in the following year by the elder Robinson who won the Bantam Division.

The fact remained, however, that sport of any kind was played only 'by a minority of the School'. This admission, made at Prize Giving in 1902, was equally valid when the Board of Education Inspection took place in 1920: 'Only a small percentage of the boys take part in any school games. There is no system of grouping the boys into teams or houses

1st XI Soccer Team, 1900.
Back row: E. G. M. Cox (Secretary), G. F. Wilson, C. J. S. Taylor, G. S. Applegate, G. R. Lawrence, Mr. W. T. Underwood.
Middle row: E. J. C. Harbutt, W. H. Monk, C. H. Corbett (Capt.), W. R. Elloway, J. H. Gover, W. E. Allan (linesman).
Front row: A. E. Crew, A. M. Goodman.

to encourage them to join in this branch of physical training. It is a matter for regret that school games do not take a greater place in the general life of the School.' Sport was, in fact, played on the two half-day holidays (Wednesdays and Saturdays) and was purely optional. The problems were, of course, real for travellers from outlying parts and for the sons of shopkeepers and farmers, who expected their assistance at work. L. R. Bence remembers the attempt to stage an inter-form soccer competition, in which older teams played under a handicap of so many goals when they met a younger team. By 1911 this tournament had been confined to Forms 1–4 in an attempt to encourage the younger boys to play. The First Form actually won the Challenge Shield in 1913, but not before the Third Form had beaten the Prep two years' earlier by the rather convincing score of 27–4. Furthermore, the Prep team had actually been given a four goal start!

Extra-curricular activities also suffered, in the same way as sport, from a lack of general interest and enthusiasm. The Chess Club, the Philatelic Society and the Field and Camera Club all fizzled out rather quickly after inauguration. Apart from the Cadet Force (see below), the greatest exception to this general trend was the Debating Society, which held regular fortnightly meetings during the winter months on Saturdays and attracted respectable gatherings.

A keen start had also been made in developing a personal involvement in the work of charity. From 1900 the School had become a Lodge of the Young Helpers' League Branch of the National Waifs' Association. By 1902 they were entirely responsible for maintaining one orphan. From these early beginnings there grew a lasting connection with Dr. Barnado's Homes, for which an annual collection was regularly taken.

Occasionally, too, the School became involved in a much larger event in the City itself. N. V. H. Symons recalls one such occasion in 1909 when Bath staged its Historical Pageant in the Royal Victoria Park, which was opened by The Duke of Connaught:

'I paraded with the School O.T.C. with rifles and bayonets and we marched to the G.W.R. Station in Manvers Street, where we helped to line the street up which the Duke drove to the Park. We marched back to the School and dismissed. Those of us who were taking part in the Pageant went home and changed from our uniforms into our Pageant Costumes.

We took part in an Elizabethan episode and our costumes were similar to those of Christ's Hospital today—black shoes, yellow stockings and a long skirted blue coat coming down to the ankles with a white ruff at the neck. There were 30 or 40 of us and we were drawn up by the side of the road along which the Queen was to come riding into Bath on a horse. All we had to do was to cheer and wave a welcome to her as she passed.

Opposite to us was the Town Pillory in which there was a malefactor. Actually he was a most respectable and law-abiding citizen named Calloway who had a watchmaker's shop in Northumberland Passage. He was a large man of about 60 with a bald head and white hair. I was detailed by the Pageant Master to run up to the Pillory and throw vegetables at him. I well remember the agonised look on his face as I approached, imploring me not to hit him. I suppose I obliged, because we became good friends. The Pageant lasted for a week or two with daily performances and was a great success, besides being very popular with us boys who got out of School early.'

The establishment of the Cadet Corps in 1900 in many ways transformed the corporate life of the School. This was essentially the brain-child of Mr. Symons himself. Against the

The Cadet Corps shortly after its foundation in 1900.

School Archives

backcloth of the Boer War, the Headmaster quickly rallied the support of both parents and Governors. By the end of the first year, no fewer than 65 boys had enrolled under the command of Lieut. Mason. Parents were required to pay £1 5s. towards the cost of providing a uniform, plus 5s. 0d. a term. Captain Skinner, who took over as Commander in 1905, was still in charge of the Corps in December 1908, when it became officially recognised as an Officer Training Corps. From then on, its activities multiplied and flourished.

School Cadets in Bath, 1905.

School Archives

Annual Camps at Aldershot or on Salisbury Plain were supplemented by regular Field Days and 15 mile route marches. Many local manoeuvres and night operations were conducted jointly with the O.T.C's from Bristol G.S., Clifton, Monkton Combe and Downside. Whenever the demands of sport permitted, half-day holidays on Wednesdays and Saturdays were also used to get further afield than time normally allowed. 'On these occasions', reported *The Edwardian* in 1915, 'the Cadets have left school at 12 o'clock, taken their lunch with them, and arrived back at school either at 5 o'clock or 6.30.' For the most part, however, drill and training were usually confined to the playground at Broad Street or to the Recreation Ground, where regular parades took place. The O.T.C. were inevitably involved in many local ceremonial occasions—the annual Church Parade, a Memorial Service in the Abbey for the late Edward VII, the Civic Procession on Coronation Day in 1911, street-lining in Bristol for the King's visit in 1912 etc. These public appearances became much more impressive, of course, after the formation of the O.T.C. band in 1913. 'From henceforth,' reported *The Edwardian*, 'our marching through the town will be less at the mercy of the casual barrel organ.' The musical repertoire of drums and bugles was extended even further in 1917 with a gift of a dozen fifes. Perhaps the most moving purpose for which the band was ever used was in 1914, when it was detailed to meet recruits of the Devon and Cornwall Regiments at the Station and play them to their billets in Bath. Then, after completion of their training, the fully-equipped recruits were marched back to the station again to the accompaniment of the King Edward's School band. According to *The Edwardian*, it was also used to 'enliven' two recruiting meetings which were held in Bath during the same year.

From the early stages, shooting became a popular feature of life in the O.T.C. Open range musketry took place at the shooting butts under Kingsdown, near Box. A miniature shooting range had also been established in the covered playground at Broad Street, where an annual competition was held for The Sheppard Cup. The first-ever Shooting VIII was formed in 1910, competing on a regular basis locally against other schools. Its initial entry into the *Country Life* O.T.C. Miniature Rifle Shooting Competition occurred in 1913. Success was almost immediate. Gaining second place in 1919, they went on to win this national competition the following year—much to everyone's delight.

Competitions within the O.T.C. itself also increased. From 1914, experts in shooting, signalling, bugling and drumming could all demonstrate their various skills at the annual Competition Day on the Recreation Ground, which attracted large crowds of visitors. Meanwhile, command of the unit had passed in 1912 from Captain Skinner to Captain Langley, who was assisted in succession by Lieut. Ince, Lieut. Jago and Rev. F. Hardy. Cadets during this period were frequently inspected by nationally-famous figures, such as Lord Kitchener and Lord Roberts. Furthermore, they took part in the great review

of all O.T.C. Divisions held by King George V in 1911 at
Windsor. Present, on that occasion, was N. V. H. Symons, son
of the Headmaster. His personal account of that occasion and
the subsequent years is a sombre reminder of the speed with
which boys from the School found themselves caught up in
war, death and glory:

'It was in 1911, when I was nearly 17 and the new King
George V ordered a Review at Windsor of all the O.T.Cs. We
went off by train and, in the Great Park, there was a forest of

A 'Cyclist' Company of the Cadet Corps, 1905.

School Archives

tents already pitched for us by the garrison. The review took
place the next afternoon and started by the King riding on
parade in the blue uniform of a Field Marshal, complete with
cocked hat and feathers and accompanied by his Staff. He
looked splendid and the sun shone on his beard turning it to
gold and making him look like a Viking. In an open carriage
behind were Queen Mary, the Prince of Wales in the uniform of
a Naval Cadet (and looking such a very little boy in spite of
being 17) and Princess Mary, a girl of about 14 with her hair
down her back. Then the Review took place with its Royal
Salutes and marching past in various formations. It was a

wonderful gesture by the King and the Royal Family and was very much appreciated by us all.

The next time I was to be reviewed by the King, although it was only about three years later, was a grim and very different affair in November 1914 on Morn Hill, Winchester, when it was bitterly cold with a high wind and rain. It was the King's farewell to the 27th Division, which was the eighth division to go out to the B.E.F. in France. The King did it all on foot and looked very unwell and haggard. Behind him strode the gigantic Kitchener with his blue eyes looking as happy as the King looked miserable. I was in the front rank and so had a perfect view.

The next time I was to see the King was two years later when I was in a London hospital with my second wound. He had about 30 officers who had been given decorations to a special investiture in Windsor Castle. We went to Windsor by train and then—oh glory!—we were driven to the Castle in open royal carriages. The King shook hands and pinned on my Military Cross and said a kind word or two to me. After the investiture, we had a magnificent lunch in Windsor Castle and then back in glory through the streets of Windsor in the royal carriages. What a day that was!

I remember my father writing to me when my decoration was gazetted saying: 'the boys will rise up and call you blessed when I announce a half-holiday in your honour'. And in due course he took me round all the forms and I handed my M.C. in its beautiful leather and velvet case round for the boys to look at.

Five hundred and sixty Old Edwardians served their country in the War, many of whom had received valuable training in the O.T.C. Of these 74 lost their lives, including Captain Skinner (former Commander of the O.T.C.) and Lieut. C. A. Symons, the third son of the Headmaster. Twenty-nine of those who served were awarded decorations and many more were mentioned in despatches. The Governors launched an appeal in 1919 for £1,000 to provide a fitting War Memorial. This was to consist of a stone Memorial Tablet (recording the names of the fallen) to be erected in Big School, a bronze tablet (recording the number of the fallen) to be placed on the School front and a framed Roll of Service (written on vellum) to be hung in Big School. The War Memorial was eventually unveiled on 11th November 1922.

Cadets leaving Bath Station for the Swanage Camp, 1905.
School Archives

E. W. Symons: His Achievements

The concluding remarks of the Inspectors' Report of 1920 fairly summarise the extent of Mr. Symons's achievement in the twenty-five years of his Headmastership: 'In spite of the unfavourable conditions as to buildings and equipment under which the School is conducted, it is doing in many respects sound and useful work on somewhat old-fashioned lines, and in the main essentials is in a healthy condition.' Fighting endlessly against shortage of funds and the lack of space, he managed to re-establish the School's respectability on a local level and to provide a sound footing for future developments.

Facilities were certainly improved to satisfy the requirements of both Governors and Inspectors alike. A Science Laboratory, housed over the Big School Room, was established in 1897 to accommodate classes of the new full-time Science Master, Mr. E. A. Eden. This was a most important step forward in providing an adequate 'Modern' side to the School's curriculum. The Governors later agreed to employ a senior boy as 'Demonstrator' to assist Mr. Eden in preparing experiments. In return, the boy was paid thirty shillings a term and his School fees halved. After criticism raised in the Inspection Report of 1904 about the lack of library facilities, Dr. Blake Ogers (an Old Edwardian) presented the School with a bookcase to form the nucleus of a School Library. He later donated a hundred of his own books as a start towards stocking it and encouraged other Old Boys to do the same. By the time the Inspectors re-visited the School in 1920, they found 'an excellent lending library, mainly of fiction' which opened twice a week.

Perhaps the most noticeable innovation, however, was the establishment of a Boarding House in 1913. This was very much due to the enterprise of the first House Master, the Rev. F. Hardy. It was opened at 19 Portland Place under Licence from the Governors, who remained responsible for its control. It turned out to be a most suitable site with dormitories, a sick ward, a dining room, a day-room for reading, a billiard room, a large school room for prep and a covered playground at the back. Although numbers were initially restricted to 25, demand for places became so great that by 1919 no fewer than 40 boarders were in residence. Fees, which had been fixed at £31 10s. per annum for older boys in 1913, had rocketed to £60 by 1919. During these years the Boarders contributed richly to the life of the school, playing a major part in both games and the O.T.C.

When the Governors had appointed M. Symons in 1896, they made their feelings abundantly clear over what was expected on the question of examination results. They were ambitious not only for greater numbers within the School, but also for more measurable success from the boys who entered. As we have already seen, Mr. Symons quickly and effectively built up the size of the School Roll. He was to achieve equal satisfaction from the attainments of his pupils in public examinations. It was the School's policy to enter the bulk of boys in Forms 3, 4, 5 and 6 for the Oxford or Cambridge Local Examination in December each year. By 1897 the Governors were already beginning to congratulate their new Headmaster on the dramatic improvement in performance. They even awarded the School a day's holiday in 1899 in recognition of the fact that 33 boys had passed (thirteen with honours) and that Norris had emerged first in Mathematics out of 6,249 candidates. This achievement, however, was nothing compared with that of C. J. Gadd. One of his contemporaries, A. W. Spence, recalls: 'The star scholar in my day was C. J. Gadd who in 1912 was 1st in order of merit in the Oxford Senior Local Examination and was bracketed 1st in Religious Knowledge, 1st in English, 1st in Politics, bracketed 1st in Latin, bracketed 1st in French, 1st in Greek, bracketed 8th in History and bracketed 13th in Mathematics—a record which I doubt has been equalled before or since. He subsequently became Professor of Ancient Semitic Languages and Civilization at London University.' The Inspectors of 1904 were doubtless conscious of the fact that 48 out of 50 candidates had passed the Cambridge Local Examinations in that year when they commented: 'the results are such as to show conclusively that the boys are well prepared for examination by their respective Form Masters.'

To all outward appearances, therefore, the School was achieving considerable academic success. According to the Inspectors, however, this was achieved at the cost of good teaching methods. First of all, the masters tended to concentrate entirely on examination requirements: 'The value of the teaching at this School is much detracted from by the fact that the chief aim of the curriculum is to help in passing pupils in the Cambridge Local Examinations. This ties the hands of the Master and tends to cramming the boys with undigested facts.' This exam-conscious attitude was most noticeable in English and French. The Inspectors detected a neglect of literature in favour of routine grammar—'The course of reading provided by the syllabus is not altogether satisfactory—e.g. three Forms are reading Robinson Crusoe.' Similarly, because the French exam did not include any oral exercises, spoken French was largely ignored—'In more than one Form reading aloud in French was so new and strange an exercise that the Masters did not, as the Inspectors suggested, bid the boys read, but invited them, with evident misgiving, to 'try to read".'

In the second place, teaching at King Edward's was based firmly on the Form Master system. This meant that all the

Staff (with the exception of the Science Master, who was the only specialist) were expected to teach their Forms in every subject. The Inspectors were extremely critical of this approach feeling that it caused 'a certain lack of freshness' and encouraged the use of old-fashioned teaching methods. The use of specialist teachers would bring onto the scene far

Staff Group, 1910.
Back row: Mr. Stuart (Form 1B), Mr. Dunn (Form 2), Mr. Annaheim (German), Mr. Hardy (Form 1A), Mr. Nourd (French).
Front row: Mr. Langley (Science), Mr. Underwood (Form 3), Mr. Symons (Headmaster and Form 6), Mr. Stewart (Form 4), Mr. Skinner (Form 5).

greater expertise and enthusiasm for individual subjects. Mr. Symons steadfastly resisted any move in this direction. Quite apart from the problem of financing such a scheme, he informed the Governors that he would be 'loth to have a Staff composed of specialists'. Maths teaching during this period was arranged on a slightly different basis. The whole School was divided on ability into nine sets with lessons taking place concurrently. Promotions and relegations occurred once a year.

Mr. Symons kept a close personal eye on the work of the School and threw himself wholeheartedly into teaching. The 1904 Inspectors were full of praise: 'He is himself an excellent teacher, and takes a very full share of the teaching work. Besides being responsible for the bulk of the VIth Form work, he takes every Form in the School once a week, and keeps himself closely acquainted with the conduct and progress of every boy by means of full weekly reports submitted by the Form Masters.' Much of his own teaching with the Sixth Form took place in the big School Room, where a junior Form was being taught at the same time. An extremely able scholar himself, he took great pleasure in teaching his brighter pupils up to the highest Scholarship standard in either Classics or Mathematics. A former pupil later wrote of him: 'Boys will remember his extraordinary facility for taking the work of two sets of boys at once—in a room, too, where other Form work was in progress. They will remember his Weekly Reading of Marks in Big School, with his stimulating exhortations and his words of praise or castigation bestowed where merited.'

Perhaps his greatest regret was their inability to revive that great tradition, which the School had originally enjoyed, of sending large numbers of pupils to both Oxford and Cambridge. There were, of course, very good reasons for this. In the first place, the School no longer attracted pupils from the higher, more cultured social class. The majority of boys in 1904 came from the homes of retail traders and clerks, whose own educational horizons were limited. Mr. Symons himself admitted in 1920 that it 'would be difficult to make the school a school of very high class, as parents were inclined to send their sons to Boarding Schools away.' Secondly, the new Scheme of 1872, in relegating the School in status to that of the Second Grade, gave it the task of preparing boys, not for university, but for the world of business. Furthermore, Greek (essential for Classical Studies at the ancient universities) was removed from the list of compulsory subjects. At the same time, the leaving age was fixed at seventeen (although this could be extended with special permission)—a further discouragement to university ambition. Thirdly, the opening of

Bristol University in 1909 provided a much more attractive local alternative to parents of limited means. The New Scheme for the School, published in 1914, rather appropriately recognised this growing connection by allocating a place on the Board of Governors to a representative from Bristol University.

It is true that a steady trickle still found its way to Oxford and Cambridge during these years. Indeed, in 1908, the Governors recorded with obvious pleasure a series of outstanding successes by Old Edwardians in their Final Degrees—H. Alcock (1st Class in Modern History at Magdalen College, Oxford), A. M. Goodman (1st Class in Mathematics at New College, Oxford), C. G. Broom (1st Class in Classics at Brasenose College, Oxford), D. D. B. Jay (2nd Class in Natural Science at Selwyn College, Cambridge). The majority of university candidates, however, now looked to Bristol, where many of them studied science.

Opportunity for higher study of this kind was made available to them through the generous provision of School Leaving Exhibitions. In 1920 the *Robert Dyer Commans Fund* (established in 1906) was helping to support three boys at Bristol and one at Oxford, the *Edmund White Fund*, (established in 1895) was maintaining three boys at Bristol and the *Nahum Nurnberg Fund* (established in 1919) a £60 exhibition for one boy at Bristol. The 1920 Inspectors stressed that, whereas a few boys occasionally proceeded to university, there was 'at present no class doing advanced work'. The New Scheme of 1914, for which the Governors had successfully applied had, at least removed three of the major stumbling blocks for future development—the maximum leaving age had now been raised to eighteen, Greek could again be restored to the curriculum and, most important of all, the School was re-instated as a School of the First Grade.

The educational ladder, which extended upwards to the Universities, also extended downwards into the local Elementary Schools. Mr. Symons made a point of meeting the headmasters from these schools to establish close personal contact. Furthermore, in 1914, the Chairman of the Bath Local Education Authority became an ex-officio Governor of the School. By 1920 there were seventeen boys holding free scholarships from Elementary Schools, including five awarded under the new Free Place Scheme of the Board of Education. The remainder were financed from the original Foundation Funds or from the *Edmund White Fund*. All applicants were, of course, required to fulfil the academic demands of the entrance exam. Bath Education Committee had also shown an earlier interest (in 1903) in sending up to eight 'pupil teachers' a year from their Elementary Schools on local authority scholarships. Once in King Edward's, pupils from all backgrounds were encouraged to work hard through an increasing number of prizes offered annually. To those already mentioned were added, during this period, the *Nahum Nurnberg Prizes* (from a fund of £3,385 bequeathed in 1919), the *Tutell Science Prizes* (bequeathed in 1914 by T. J. Tutell, a former Foundation Scholar) and the *Laurence Cook Prize* for High Endeavour 'in recognition of character and a good spirit rather than ability alone' (provided in 1921 by Councillor R. G. Cook in memory of his son, who was killed in the war). Meanwhile, the *Brodrick Medal* had been revived, struck in bronze and offered as a prize for Mathematics.

When Mr. Symons retired in 1921, he could just look back on his term of office with satisfaction. He had largely achieved the targets set for him by the Governors, at least by implication—a substantial increase to the number of boys in the School, a sound basic education for the sons of local people, success in public examinations, firm disciplinary control, the broadening of the curriculum to accommodate Science and other 'modern' subjects and the creation of a Boarding House. It was, therefore, curious that, when the Governors presented him with a decorated scroll as an expression of their thanks for his twenty-five years of devoted service, they should highlight two of his other achievements: 'Two of the outstanding features that mark his headmastership', they recorded, 'are the establishment of the Prep School and the Officers' Training Corps, started as a Cadet Corps in 1900'. It is certainly true that he had done far more than ever they had asked. The growth of a distinctive School spirit owed much to his inspiration and reform—a spirit which spread outwards through the ranks of the Old Edwardians' Association and through the pages of *The Edwardian*.

Viscount Simon (Old Edwardian, who left School in 1887); Attorney-
General, 1913–15; Home Secretary, 1915–16; Foreign Secretary,, 1931–35,
Chancellor of the Exchequer, 1937–40; Lord Chancellor, 1940–45.

National Portrait Gallery

He had had the gratification of reading three commenda-
tory Inspectors' Reports on his School in 1904, 1912 and 1920
and of witnessing the granting of First Grade Status in 1914.
He had taken pleasure in the progress of humble boys as they
climbed the educational ladder to University—just as he had
rejoiced in 1910 when Sir John Simon, a pupil of his predecessor, had been appointed Solicitor-General. It was, without
doubt, a reminder to him of the School's long traditions of
service, to which he had contributed so richly himself. If his
aims had been limited, then they had essentially been limited
by the difficult situation in which he had found himself. Much
undoubtedly remained to be accomplished in the future—the
revival of real scholarship through the links with Oxford and
Cambridge, the recruitment of a more highly qualified and
specialised teaching staff, the development of sport and
extra-curricular activities and the re-housing of the School
itself.

Throughout his term of office at King Edward's, he was
loyally supported by his wife Katherine E. Symons. A charm-
ing and erudite lady, she was the sister of the poet, Professor
A. E. Housman, author of *The Shropshire Lad* and Fellow of
Trinity College, Cambridge. Mrs. Symons subsequently
wrote the first history of the School, which was published in
1934 and entitled *The Grammar School of King Edward VI, Bath,
and its Ancient Foundation*. According to a later tribute paid to
him by an Old Boy, Mr. Symons took little part in the public
affairs of the City. 'He was a man of retiring disposition and
made few friends outside the circle of his School. His working
life was spent in those duties, in his home and in his books.'
When, in January 1921, he announced to the Governors his
plans for retirement, he put forward two reasons. First, the
changes required under the terms of the newly-acquired
Recognised Status would call for 'further energy than he could
afford'. Secondly, his retirement would free his residence at 20
Belmont for use as a Prep School and thus help to ease the
problem of overcrowding at Broad Street.

After seven years of retirement in Bath, he and his wife
eventually moved down to Exeter, where he died in 1932 at
the age of 75.

CHAPTER FIVE

Broad Street—Years of Consolidation, 1921–1961

'Some solid work is done in the School, but in the main the general standard is far from being as high as it ought to be in a school of standing. It is hoped that . . . the School will rise to a position worthy of its traditions and of the place which it ought to occupy in the City of Bath. At present there is a tendency to accept and acquiesce in the present standard, which is too low. The School should aim at taking a leading position, sending on the best of its boys with good prospects to a University.' (Report of the Board of Education Inspectors, 1920.)

City, State and Education, 1921–1961

This period was to witness nationally the post-war depression, the General Strike of 1926, the first Labour Government of 1924, the economic slump of the 1930's, unemployment, the rise of Hitler and the Second World War. Locally, Bath escaped most of the extreme consequences of these events. Unemployment reached a peak of a mere 2,739 in 1932; population declined slightly; industry expanded modestly at Stothert's, Horstmann's, Pitman's and Lock's; tourists attended the Spa steadily; the Corporation cleared slums gradually and built some two thousand council houses between the wars. Bath's comfortable existence was temporarily halted in April 1942 when the 'Baedeker' bomb attacks killed 417 people and damaged over 1,900 properties. Of even greater significance to the future development of the City, however, was the arrival in 1939 of the Admiralty from London. Taking over the Empire Hotel as its first headquarters, it subsequently expanded into a hutted site at Foxhill and eventually became the biggest single employer in Bath.

Meanwhile, the educational system had, by 1945, developed a distinctive shape. Although the Education Act of 1918 (The Fisher Act) had remained largely ineffective due to post-war economic problems, the Hadow Report of 1926 clearly outlined a pattern for the future. Secondary Education was to become available for all children whether in 'grammar' schools, 'modern' schools, 'senior classes' or in 'junior technical' schools. The Education Act of 1936 did its best to assist in the reorganisation of schools along these lines. It was not until 1944, however, that theories were effectively put into practice. Based on an all-party desire to make educational facilities more adequate, the Butler Act of that year made sweeping changes. The Board of Education was replaced by a Ministry of Education; Local Education Authorities now became responsible for both primary and secondary schools; 'elementary' schools were abolished; education was henceforth to be organised in 'three progressive stages'—primary, (from 5 to 11 years), secondary (from 11 to 16 or 18 years) and further; schools were to commence each day with an act of collective worship; the school-leaving age was raised to fifteen; fees in maintained secondary schools were abolished; school meals were to be provided. Direct Grant and Independent Schools were allowed to exist outside the System and to continue charging fees (except, of course, to those pupils who held 'free places'). During this period, Bath Education Authority showed considerable vigour in expanding the local service. In 1921 Oldfield Boys' and Girls' Schools were raised in status to Senior Schools; two Grammar Schools were built; and a Technical College was established in 1936 in the former premises of the Royal United Hospital.

Captain A. W. Annand, 1921–1945

The man selected by the Governors to take over as Headmaster in 1921 was Captain A. W. Annand, M.C., M.A. It proved to be a wise appointment. After completing his early education at Shrewsbury School, he became a scholar at Pembroke College, Cambridge, where he studied both Classics and History. Having gained wide teaching experience in schools of good standing, he was elected Headmaster of King's School, Peterborough in 1913. War, however, was to interrupt his career. In 1915 he obtained a commission in the Army, serving in France for sixteen months with the Gordon Highlanders. He was wounded twice and received the Military Cross in 1917.

Captain A. W. Annand, Headmaster 1921–1945.

School Archives

To Captain Annand, therefore, fell the task of implementing the changes suggested by the 1920 Inspectors' Report. This was to include the transition from complete financial independence to a situation in which public money was accepted as a fact of life. Faced with rising costs and the establishment of the Burnham Scale of salaries for schoolmasters, the Governors had finally bowed to the pressure which Board of Education Inspectors had steadily exerted in their Reports of 1904, 1912 and 1920. Urged to upgrade the School into the sort of establishment 'of which they and the City of Bath might with more just reason be proud', they somewhat reluctantly applied for official Recognition in 1920. The immediate assistance received locally from the Bath Education Committee (see above) was substantially augmented in 1921 when Direct Grant status was conferred on the School. This enabled the Governors to receive grants from the Board of Education in return for accepting a maximum of 25 per cent of their intake as Scholarship (or Free Place) boys from the local Elementary Schools.

Consequently, the post-war financial crisis had been somewhat lifted by 1922. The situation was further eased by the paying off of two earlier loans, by the increase of rents for certain properties in the City and by the raising of School fees from £5 to £7 7s. per term. This released a greater supply of ready cash to modify the Broad Street buildings in accordance with the Inspectors' recommendations. Certainly by the time of the next Inspection in 1927, it was possible to report that 'the financial situation of the School has improved substantially' and that 'the general prospects of the Foundation for the future appear to be quite satisfactory'. Nevertheless, this meant little more in reality than ensuring for the School a state of mere survival in its Broad Street premises. Any hope of finding the capital to transfer King Edward's completely onto a new site remained a pipe dream for years to come.

Meanwhile, the 'Free Place' boys began to trickle into the School from the local Elementary Schools. By 1927 there were twenty-seven such boys receiving support either from the Local Authority or from the School's own endowments (that is, the funds established by Nahum Nurnberg, Robert Dyer Commans and Edmund White). Although it took some time for the system to become fully operative, its real potential was evident right from the start. Over the years, King Edward's was to benefit richly as able boys from humble backgrounds were given opportunities, through the Direct Grant System, to climb the educational ladder. At the Prize-Giving of 1928, Capt. Annand reported with evident pride that 'three boys who obtained Free Places in the School in 1921 have been able . . . to go up to Oxford or Cambridge, where they have every prospect of taking a good Honours Degree'. His prophecy came true. Three years later, he was able to announce that all three boys had gained Second Class Degrees. 'It is doubtful', he continued, 'whether any of these boys could have proceeded to the University at all without the very substantial assistance which they received from the Exhibition funds of the School: and it must be a matter of satisfaction, both to the Governors and to the City Authorities, to learn that they have turned out so well, and made the most of their chances.'

By 1922, Captain Annand had not only found relief in financial matters, but also on the question of over-crowding. The Inspectors had been adamant that the Preparatory School must be found accommodation of its own in a separate building in order to release much-needed space for the senior classes. The retirement of Mr. Symons in 1921 provided the opportunity. His official Headmaster's residence at 20, Belmont, which the Governors had purchased in 1899, was quickly ear-marked for conversion into the Preparatory School—a process which had been completed by 1922. In taking this decision, the Governors at the same time ruled that it was no longer their function to provide a house for the Headmaster—probably the first time in the School's history that this had been the case. Capt. Annand was nevertheless delighted at the freeing of three additional rooms, on the first floor at the front of the school, caused by the evacuation of the youngest boys. One of these was quickly adapted into a Junior Science Demonstration Laboratory and another into a Form Room for the Fifth. The smallest room was later converted (in 1923) into a Reference Library.

The Preparatory School itself, which had originally been established in 1898 under Miss Neal and Miss Shum, was now placed under the care of Mr. J. H. C. Dunn, who was made

Master-in-Charge. Originally Second Form Master in the main School, he was (as J. F. Langley recalls) a man 'of bucolic complexion, addicted to good tweed suits who carried an air of agriculture about him'. He continued to be assisted by Miss Neal, who was 'a trifle eccentric and the butt of much young humour', and Miss Shum 'who was rather more shy and subject to sudden hot flushes, which you took for rage but which were not so'. When Miss Neal retired in 1927, after nearly thirty years devoted service, she was replaced by Major W. Lewis, M.C., who eventually became Master-in-Charge in 1937 on the retirement of Mr. Dunn.

B. Henson recalls the happy life he experienced in the Preparatory School during these years. The Gardening Club, held in the Conservatory after School; the Stamp Club, organised by Mr. Dunn; and Miss Wood's singing lessons (there was no piano—just a tuning fork) all helped to enliven the proceedings (though Miss Wood's large baton was frequently used as a cane by Maj. Lewis). The Inspectors who visited the School in 1927, however, were less enthusiastic about the singing lessons, complaining that the boys 'slouch and sing with their heads down'. On Sundays, the Prep boys were required to wear Eton Collars and (in summer) straw boaters. Inventive young minds, needless to say, quickly discovered that these could be put to more enjoyable use by skimming them over any available water. Miss Shum, who expected the highest standards of behaviour, would certainly have disapproved. Boys who met her in the street were expected not merely to touch their caps, but to remove them completely as they passed her by.

H. M. Porter recalls the extent of the new accommodation provided for the Prep School. 'At 20 Belmont, the Master-in-Charge had a Study on the ground floor facing the street, and his large and sunny classroom, where he taught the top form, was also on that floor, with a fine view across country to Bathampton Down. On the first floor there was another large classroom of the same dimension for Form PII, and a small classroom, above the Study and facing the noisy street, housed the lowest Form PI, which was always kept small. Cloakrooms and lavatories were fitted out in the basement, heating apparatus and electric light were installed, and the garden became a small asphalt playground. The top of the building was let by the Governors as a flat, the first tenant being a master, Mr. Holland. The Preparatory School, more accurately re-named 'King Edward's School, Bath, Junior School' in 1959, remained the responsibility of the Headmaster of the whole school. He visited it regularly to read out the fortnightly marks and to administer praise and blame, as occasion arose. He took part in the admission interviews and retained the right of final decision on admissions.' Numbers varied between 40 and 72 throughout this period.

Captain Annand's Reforms, 1921–1923

Assured of both financial stability and reasonable space, Captain Anand threw himself whole heartedly into the task of introducing the improvements recommended by the Inspection Report of 1920. His first two full years of office witnessed, in consequence, a great variety of exciting changes, which generated a considerable amount of enthusiasm and spirit amongst all those connected with the School. The new Headmaster's qualities of charm, decisiveness and tact ensured that the reforms were carried out with maximum speed and minimum opposition. In drawing up his plans, he demonstrated clearly both an organising ability and a capacity for working out those minute details which are essential to the success of any administrative reform.

His first assignment was to dismantle the Form Master system, which had been heavily criticised by the Board of Education Inspectors, and to introduce a system of specialist teaching. Whereas previously the Form Master had been responsible for teaching his Form in practically every subject (except Science), in future his role would be somethat different. This is described by H. M. Porter: 'A Form Master would be a sort of "moral tutor" exercising "pastoral care". It was, of course, necessary that he should take his Form for at least one subject. His most definite task was to add up marks handed to him by subject masters at the end of every fortnight, to make out the Form Order and to write comments, and similarly at the end of each term. These marks and comments, with the comments of the subject masters, were read out in front of Mr. Annand on alternate Monday afternoons. (His sight was very defective.) A succession of adverse comments indicating laziness led to a caning, often with very salutary effects.'

Needless to say, the Form Master system could not be completely replaced overnight. There was little room for such flexibility in a one-stream school, where different subjects were allocated varying amounts of teaching time each week. Existing staff were, therefore, required to specialise as best they could and, instead of teaching the full range of subjects, to concentrate rather on their strengths. Mr. Jago, for instance, taught History, Latin and English, whereas Mr. Kent taught both Geography and Mathematics. Gradually, however, specialised 'Departments' began to emerge as individuals were made responsible for the organisation of particular subjects within the school—Mr. Langley for Science, Mr. Williamson for English, Mr. Jago for History and Mr. Kent for Geography. This process could only be speeded up by the appointment of new staff who, in future, came not as Form Masters, but as subject specialists. Captain Annand was at least able to make a start in this direction in 1922, when he appointed Mr. E. T. Symons to be responsible for 'the teaching and organisation of Mathematics throughout the School', Mr. R. H. Hollowell to teach Modern Languages, and Mr. W. A. Holland to teach French. All three were graduates of Oxbridge. Opportunities for later reinforcement, however, proved to be few and far between.

While these changes were taking place in the teaching structure, a series of further reforms was being applied to the organisation and content of the year's work. The School Year itself, which had previously been brought to a climax in December with the taking of the Senior Cambridge Local Examination, would in future be reckoned from September to July. To meet the requirements of the Board of Education, a completely revised syllabus of work in each subject was drafted and the timetable reorganised accordingly. Sets were remodelled for the teaching of Mathematics throughout the school and formed for the first time in Latin and French for the Junior Forms. The new scheme, which came into operation in September 1922, provided for a four-year course leading up to the Cambridge Senior Local Examination (re-named the 'School Certificate' in 1923). Taken in the Fifth Form, it was no longer to be regarded as a leaving Certificate, but as 'a first examination'. Capt. Annand expressed the hope, in his Prize Giving Speech of 1922, 'that a sufficient number of boys will remain at the School, after passing the First Examination, to take a full Two Years' Advanced Course in the Sixth Form, and pass the Second Examination [soon to be called the 'Higher School Certificate] before entering into business or going on to a University'. This was, in effect, the beginning of the idea of the modern Sixth Form with a purposeful and clearly-defined two-year course. Only boys who had passed the Senior Local Examination in the Fifth Form would in future be allowed to proceed into the Sixth.

Boys at King Edward's School, during the period 1922 to 1945, had the opportunity to gain the Cambridge School Certificate in Religious Instruction, English, History, Geography, French, Mathematics, Chemistry and either Latin or Physics. (This choice had to be made at the end of the third year). In the Sixth Form, boys taking 'Arts' subjects could choose from a rather short list of English, History, French and Latin. Scientists, however, normally took Mathematics, Physics and Chemistry *or* Mathematics as a 'double subject' and Physics. Teaching resources were such that boys in the Upper and Lower Sixth Forms were taught simultaneously.

The reforms of Capt. Annand, however, were by no means limited to the academic sphere. Much criticism had been raised by the Board of Education Inspectors in 1920 about the dreadful lack of opportunity available to the boys in sport (see above). Capt. Annand, a keen lover of games himself, applied himself to this particular challenge with abundant relish. Perhaps his most significant introduction was the establishment of a House System in 1922. The Day Boys were divided into three Houses, which were named after their Housemasters—Mr. Jago, Mr. Williamson and Mr. Symonds. The Boarding House, under Rev. Hardy, already existed as a ready-made unit to provide the fourth grouping for a wide range of activities and competitions. House Notes, which made their first appearance in *The Edwardian* of December

1922, give some idea of the initial interest and enthusiasm which the new system aroused. Inter-House matches in cricket and rugby at least provided far more boys of all ages with the opportunity of taking part in competitive sport.

Other athletic events were quickly added to the sporting calendar of the four Houses. Inter-House Cross Country races first made their appearance in the Spring of 1922, with courses usually based on the route from North Road to Sydney Gardens (via Brassnocker Hill, Monkton Combe, Monument Fields and The Tyning!). House Paper Chases were also tried in the following year. The annual Athletic Sports were first held on the Recreation Ground in April 1923. Challenge Cups were offered for the best senior and junior athletes, whereas the Houses themselves competed for the Hooper Inter-House Cup. This also became the centre of a new idea in 1925 to stimulate more active support for the School 1st XV on Saturday afternoons, a scheme outlined by *The Edwardian*:

> 'Owing to the slackness of attendance at School Matches, it was decided this term to introduce a system by which attendance counted points for the Hooper Cup. The House which had the greatest number of members present at certain matches gained five points. This has certainly ensured much needed support for the School XV, as the system is working well up to the present.'

Later still, in 1938, points were awarded to boys who obtained minimum 'standards' in athletic events prior to Sports Day itself. These points, which were added to those gained in the actual competitions when assessing the eventual winners of The Hooper Cup, enabled all boys to feel that they were contributing in some way to the success of their House. Greater variety to the races was ensured in 1927, when the Mayor of Bath generously donated a set of adjustable hurdles to the School. From these early beginnings, athletics gradually established itself as a sport at King Edward's, with teams regularly taking part in the annual inter-school Rotary Club Competitions on the Recreation Ground.

Swimming, on the other hand, had already made its mark, thanks to the enthusiastic lead given by the Rev. F. Hardy over several years. By 1922 the School had regular bookings at the Royal Swimming Baths on Thursday and Saturday evenings for lessons in basic swimming, life-saving and water polo. Furthermore, as *The Edwardian* suggested; 'If a boy is an aspirant for long-distance swimming in the Avon, he has only to mention the matter to Mr. Hardy and every facility will be given him.' So accomplished did the boys become, that they were frequently called upon to give exhibitions of swimming and diving or to take part in local galas. School Swimming Sports had already been established as a major Autumn Term event before Capt. Annand's arrival, although they had essentially provided races for individual competitors. In 1925, however, they were organised for the first time on an Inter-House basis. Quite apart from the normal swimming events, competition were included for fancy costume, survival on the 'greasy pole' and life saving. The Sports usually ended with a water polo match often between the School and the junior team of the Bath Dolphins.

The House system quickly gained momentum and was noticeably successful during this period. Matters of internal House policy, including the award of House Colours, were decided by the House Master, the House Captain and three House Prefects. House blazers were introduced some time later, but had virtually disappeared from the scene by 1938. According to H. E. Norris, writing later in *The Edwardian*, 'boys had to wear cross clubs of the colour of their House on the ordinary School Cap, but it was sometimes feared that not every boy did so. As a consequence it was no unusual practice for the powers to hold a House Cap inspection, and take steps to ensure every boy displayed his colours.'

The impetus given to sport by Capt. Annand's reforms was not confined, however, to the introduction of a House System. He was most anxious to pay immediate attention to the physical development of younger boys. With this in mind, he started the practice in 1923 of allowing the junior Forms to play games, under the supervision of a master, as part of the time-table on Thursday afternoons. Games for the majority of the boys, of course, continued to be voluntary on the Wednesday or Saturday half-days. By this time, the Headmaster had already made radical alterations to the organisation of gymnastic classes. Previous arrangements had proved unsatisfactory with infrequent lessons and large mixed-age groups.

From 1922, classes were reduced in size and limited to boys in the ten to thirteen age bracket, who now received instruction twice a week. Older boys were expected to join the O.T.C. where, according to Capt. Annand, they would be taught 'military drill and other exercises' as a form of compensation.

Later, in 1934, when new Board of Education Regulations made Physical Training compulsory for all boys, two periods a week were also allocated to senior Forms. This was only achieved, much to the Headmaster's disgust, at the expense of other subjects. Mr. Brewer, who was hurriedly sent off during the holidays on a crash-course at the P.T. Centre in Barry, valiantly covered the additional lessons involved. Junior classes continued throughout this period, however, to receive instruction from Capt. Olssen in his private Gymnasium based in The Paragon. Such was the enthusiasm aroused that, by 1923, annual Gymnastic Displays were being arranged in aid of the Sports' Fund. Three years later these were merged into the Inter-House Gymnastics Competition for the Bird Challenge Trophy, which henceforth became a regular event in the Spring Term. Groups of boys were often invited to give displays at local fêtes or to raise money for charity through their growing reputation for Gymnastics.

Probably the most dramatic reform made by Capt. Annand at this time was the introduction of Rugby in 1922 as the School winter game in place of Soccer. Reasons for the change were outlined in *The Edwardian*:

> '. . . For some years the School Fixture list has been growing more and more unsatisfactory. By degrees nearly all our old opponents on many a hard fought Soccer field have gone over to the Rugby game, until last term the School was forced to give fixtures to teams which were not suitable in School Football . . . Another reason in favour of Rugby is that more men are wanted to compose a team than in Association, and consequently a larger number of boys will be able to take a share in playing games for the School, as thirty boys will be wanted for the First and Second Teams instead of twenty-two.'

Prompted and encouraged by the Bath Rugby Club, the School therefore embarked on its first full season with somewhat limited success, winning only 5 out of its 18 matches. Its first recorded fixtures against local School rivals took place as

1st XV Rugby Team, 1922.
Back row: J. L. Coulter (touch judge), J. N. Buse, H. C. L. Morris, J. W. S. Ryan, M. G. Wood, C. H. Illidge, J. K. Chappell, D. C. Leaman, A. E. Abel.
Front row: C. T. Leaman, P. Dalsell, F. F. Jones, F. D. Biggs (Capt.) B. E. Ireland, C. L. Pinnegar, V. C. Pyster.

follows: Bath City Secondary School (1922), St. Brendan's (1922), Cotham School (1922), Kingswood 2nd XV (1923), Prior Park (1924), Downside 'A' (1925) and Colston's 2nd XV (1925). Junior teams commenced playing against Monkton Combe Junior School and Kingswood in 1923 and against Downside in 1924. In spite of the newness of the game, two outstandingly good seasons were enjoyed during this period. In 1926–27, the 1st XV won eleven out of its fourteen matches (with one drawn), while the 1931–32 team did even better by winning sixteen out of ninteen games (also with one drawn).

The growing variety of sporting activity is further illustrated by the growth of Boxing within the School. This was again inspired by the Rev. F. Hardy as an activity largely available for boys in the Boarding House. Instructors were brought in to coach those who showed interest and regular competitions were held. In 1921 an Exhibition Match was staged at the Boarding House between the boarders and a team of 'visitors'. This was followed a year later by a Tournament between the School and the Fairfield Park Club and, in 1924, by a match against members of the 4th Somerset Light Infantry. Individual boys were able to carry their boxing skills into competitions staged annually at the O.T.C. summer camps. The Sport, which suffered greatly from the departure of Mr. Hardy in 1925, gradually died out in later years.

Sport within the School was co-ordinated by means of the School Games Committee, another of Capt. Annand's creations. This was composed of representatives of each House, who sat with the masters who were in charge of the particular games, under the Chairmanship of the Headmaster. The Committee was responsible for electing team officials at the beginning of each season, drawing up rules for internal Competitions, making fixtures and awarding Colours. A system of Half Colours for Cricket commenced in 1925 to encourage loyal team members, who were not necessarily outstanding. Boys awarded Half Colours would be entitled to wear the maroon and white cap and blazer (without a badge). If, at a later stage, they were awarded Full Colours, the Tudor Rose badge would be added to both garments, together with the date of award.

In various other ways, too, Capt. Annand brought new life and interest onto the scene. In 1922, for instance, he started a series of Evening Lectures at Broad Street, partly with the aim of raising money for the Sports Fund. These continued over several years, attracting sizeable audiences drawn from the boys, their parents, Old Boys and groups from other schools. B. Henson recalls that boys paid 4d. for a ticket and were excused homework into the bargain. Certainly the lectures, many of which were illustrated by lantern slides, covered a wide range of colourful topics—'Adventures as a Spy', 'Frauds and Forgeries', 'The Royal North-West Mounted Police', 'Two Years in the Antarctic', 'The Buried City of Pompeii', 'The Zulu of the African Veldt', and so on. In 1923, a much-needed Reference Library was established in a small

room on the first floor. The balance of £232 from the War
Memorial Fund was made available for the purchase of books.
Two years later, Mr. Heap started a secondhand book store
for text-books, thus enabling boys to purchase essential books
at lower prices (and, of course, to sell them back again later
when no longer required). Electric lighting was installed
throughout the building during the winter of 1926–27, bringing considerable benefit to the depressingly dark classrooms
throughout the School. Clubs and societies also began to show
a flicker of life. A Chess Club was formed in 1922 and the
Debating Society revived in 1927. Perhaps the only really
successful group during these early years, however, was the
Wireless Club, formed in 1924. Meetings were held at School
each Wednesday evening to listen to broadcasts, to make
modifications to the School wireless set and to read technical
publications which were bought out of the subscriptions.

The Wireless Club also contributed to a most enterprising
project launched by some senior boys in 1926. This is
described by H. E. Norris, one of the participants:

'During the General Strike of 1926, when the Press was
paralysed, and the only news was that contained in broadcast
News Bulletins, it was thought that capital might be made out
of this, and a paper produced for the benefit of Dr. Barnardo's
Homes. So for six days *The K.E.S. Gazette* was produced . . .

Produced on the first day as a single broadsheet, the subsequent issues boasted four pages, and it was printed on the
duplicator used ordinarily for the reproduction of examination
papers. The Editorial and Printing Offices, by courtesy of Mr.
Jago, were in the Corps Orderly Room, which we were allowed
to have after the Masters, not realising the importance of our
work, had refused us the use of one of their Common Rooms.
We had a leading article each day, and two of these articles
were written by the Headmaster; a cartoon appeared on four of
the days. Any space not so occupied, or by news (provided by
the Wireless Club in conjunction with the B.B.C.) we filled up
ourselves as best we could.

The price was fixed, hopefully, at a minimum of one penny
and all our takings were to be given to Dr. Barnardo's. I
remember that one Master gave us 6d. for our second issue.
Modesty, or greed, prevented us from offering change, but we
felt rather hurt when he treated this as a life subscription and

received free copies of the remaining issues. Our gross takings amounted to £1 10s., but whether in a strictly business concern this could be called pure profit, I am very doubtful, for we had some caustic remarks from Mr. Jago, on whose chair in the Orderly Room we had, as we were told, spilt hectographic ink, and so caused the ruin of his uniform breeches.'

This growing spirit and liveliness in the community quickly spread across into the ranks of the Old Edwardians' Association. These were, without question, the golden years of that particular organisation. Social activities of all kinds flourished. A regular series of dances in the Assembly Rooms was launched during the winter of 1923–1924 with gatherings in October, December, January and March. Two years later, the first Christmas Ball was held in the Pump Room. This became a most popular annual event for years to come, normally taking place on Boxing Night. An Easter Dance (on Easter Monday) soon followed. Whist drives were staged at the Red House; occasional 'Theatre Nights' were arranged at the Theatre Royal; a summer outing to Bournemouth was organised in 1927; the Annual Dinner was held at either Fortt's or the Red House; a Club Room in the City was considered in 1927; a Dramatic Section was proposed in 1934. Great celebrations surrounded the Coming-of-Age Dinner arranged at Fortt's in May, 1928 to mark the foundation of the Association twenty-one years earlier.

On the sporting side, too, the Old Edwardians showed great enterprise and initiative. A Sports Section Committee had been formed in 1925 to co-ordinate its activities. Developments followed with break-neck speed. The O.E.'s Rugby Club was officially formed in 1926, although a few matches had been played during the previous year. Sharing a ground with the Bath Avon Rowing Club at Odd Down, opposite the Burnt House, the team quickly established a full range of twenty-seven fixtures during its first season and a fine reputation. They were even strong enough to form a 2nd XV in 1927. Meanwhile, a Tennis Club had been set up in 1925, using four courts on the Recreation Ground until a move was made to the Lansdown Grove Hotel in 1935. Mens' and Ladies' Teams took part in local competitions. In 1926 not only did an Old Edwardians Cricket team take the field in the first of a series of regular fixtures against local clubs, but there was also serious talk of forming an O.E.'s Platoon of the 4th Battalion of the Somerset Light Infantry.

Further afield, the London Association of Old Edwardians, which had been originally formed as an independent group, finally became affiliated to the parent body in 1924. This put an end to the ill-feeling which had gradually developed between the two organisations.. Regular dinners and smokers were held at The Old Cheshire Cheese in Fleet Street, whereas the more formal dinner/dances took place at the Hotel Belgravia. A local newspaper reporter witnessed, by chance, the comradeship and spirit which characterised the Old Edwardians Association in 1923:

> 'Boat Race night found me in a crowd in Leicester Square. I went over to the Monico and in crossing the hall to go into the Cafe, a board with the magic words, "Bath Old Edwardians" caught my eye. I walked up the red-carpeted stairs and as I neared the top, I heard lusty voices joining in the chorus of a song about "We'll all come up from Somerset". The door was slightly ajar and I was able to see a number of boys from the Old School enjoying what apparently was an impromptu smoker, after what I learnt had been a good dinner. The Chairman was of youthful appearance, but was supported on his right-hand side by a venerable gentleman, I should say, of nearly 80 summers. Unobserved, I listened to their little speeches and the good humoured chaff that was bandied across the table, and I realised that I, an old Bathonian, was in the presence of some sons of Somersetshire who occasionally met in London to renew old friendships and keep alive in the great metropolis the tradition of the grand Old School at Bath. I hastened away and soon found myself in the usual excited Boat Race crowd of Leicester Square again, but ever present in my ears were the sounds of voices singing, "We'll all come up from Somerset".'

The Inspection of 1927

By 1926, the Governors had good reason to feel more than pleased with the enthusiastic contribution made by Capt. Annand during his first five years in office. Essential reforms had been accomplished; new life and vigour had been generated throughout the School; the crisis of 1920 was clearly a thing of the past. This atmosphere of calm satisfaction was completely shattered, however, by the Inspection Report of 1927, which was scathing in the extreme. While recognition was given to the removal of the Preparatory Department and the reorganisation of the curriculum, most aspects of School life came in for severe criticism at the hands of the Inspectors.

In spite of minor modifications which had been made, the buildings could 'never be really adequate for the full needs of the School'. There was no proper library or reading room, no Art room and no room for 'Manual Instruction'. The accommodation for teaching Science was still inadequate; classroom walls were 'dingy' and in need of redecoration; there was a noticeable lack of pictures and illustrations; and 'the whole school should be furbished with suitable desks to replace the present clumsy benches'. Nor was it just material provision which seemed to be deficient. Although the Headmaster himself had 'very high academic qualifications', a stronger teaching Staff was urgently required for the future. The Inspectors observed: 'The older Masters have done useful work and have given faithful service to the School, and there are some good and effective teachers on the staff. On the whole, however, the staff is not very distinguished for a school of this standing, and as occasions arise it is essential that Masters with higher qualifications should be appointed.' The most immediate needs were for top-class specialists in Mathematics, Art and English, which was 'notably weak' in the school. Urgent provision should be made for at least some teaching of Art, Singing and Woodwork in the Senior School.

It was almost inevitable, therefore, that academic standards also came in for attack. 'The impression of the Inspectors that a higher standard ought to be reached in a school of this standing was confirmed by a consideration of examination results in the last three years which have been far from satisfactory. Of 54 boys entered for the School Certificate in these years, 28 (52 per cent) have failed, and of the present Sixth Form (15) it appears that only some two or three qualified for Matriculation at the School Certificate Examination.' Far too many boys were allowed to leave at an early age. In 1925–1926, for instance, half of those who left were under sixteen. 'Most of the boys who leave,' the Report noted, 'go into business. Very few (in the last three years only four) go on to a University, and not many enter the teaching profession.' The School was failing to offer sufficiently good prospects 'to really able and ambitious boys'. No University Scholarships had been won 'for a very long time'; a large surplus, therefore, remained untapped in the fund of Leaving Exhibitions.

In conclusion, the Inspectors urged the School to 'make a very definite effort' to stir itself out of its mediocre state. Above all it needed to re-discover its old ambition of excellence. 'A good deal of steady (if not very inspiring) work is done . . . The School has advantages; it should raise its whole aim and endeavour . . . At present there is a tendency to accept and acquiesce in the present standard, which is too low. The School should aim at taking a leading position, sending on the best of its boys with good prospects to a University.' Only then would the School 'rise to a position worthy of its traditions and of the place which it ought to occupy in the City of Bath'.

Capt. Annand was far too big a man to resent criticism. With the backing of the Governors, he immediately set about the task of correcting the faults, as far as was humanly possible. By the end of 1928, he was able to report at Prize-giving that the Science Laboratories had been 'completely transformed' with up-to-date benches, equipment and apparatus; class singing had been introduced to the two lower forms; a fine Steinway Grand Piano had been procured; a certain amount of handwork had been introduced into the Preparatory School; arrangements had been made with the Local Authority for two voluntary classes to be sent each week to the Technical School for instruction in woodwork; art classes had been started in Big School for the first three Forms. In 1929 a major programme of re-decoration was carried out; the old long desks in the Sixth Form Room were replaced with two large oak tables and leather chairs; a wide variety of pictures appeared all over the School—team photographs, Medici prints, engravings of Bath, time charts, British Museum photographs, reproductions of historic events; small plaster copies of Greek statues were purchased for classrooms.

These material improvements were, of course, comparative-

ly easy for a man of Capt. Annand's determination to achieve
in a rather short space of time. What was far more difficult
was to solve the essentially human aspects of the situation—
the problem of a staff that was 'not very distinguished', the
problem of early leavers; the problem of poor examination
results; the problem of ambition. Capt. Annand certainly did
his best. Circumstances enabled him to make two significant
new appointments in 1928. On the death of Mr. Williamson
and the departure of Mr. Hollowell, he recruited Mr. H. M.
Porter, M.A. (Cantab.) as Senior English Master and Mr. S.
A. Brewer B.A. (London), to take charge of French. They
quickly made an impact both in the academic sphere and in
the general life of the School. Mr. Porter was later to start a
Rambling Club and a Literary Society, to become a prominent officer in the O.T.C., Editor of *The Edwardian*, and
Treasurer of the Old Edwardians' Association. As J. F.
Langley recalls: 'His gusty personality made a great impression and brightened things up no end.' It was, perhaps, no
coincidence that examination results in English improved in a
rather dramatic manner. At the same time, Mr. Brewer
'taught us French so well that success in examination was
comparatively easy'. For about thirty years he devoted himself
wholeheartedly to School Rugby and Cricket, seldom sparing
himself a half-holiday. The opportunity to strengthen his team
even further by making additional Staff changes was, however, denied to Capt. Annand throughout the remaining years
of his Headmastership. Indeed, until his retirement in 1945,
only one new appointment was possible. In 1936, Mr. J. H.
Kent, the Senior Geography Master, retired after over twenty
years' service and was replaced by Mr. C. J. E. Betty, B.A., a
Cambridge Athletics Blue.

Capt. Annand, throughout these years, lost no opportunity
to preach to both parents and boys the advantages of staying
on at school. In his Prize-Giving Speech of 1935, he urged
parents to consider the advantages of Sixth Form education.
'Many a boy who has left school at 16 might have done so
much more if he had stayed a couple of years longer. He might
have obtained a place in the Football or Cricket team; he
might have become a Monitor or an N.C.O.; he might have
obtained his Certificate A or won the Cross Country Run.

Believe me, these things are of value; they give a boy a sense of achievement, a chance of leadership, an experience of responsibility, which not only gives him something to look back upon, and binds him closer to the School, but earns him individual recommendation for the qualities he has shown, when he comes to seek employment.' During the difficult years of the economic depression, a boy's 'future economic position and salary will depend on the knowledge he can command, and the qualities he has developed'. But Capt. Annand not only encouraged budding local businessmen to join the Sixth Form for their own material advantage, he also did his level best to persuade boys of ability to consider the prospects of University. In 1939, for instance, he pointed out to parents that it was possible to obtain 'substantial assistance from the Exhibition Funds of the School and usually additional grants from the City Authorities'. With care, a boy could pay his way on £175 a year at Oxford and Cambridge—half of which could be raised from public funds.

Gradually, with patient application, the Headmaster injected a small dose of ambition into the academic life of the School. It was hard work. The economic situation in the country at large was not in his favour. Local ambition did not run at a very high level in the City of Bath during the 1930's. But, by 1939, the average age of leavers had been raised to 16·9 years from just under 16 years in 1925–1926. The success rate in the School Certificate had improved from an average of 52 per cent during the years 1924–1926, to an average of 81 per cent during the years 1934–1936. Even as early as 1931, Capt. Annand had been able to report that only one boy had failed during the course of the year and that the pass-rate *with credit* in every subject had exceeded the national average by at least 10 per cent.

His hopes of persuading large numbers of boys to stay on into the Sixth Form to pursue the new advanced course, however, were totally frustrated. During the eighteen years which spanned the period between 1928 and 1945, only 33 boys were successful in gaining their Higher School Certificate (averaging a mere 1·8 passes a year). There was, nevertheless, a slight glimmer of better things to come as far as University entrance was concerned. Of the seven boys who composed the

The Sixth Form, 1936; taken in the Sixth Form Room (later to become the
Staff Common Room).
Back row: J. G. Webley, D. E. Oliffe, J. M. Smith (Head Boy), D. S.
Bidmead.

Front row: J. W. A. Lovell, R. F. Clark, S. J. Sutton, L. Weiner.

Photo by J. W. A. Lovell

Sixth Form in 1928–1929, no fewer than four eventually proceeded to Cambridge. Three of these gained Firsts in the Tripos exams of 1934. N. J. G. Pounds going on to become Professor of Geography at the University of Indiana. Scholarships, too, re-entered the scene after a lapse of many years. S. H. Tallamy won a War Memorial Scholarship in History at Oriel College, Oxford in 1934; J. Curtis gained an Open Exhibition in Latin and French at Christ's College, Cambridge in 1944; and D. E. Coombe was awarded a Major Scholarship in Natural Sciences at Christ's College, Cambridge in 1945, (where he later became a Fellow). It is true that these successes were only intermittant but, together with the steady trickle of boys entering Bristol University, they represented an encouraging turn of the tide.

The Never-Changing Scene, 1928–1945

'In retrospect, the feature which stands out most in my mind,' recalls Dr. J. B. Tucker (1934–1941), 'was that at K.E.S. nothing significant ever changed, and you could rely on that, for good or for bad—everything was utterly predictable.' Once Capt. Annand had completed his essential reforms, following the Inspections of 1920 and 1927, life at King Edward's fell into a very precise pattern. With one exception (see above), the Staff remained the same. Numbers remained the same (216, including the Prep, in 1928; 228 in 1945). The annual routine remained the same—Rugby in the winter, Cross Country and Athletic Sports in the Spring, Cricket in the Summer, Swimming Sports in the Autumn. July each year saw the School Certificate, the O.T.C. Inspection and the Inter-Platoon Competition with tea on the Recreation Ground (the only social function to which parents were invited). December heralded Prize-Giving in the Banqueting Room at the Guildhall. Chaired by the Mayor, complete with robes of office, it included a ritual singing of the School Song and the National Anthem. The ceremony ended with a round of cheers, led in turn by the six Prefects, for the King and Queen, the Mayor and Corporation, the Governors, the Prize-Giver, the Headmaster and Staff, and the Ladies. The pages of *The*

Edwardian, then a termly magazine, follow a predictable course—School Notes, O.T.C., The Rambling Club, The Literary Society, Rugby (or Cricket), House Notes, News of Old Boys, Old Edwardians' Association. Innovations hardly ever appeared on the scene to excite or to provoke.

Capt. Annand pursued a consistent line, too, with matters of discipline. J. W. A. Lovell recalls: 'He was held in great awe, although actually his rather forbidding appearance covered a rather retiring character. He had been gassed in the 1914 war, and thereafter suffered from poor eyesight. It was said spectacles were of no use to him and he rarely wore them. Instead he had a habit of peering at all documents from a distance of two or three inches only. I do not think he was a lover of corporal punishment, although I know my brother was once caned by him.' Dr. J. B. Tucker remembers, however, that boys whose names appeared three times in the 'Book' in one day for misbehaviour received an automatic beating 'and to give power to his arm, the late Capt. A. W. Annand was wont to take a short run, or perhaps amble, to the beating desk'.

During this period, the Headmaster continued to be assisted in matters of discipline by six Monitors. These were responsible, as J. W. A. Lovell describes, for a variety of tasks, including the marching of junior boys to Capt. Olsson's Gymnasium in The Paragon: It was never a popular duty escorting the crocodile to The Paragon, especially from Lansdown Road down Guinea Lane. Other duties of prefects included reading the Bible Lesson at morning prayers and calling the roll (all 7 forms or about 200 pupils), to be followed later by a check of absentees round all forms. Another duty was clearing the school rooms of all pupils at break times, when all members of the lower forms were securely bolted out in the playground. Masters were not involved in these events, being securely tucked away in their common rooms'. The only compulsory item of School uniform was the cap, although a School blazer (in navy blue, with chromium buttons and Tudor Rose badge) was made available in 1938.

Nor did the actual School premises at Broad Street witness any changes in structure or usage between 1928 and 1945. Life within became increasingly static. On the left of the front door

The School in the 1930's.

Photo by William Morris

was the Headmaster's Study (also used for Governors' meetings), which had been completely redecorated after a small fire in 1929. Immediately opposite was the Sixth Form Room under the care of Mr. S. A. Brewer. 'Big School,' the original School Room, was used as the Fourth Form Room (controlled by Capt. E. O. Jago) as well as for both Assembly and Art. It still housed a high desk along each wall to accommodate four masters—a relic of earlier days when most classes were taught in the same room. The Third Form, under Mr. J. H. Kent, occupied the original boarders' dining room on the ground floor. Rooms at the front of the School on the first floor, previously used as bedrooms by the Headmaster's family, had been converted into a Fifth Form Room (under Mr. H. M. Porter), a Junior Science Laboratory (controlled by Capt. J. C. McKee) and a Reference Library. At a slightly higher level, in rooms which had formerly been used as dormitories, were Mr. W. A. Holland's Second Form Room (which

contained the grand piano for singing lessons), the large
Chemistry Laboratory (under the watchful eye of Mr. E. T.
Langley, the Second Master and Senior Science Master) and
the smaller Physics Laboratory. On the top floor of all were
two classrooms used as First Form Rooms by Mr. J. S. Heap
(Form 1B) and Mr. J. Morgan (Form 1A). Off the landing
were five rooms, previously employed to house domestic
servants or, latterly, the caretaker and his family. These had
been converted by Capt. Annand into a Top Common Room
for Staff, a room for the Wireless Club and O.T.C.
signallers, the Sand Table Room (used by the O.T.C. for
teaching tactics to Certificate 'A' candidates), the Orderly
Room or Corps Office and a Quartermaster's Stores. There
was also a Band cupboard full of drums and bugles.

Finally, back on the ground floor, there was an additional
small room which had at one time been the Headmaster's
Study, but was now officially the caretaker's base. H. M.
Porter describes its importance:

'Here sat Sergeant Cadby, ready to answer the front door bell
and to ring the hand-bell, kept on a table under the clock (along
with the Detention Book) at the end of every period. But few
realised that this was not the Masters' Room. It was used as
such because masters could not possibly climb up to the Top
Common Room to dump a pile of books or for a few minutes of
Break: they crowded into this small room, shut the door and
smoked. (Morning coffee was unknown in those days in most
schools.) Many Old Boys will remember the vast billows of
smoke that suddenly burst forth from the doorway when a boy
knocked and asked if he could speak to a master. The official
Top Common Room was seldom occupied except during the
dinner hour, when Mr. Morgan and Mr. Dunn ate their
sandwiches there. When Mr. Heap came back from lunch at
the Red House, they all played Bridge, in a jocose-quarrelsome
manner.

It is worth noting that from the departure of the Symons
family in 1899 until the provision of school dinners became
compulsory in 1946 (under the Act of 1944), no meals were
cooked or provided in the School. Apart from sandwiches
brought by two masters and a handful of boys, the only food
consumed on the premises was buns and doughnuts sold by the
School Sergeant/Caretaker in the "Bun Room" in the basement

at Break. They came from Sturtewagen's shop three doors away, a shop famous for making the best cream slices in Bath. Visiting teams after matches were taken to a Cafe, Norton Dairies, in Argyle Street, for tea . . .'

The School Sergeant was also responsible for tolling the School Bell at ten minutes to nine, operated by a rope pulled in the basement. That part of the basement, which was situated under Big School, was used as a covered playground paved with large stones. Under the Third Form Room was a long, dark room, which Mr. Macleane had converted into a classroom in the nineteenth century. After use during the 1920's as a bicycle shed, it was fitted out as a changing room for P.T. in 1939. The miniature range was located in a long, stone tunnel under the School's front terrace.

In spite of repeated criticisms of the building by a long line of Inspectors from the Board of Education, the Broad Street premises had proved themselves capable of dealing with most of the changing needs of a Grammar School over nearly two hundred years. H. M. Porter later wrote: 'What strikes one most forcibly is the almost infinite adaptability of the Broad Street building.' Capt. Annand expressed his own affections at Prize-Giving in 1927:

'Admittedly, the buildings are old and not of a type which would be constructed nowadays for the purpose, but they enshrine a tradition which I, for one, should deplore to see tampered with. Tradition is a thing which cannot be built up in a day, or even in a generation: it is the heritage of the past; and the value which a boy gets at school is not the value of the bench on which he sits, however comfortable or hygienic, but the value of the instruction which he receives, and the example which he imbibes.'

It was nevertheless true that many boys in this period continued to sit on benches which were decidedly uncomfortable and were, in fact, relics of the previous century. Long desks, made to accommodate five boys, were permanently attached to the benches by means of metal supports and give little room for manoeuvre.

One of the most stable School activities throughout Capt. Annand's term of office was undoubtedly the Officer Training

Corps. Perhaps more than any other pursuit, it involved boys in a most purposeful and enthusiastic manner, bringing a unity and spirit to life in the School. Bearing in mind that the strength of the Senior School seldom exceeded 160 and that entry into the O.T.C. was not permissible until a boy reached the Third Form, it was remarkable that the number of cadets never dropped below 60 and at times reached 100. In 1922 command of the Corps passed from Capt. Langley to Capt.

The O.T.C., led by its band, parading down to the Recreation Ground.
Photo loaned by B. Henson

Jago, who was himself replaced by Capt. (later Lieut.-Col.) McKee in 1931. Sergeant A. Cadby, who possessed 'a fearful voice', was appointed School Caretaker and Sergeant-Instructor in 1925.

The O.T.C. paraded twice a week, on Tuesdays and Fridays at 11.45 a.m., and marched down to the Recreation Ground for a training parade of about 45 minutes. Cadets in full uniform (tunics, puttees, pouches, peaked caps, rifles and bayonets) were led by the band with drums beating and bugles blowing. This proved to be quite a local attraction, especially to mothers with small children. Trams and other traffic simply had to wait while the parade made its way down Broad Street. As it passed by Mallory's corner, a crippled newsvendor used to call out: 'Why should England tremble?'

Dr. J. B. Tucker remembers one such parade 'led by Capt. J. C. McKee in his breeches and Lieut. H. M. Porter in his impeccable puttees'. During the march 'one drummer by the name of George Graham, sadly killed later, managed to lassoo with one of the white trailing lanyards of his kettle drum, the small parking light which in those days used to sit on the top of the wings of cars (with a little red reflector at the back). The car remained immobile and Graham's drum came off the hook and rolled down the street, just opposite the jewellers, Mallory's. Maggie could scarcely fail to notice the rumpus and at the back of the column of marching troops could be clearly heard to say, "What's that great fool Graham doing playing football with his drum?" Delivered in Irish, it brought the house down, and many sloped arms were seen to waver.' When, in the 1940's traffic eventually became too heavy, marching to the Rec was abandoned and boys made their way down in plain clothes.

In addition to field-day once a term and open-range shooting twice a year, annual events consisted of the Inspection, the Inter-Platoon Competition, the Summer Camp (usually at Tidworth or near Aldershot) and the Certificate 'A' Examinations. The Camp of 1932 proved to be particularly significant. The official War Office Camp had been cancelled owing to the economic crisis. Instead, the School accepted an invitation to attend a Camp in Guernsey organised by the O.T.C. of Elizabeth College, whose Headmaster was the Rev. F. Hardy (previously a master and O.T.C. Officer at King Edward's). Although the programme was greatly enjoyed, H. M. Porter recalls that 'we were beaten wholesale in the competitions and our uniforms looked terribly shoddy and shabby'. As a result, Capt. McKee decided to smarten up the Corps by ordering new uniforms of woollen serge and to adopt 'plus fours' and puttees instead of walking breeches. The whole experience in Guernsey helped to revive standards and to increase enthusiasm.

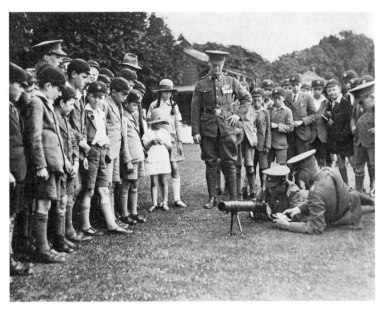

Inter-Platoon Day on the Recreation Ground, 1928; Lewis Gun Demonstration watched by Serg. Cadby.

Photo by Bath Evening Chronicle

In 1940, after the outbreak of the Second World War, the title of the Officers' Training Corps was changed in all schools to the Junior Training Corps. Cadets were no longer given the privilege (which they had received in the First World War) of proceeding automatically into Officer Training Units in the Army. A preliminary period in the ranks, followed by a War Office Selection Board, was necessary before Commissions were granted. Except in name, however, little seemed to change. Activities perhaps became a little bit more varied. Senior cadets were called upon to instruct Local Defence Volunteers (later the Home Guard), to work in the Admiralty or to guard the Post Office against invaders. Rifles were loaned to the Home Guard; Battle Dress suits were adopted for the first time (on free issue from the War Office); and the Contingent gave maximum support to 'Salute the Soldier' week in 1944. The Band, in particular, was in great demand during that week, performing daily in the Abbey Churchyard and making special appearances at Combe Down and Weston. School buglers were even given a star billing at the Odeon Cinema on two evenings. According to *The Edwardian*, the vigour of the Band on these occasions resulted in the fracture of the heads of four side-drums, one tenor drum and the bass drum. 'The disappearance of a bugle mouthpiece down a

Cadets inspected by the Marchioness of Carisbroke, 1926—attended by Capt. Jago.

School Archives

rathole on the Rec was, in comparison with the foregoing, of little import.'

Capt. Annand threw himself whole-heartedly behind the Corps, urging boys to join and encouraging them to stay. He regularly used Prize-Givings as an opportunity to stress the merits of the organisation to business-minded parents:

'Apart altogether from any question of military efficiency, I am more than ever impressed—in common with other Headmasters—with the practical utility of the O.T.C. in training a boy for a business career. It is not only in general alertness, of mind and body that the value lies, but in the habits which are enforced. Quickness to obey unhesitatingly, the power to control others and exact obedience from them without friction, above all the knowledge that co-operation is essential to success, and that self must be sacrificed to service—are there any finer lessons to be taught in the whole of a School curriculum? Book-learning may teach habits of thought, but surely habits of action are no less the essential basis of any sound system of education or morality.'

One other institution continued as part of the regular scene throughout the majority of this period. The Boarding House, opened in 1913 at 19 and 20 Portland Place by the Rev. F. Hardy as a private venture, accommodated between thirty and forty boys. The majority of these came from the area around Bath—Chippenham, Trowbridge, Keynsham, Midsomer Norton—where few secondary schools existed. A small minority were the sons of civil servants or tea planters in India, where advertisements for the Boarding House appeared regularly in the *Weekly Illustrated of India*. Life was hard for small boys. B. Henson remembers how they used to go to bed at night wearing gym kit ready for the early-morning run. Dragged out of bed by a Prefect at 6.45 a.m., they dutifully trotted round Victoria Park before breakfast. This effort in training clearly had the desired effect. Boys from the Boarding House provided the backbone of all the School teams and frequently carried off the Inter-House Championships. He remembers, too, his experiences as a 'fag' for Ronald (later Sir Ronald) Fairfield—how he cleaned his shoes, made his toast and sat on the stairs waiting for his call.

Mr. Hardy certainly made great efforts to keep the boys occupied in an interesting and constructive manner. Quite apart from their involvement in Rugby, Cricket and Athletics, he provided them with a real opportunity to learn both Boxing and Swimming (see above). House Notes in *The Edwardian* emphasise the remarkable variety of other activities which were made available to them—rowing, billiards, chess, mock elections, concerts, end-of-term suppers, whist drives, etc. When he left in 1924 to become Headmaster of Elizabeth College, Guernsey, the School lost one of its most lively influences (although, from the boys' point of view, not one of its most popular characters). He was succeeded as House Master by Capt. E. T. Langley, who was horrifed to discover, during the latter stages of negotiation, that Mr. Hardy had persuaded a number of existing boarders to go with him to Guernsey! Mr. W. A. Holland, who took over control from Capt. Langley in 1929, was himself succeeded by Maj. W. Lewis in 1935. The days of the Boarding House were, however, numbered. When it finally closed in July, 1939, it was no longer financially viable. By September, the situation had been completely transformed by the arrival in Bath of a large part of the Admiralty. A new market for boarders had been created almost overnight. This mobile population of Admiralty parents looked in vain for the stability of boarding facilities at King Edward's whenever a posting came their way. Quite a few boys, therefore, were subsequently taken away by reluctant parents through sheer force of circumstances.

Even the Second World War itself failed to cause any significant change to the life and daily routine at King Edward's School. There was little risk of compulsory evacuation and, because of the cramped nature of the site, there was no possibility that any other school from a more vulnerable region would be billeted on them. Perhaps surprisingly, the composition of the Staff also remained virtually unaffected throughout the course of the War. The most elderly members, Capt. Annand, Mr. Langley, Mr. Morgan and Mr. Heap, unselfishly worked on beyond retirement to help the School through this difficult period. Only Mr. Betty, a Corps Officer on the T.A. General List, was called up to serve with the Welsh Regiment. Nor did the German bombers, which raided Bath on the nights of 25–27 April, 1942, make any real impression on the School. The total damage sustained amounted to one or two cracked windows and an injured boy.

Air raids were, however, taken seriously. Mr. Holland, an A.R.P. Warden, was made responsible for the School's Air Raid Precautions. H. M. Porter recalls the scene:

'Of course, we had, like everyone else, to provide black-outs for windows and stirrup-pumps, to practise going to shelters (various Broad Street basements) on hearing the Alert and to arrange fire-watching rotas for the masters. The Governors appointed A. M. Ghyselinck, an Old Boy, as a permanent fire-watcher at night and there was always available to assist him, if required, one master, who slept in the old Signalling Room behind the flagstaff. If the master woke in the night, he might well hear Alphonse Ghyselinck very quietly practising on his flute in the Top Common Room.'

Dr. J. B. Tucker vividly remembers the practical use of those shelters in the basements of neighbouring property:

'To the younger boys, the sounding of the "Alert" was a God-send—it terminated the lesson and part of the School scattered to various shops etc. in the neighbourhood of Broad Street. Good billets were much sought after and I was able to organise my own at Ferey's the hairdresser/tobacconist at the top of Broad Street on the right, adjacent to the Y.M.C.A. Here the cigarettes were on the house (Player's Weights as a sop to authority).'

One permanent change was made to the routine, however. In order to ensure that boys reached home before the blackout, the times for afternoon school were altered from 2.30–4.30 p.m. to 2.00–4.00 p.m.

The War Record of Old Edwardians was very distinguished. 428 former members of the School served in the Armed Forces, of whom 210 received commissions and 45 were killed on active service. Decorations awarded during the course of the war included C.I.E. (1), C.B.E. (1), D.S.O. (2), O.B.E. (2), M.B.E. (3), D.S.C. (1), M.C. (7), D.F.C. (5), A.F.C. (3), D.F.M. (1), G.M. (1), B.E.M. (1). In addition, 13 Old Edwardians were mentioned in despatches.

The Retirement of Capt. Annand

With the ending of the war in 1945, a number of retirements took place. Mr. E. T. Langley, B.Sc., Second Master and Senior Science Master, retired after thirty-nine years of magnificent service. He had, in his time, been Commanding Officer of the O.T.C. and Housemaster of the Boarding House. Many Old Boys owed their successful careers in Science, Medicine and Engineering to his effective teaching. Mr. J. Morgan, M.A., Senior Mathematics Master, also retired after nineteen years at King Edward's. He had been a patient Form Master of IA and a keen supporter of Junior Rugby in his younger days. Mr. J. S. Heap, M.A., Form Master of IB, singing teacher and organiser of the book store, retired with almost thirty years to his credit at Broad Street.

The most important retirement, of course, was that of the Headmaster himself, Capt. A. W. Annand, M.C., M.A. He was, as J. F. Langley later wrote, 'an elegant and stylish man who imposed his personality on the school, though poor eyesight often made him seem and probably feel administratively ineffectual'. According to H. M. Porter: 'He was a scholar and a gentleman and had made the School a very happy community. The malefactor always knew that he would receive a fair hearing, but also, if he had earned it, proper punishment. Discipline was kindly, but firm. He was never angry and he laid emphasis on character and good manners.' A man whose 'very high academic qualifications' had been praised by the Inspectors, he delighted in teaching Latin to the Sixth Form. The quality of both mind and memory was extremely impressive. H. C. P. Burden remembers his unerring ability to give page references for detail in Kennedy's *Latin Primer* without recourse to the book itself.

By 1945, Capt. Annand could certainly look back over his period in office with a justified sense of satisfaction. He had steered the School into its new Direct Grant Status; he had moved the Preparatory Department into its new accommodation; he had reorganised the curriculum, the syllabus and the School Year; he had introduced Specialist teaching, Rugby Football and the House System; he had opened up a larger range of opportunities in sport; he had witnessed a dramatic improvement in School Certificate results at Fifth Form level. Furthermore, community spirit was probably better than it had ever been both inside the School itself and outside in the Old Edwardians' Association.

If, therefore, the School had not yet recovered its former status and former glory, the fault was not primarily that of Capt. Annand. His own plans, desires and intentions were constantly thwarted by circumstances over which he had little control. There is little doubt that he had agreed wholeheartedly with the 1927 Inspectors that the School 'should raise its whole aim and endeavour', that it should seek to acquire 'a leading position' locally which would be 'worthy of its traditions'. There is little doubt either that Capt. Annand had done his best throughout to promote those aims. But, before 1945, a transformation of that kind was really out of the question. There was no money to provide the sort of new buildings which were essential—and the economic climate of the 1930's discouraged speculation of that kind in any case. There was, in addition, no recent tradition of excellence. The School had inherited mediocre standards from the nineteenth century—Oxbridge Scholarships were tamely accepted as a thing of the past. Time was needed to change attitudes which were now inbred. The Headmaster, never by nature a dynamic force, had run out of both time and heart.

Furthermore, there was no local ambition. Bath had moved out of the mainstream of life and into a rather dull backwater. Its citizens did not *demand* the revival of their old Grammar School. They preferred, instead, to regard it as a training ground for local business. King Edward's therefore, remained at heart a Second Grade School. The Sixth Form scarcely existed. The Boarding House was never large enough to attract in a significant number of able boys from cultured homes outside Bath. The Staff still lacked a large proportion of highly-qualified specialists. Transformation of the School, in fact, could only be achieved through a transformation of the City. It finally took the Second World War to bring this about.

H. M. Porter (1945–1961): The Direct Grant Battle

The man selected by the Governors to succeed Capt. Annand as Headmaster was Mr. Henry Maurice Porter, M.A., who had been Senior English Master at the School since 1928. Educated at Taunton School, he had served a year in the Royal Artillery before going on to Trinity College, Cambridge as an Exhibitioner. With previous teaching experience at Brentwood School in Essex and Queen Elizabeth Grammar School in Wakefield, Mr. Porter had already made a sizeable impact on life at King Edward's. As an officer in the O.T.C., editor of *The Edwardian*, Treasurer of the Old Edwardians' Association, founder of the Literary Society and leader of the

Mr. H. M. Porter, Headmaster 1945–1961.

Rambling Club, his contribution to the development of the community under Capt. Annand had been rich and varied. He was now faced with the unenviable task of raising the general level of ambition which alone could restore the School to its previous status in both the city and the world outside.

He set about his work with determination and vision. His boundless enthusiasm enabled him to brush aside problems created by the ending of the war. The war in one way, however, gave him a legacy which later proved vital in his campaign to better the intellectual standards within the School. Admiralty Civil Servants, who had arrived in great numbers in 1939, were now beginning to regard the pleasant City of Bath as a desirable permanent home—as, too, did many Naval officers. This was to create over the coming years, therefore, a steady flow of applications for admission to King Edward's of boys drawn from an intelligent family background, whose fathers had all made progress in life as a result of competitive examinations. This transformation in the ability of the typical applicant to the School was considerably speeded up by a number of other factors—the improvement of transport, which greatly increased the catchment area; the advent of the commuter, who lived in Bath, but worked elsewhere; and the arrival of a new University on Claverton Down in 1964 with large numbers of highly qualified staff, who proceeded to settle in the City. Gradually, therefore, the standard of intelligence, industry and ambition was improved at the School by something of a natural process.

The ending of the war also provided Mr. Porter with the opportunity to strengthen his teaching staff by recruiting a substantial group of able young men all at the same time. This was possible, of course, because four masters had delayed their retirement, as a favour to the School, during the period of hostilities. Mr. W. E. Willett, B.A. (London) was now appointed as Senior Latin Master to take over Capt. Annand's teaching work; Mr. C. W. Eaves, MSc. (Manchester) arrived as Senior Mathematics Master to replace Mr. Morgan; Major L. J. Holman, B.Sc. (Liverpool) succeeded Mr. Langley as Senior Science Master; Major F. A. Stuart inherited Mr. Heap's teaching of general subjects. Shortly afterwards, in 1946, Mr. H. C. P. Burden, B.A. (London) was appointed to teach French, Latin, Religious Instruction and P.T. as a replacement for Mr. Holland, who retired through ill health after twenty-three years' service. At the same time, Mr. C. J. E. Betty returned from war service to resume his work as Senior Geography Master. Meanwhile, Mr. E. O. Jago, the Senior History Master, had taken over as Second Master in succession to Mr. Langley.

This sudden influx of new blood and new ideas greatly enhanced the life of the School. It also enabled the new

Staff Group, c. 1950:
Back row: W. T. Currie, F. Stubbins, H. C. P. Burden, G. R. Dawson, J. I. Peatfield, D. N. MacKay, L. G. W. Jones.
Front row: J. C. McKee, W. Lewis, Mrs. J. Ledbury, H. M. Porter, Miss M. Gardner, W. E. Willett, S. A. Brewer.
Photo by T. C. Leaman

Headmaster to commence work with his *own* team of assistants. The transformation of the Staff was completed in 1949 and 1950 when Mr. Jago retired and Major Stuart, Mr. Eaves, Mr. Betty and Mr. Holman all left for other posts. They were in turn replaced by Mr. W. E. Willett (promoted to Second Master), Mr. D. N. Mackay, B.A. Oxon. (Senior

History Master), Mr. L. G. W. Jones, M.A. Cantab. (Senior Mathematics Master), M. G. R. Dowson, M.A. Edinburgh, (Senior Geography Master), Mr. J. I. Peatfield, B.Sc. London (Senior Science Master) and Mr. W. T. Currie, B.A. London (Senior English Master, taking over his responsibility from the Headmaster). As early as 1927, the Inspectors had urged that 'as occasions arise it is essential that Masters with higher qualifications should be appointed'. This task of reconstruction—though considerably delayed—had now been achieved. Six of the old guard had retired during the space of five years. A young squad of highly qualified specialists had been drafted in with the aim of helping the School 'to rise to a position worthy of its traditions'.

On his appointment, however, the new Headmaster was immediately faced with an even more urgent problem. The Labour Government, brought into office after the General Election of July 1945, had announced its intention to reduce the number of Direct Grant Schools. The whole future of King Edward's School was suddenly at stake. Butler's Education Act of 1944, in listing the four types of Grammar School permitted—(Maintained, Direct Grant, Aided and Controlled), had imposed minimum standards on schools with Direct Grant status. It had already become apparent to the Governors of King Edward's 'that to conform to the building and equipment conditions laid down by the Act, a new School must be built and a new site chosen'. They realised, however, that this could not be done with the funds then available under the Foundation Endowment. Nevertheless, after a meeting with parents, Old Boys and Staff on 28 June, 1945, Mr. Roy Fuller, the Chairman of the Governors, announced their intention to apply to the Ministry of Education for permission to continue as a Direct Grant School. This decision was warmly supported by the Mayor of Bath, Mr. Edgar Clements, who was Vice-Chairman of the Governors and Chairman of the Bath Education Committee.

The School's application was speedily rejected by the Minister of Education, the Rt. Hon. Ellen Wilkinson. No reasons were given. The Governors lodged an immediate appeal for reconsideration of their case. The Minister refused to alter her decision. At this point, with clouds of despair already gathering, Mr. I. J. Pitman, M.P. for Bath (later Sir James Pitman), came to the rescue. He begged leave of the Minister to allow him to accompany a deputation of Governors to present their case in person. She agreed and, on 7 February, 1946, received Mr. Pitman, the Chairman of Governors, the Mayor of Bath, The Headmaster and the Clerk to the Governors in her rooms at the House of Commons. The visit, however, was to no avail. In Mr. Porter's own words, 'the deputation received a dusty answer'. But Mr. Pitman was not to be beaten. His researches had revealed a suspicion that incorrect figures had been produced by the Minister and that inconsistent standards had been applied in assessing other Direct Grant Schools in the area. Armed with this information, he threatened to ask awkward questions in the House. Suddenly, the Minister gave way. Her three previous decisions were now reversed and the School was permitted to retain its Direct Grant status after all.

Direct Grant Schools of this period were required to fulfil certain obligations, but in return enjoyed considerable financial benefits. These had gradually evolved since 1926, when such schools were first classified. They had been further modified in 1945, after a report by the Fleming Committee, and were later to be finalised by the *Direct Grant School Regulations* of 1959. Briefly they were required to reserve not less than 25 per cent of their intake as Free Places for children who had attended a state supported primary school for at least two years. The fees for these Free Places could be paid either by the Local Education Authority or by the Governors from School endowments. In addition, they were obliged to offer to the L.E.A. a further 25 per cent of 'reserved' places, which could be filled, at local expense, with pupils from any educational background. All these places were usually awarded as a result of success in the 'eleven plus' examination, although final selection was normally left to the Headmaster himself. The remaining places, known as 'residuary places', were filled at the discretion of the Governors on the basis of their own entrance examination. Although these were essentially fee-paying places, the Government introduced a 'remission of fees' scheme which, based on a sliding scale of parental income, enabled poorer families to claim back a proportion of the full fee. By 1956, King Edward's School was admitting twelve pupils on 'free places', six from the Bath Local Education Authority, three from Somerset and three from Wiltshire. Shortly afterwards, however, Bath increased its total to nine when Somerset withdrew on the building of its own grammar school at Keynsham. The majority of boys entering King Edward's School, of course, continued to be drawn from its own Preparatory School. A few of these actually qualified for L.E.A. 'free places' having passed the 'eleven plus' and having earlier spent two years at a State primary school. Indeed, from 1946, Mr. Porter encouraged all the Prep School boys to enter for the 'eleven plus' exam.

In return for this co-operation with the Local Education Authority, a Direct Grant School received *direct* from the Ministry of Education a capitation grant for each child over 11 years and an additional Sixth Form grant for each child over 17 years who was engaged in an 'A' Level course. These financial arrangements greatly increased the range of income available to a school such as King Eward's. By 1956, for instance, its total revenue consisted of £5,360 profit from endowment property, £5,398 in fees from 'fee-paying' pupils, £3,934 in fees paid by Local Education Authorities and £5,410 in capitation grants from the Ministry of Education. The School's three Scholarship Funds (the Edmund White, the Robert Dyer Commans and the Nahum Nurnberg Funds) were, by 1956, producing a combined income of just over £400 a year. Because this was no longer needed to provide scholarships for boys at School or University, it was used instead to encourage worthy Sixth Formers by the award of bursaries valued at £15 a year. Under Direct Grant Regulations, the Governing Board, which continued to be entirely responsible for school buildings, was obliged to recruit at least one third of its members from Local Authority nominees. In 1956, there were fifteen Governors at King Edwards, of whom eight were co-optative, one was nominated by the University of Bristol and six were appointed by the Bath City Council.

Quite apart from capitation grants and free places, the new Direct Grant regulations of 1945 imposed specific obligations on the School in a number of different ways. In the first place, parents were no longer required to pay for text books.

Secondly, a medical inspection had to be provided at some point in a boy's school life. The first of these took place in 1947 when Dr. D. E. Olliff, an Old Edwardian and Senior Medical Officer at Bristol University, was appointed as the official School Doctor. Dr. Oliff was eventually succeeded in this office by Dr. J. Beviss in 1952. Thirdly, arrangements had to be made for the provision of dinners at School. Fortunately, the Bath Education Committee came to the rescue and agreed to supply the school from their Central Canteen in insulated containers. The Third Form Room, on the ground floor, was hurriedly converted into a dining room (thus reviving its original function when the Broad Street premises were first opened in 1762). The bicycle store, immediately below, was turned into a scullery and connected to the dining room by means of a hand-operated lift for crockery. Tables, benches and crockery were provided free of charge at government expense.

Organisation of the new system, however, involved a considerable amount of additional work. In view of this, the Governors agreed to the installation of a telephone and appointment of the School's first Secretary, Mrs. F. H. Ledbury, the wife of an Old Edwardian. (Until this date, as Mr. Porter himself recalls, the School had had no secretary, no telephone and no typewriter. The School duplicator was 'an incredible antique'. Capt. Annand had written all his letters himself, in spite of very poor eyesight.) Mrs. Ledbury now became responsible for the management of school meals, including the control of canteen helpers, and also for the ordering of all new text-books. Her office was the old library behind the Junior Science Demonstration Laboratory. When school dinners first started in September 1946, no fewer than eighty boys chose to stay. By 1956 the number had risen to 120. W. T. Currie recalls how meals in those days were taken in almost total silence to enable canteen staff to hear the requirements of individual boys as they were served.

Developments in School Life, 1945–1961

One of the first changes made by Mr. Porter was to end the system which had enabled boys to linger for six years before they sat the School Certificate Examination. On entering the School, a boy had originally spent a year in Form 1B, followed by a year in Form 1A before finally gaining promotion to the Second Form. After criticism from the Inspectors in 1939, a modified version of the same system was introduced which made it possible for the brighter boys in Form 1B to be promoted to the Second Form at the end of their first year. Meanwhile, boys of a more mediocre standard were permitted to plod their way through what was virtually a repeat of the first year course. Mr. Porter was determined to improve the academic reputation of the School first, by raising the standard of the entrance examination and making it much more competitive, and secondly, by insisting that all boys should reach School Certificate level after only five years. Competition for places certainly increased with surprising speed. Whereas previously few applicants had been refused admission, by 1946 there were four applications for every vacancy in the Preparatory School and three applications for every fee-paying vacancy in the Senior School.

The removal of a Form at the bottom of the School had one added economic advantage. It became possible, without any further increase to the size of the staff, to utilise the teaching periods thus saved by adding a Form at the top of the School. Consequently, in 1948, the Sixth Form was divided for the first time into the Lower Sixth and the Upper Sixth. These, in future, were taught separately for the majority of their main subjects.

This increased emphasis on the importance of Sixth Form work, coupled with the improved standard of entry, gradually produced the sort of quality and ambition that Inpectors had been demanding throughout the previous years of the century. Even as early as 1949, Mr. Porter was able to claim that sixteen Old Edwardians were currently in attendance at University (compared with only 5 in 1946) and that no fewer than 18 out of the 29 Sixth Formers then at School had plans to proceed there later. By 1956, it was possible for the Inspectors to observe that roughly two-thirds of the boys now remained at school to complete the full Sixth Form course and that the average leaving age had risen from 16·9 in 1939 to 17·6, 'a very commendable figure'. They also noted with obvious pleasure that 21 boys, out of a total of 123 leavers over the three previous years, had gone to university. Furthermore, whereas in 1939 the Inspectors had complained that the limit of most boys' ambition was to go into local business, by 1956 this was no longer the case. Of those who had not proceeded to university, 21 had followed a career in Engineering, 11 had joined the professions, 11 had taken clerical posts, 10 had entered the Armed Forces and 10 had gained jobs in Trade and Industry.

This transformation and the revival of scholarship are best illustrated by a consideration of examination results. Whereas only two boys had passed the Higher School Certificate in 1945 out of a total of three candidates, in 1950 (the last year of the H.S.C. system) no fewer than eleven boys passed out of the thirteen who entered. Better still, in 1960 a record number of 63 subject passes was recorded at 'A' Level in the General Certificate of Education. During the period 1945–1961, twenty pupils at King Edward's School won State Scholarships for use at university and a further seven were awarded County Scholarships on the basis of their G.C.E. results; one Open Scholarship was gained at Southampton University; one boy came first out of 585 candidates in the 1948 Examination for the Executive Class of the Civil Service. Of even greater significance, in the seven years between 1954 and 1961, as many as twenty-four boys gained places at Oxford and Cambridge—one of whom was awarded an Exhibition. By 1959 there were thirty-one Old Edwardians in residence at a total of twelve universities throughout the country. At long last, King Edward's School had been restored to a position worthy of its academic traditions.

Apart from this revival inside the classroom, perhaps one of the most marked features of life at the School during Mr. Porter's term of office was the blossoming of extra-curricular activities. Before 1945 there had been comparatively little to arouse the interest and involvement of boys apart from the Officer Training Corps. By 1956, all this had changed. The Inspectors praised the Staff for 'their all-round contribution to the life of the School' and observed that 'the strong corporate life of the School' which resulted from 'a small, well-knit community' owed much to the leadership of the Headmaster himself. Boys were given plenty of opportunities 'to develop individuality, to show initiative and to exercise their powers of leadership'.

Almost immediately, in 1945, a Dramatic Society was formed. Two years later it was possible to stage *Scenes from the Merchant of Venice*, produced by Mr. Willett with the active

The Dramatic Society's Production of *Julius Caesar* in The Octagon, 1960.
Photo by G. D. Smith

support of no fewer than 57 out of the 160 boys in the Senior School. Thereafter, the annual production of the Society became one of the highlights of the Schools' calendar. It later became customary, under the successive leadership of Mr. Willett, Mr. Mackay (from 1954) and Mr. Rhymes (from 1960), to alternate a Shakespeare play with that of a more modern author. Plays were at times staged at the Pump Room and the Octagon, as well as at Broad Street. Meanwhile, the Geographical Society (under Mr. Dowson) and the Historical Society (under Mr. Mackay) started to combine forces at an annual summer camp. The first, organised in 1951 at Keswick in the Lake District, was attended by 28 boys. This was followed by similar expeditions to Guernsey, Wooler in North-umberland and Bude. Out of this early enterprise was eventually born The Parry Society in 1953, named appropriately after the Old Edwardian Arctic explorer. This lively Society not only continued the tradition of Summer Camps and walking tours, but also took over responsibility for the School Play and a great variety of other activities. A Photographic Group, a Stamp Club and a Music Club all emerged as off-shoots of the parent body. The creative interest of boys was further catered for by the annual Hobbies Exhibition, which was first started in 1953, by the Science Exhibition of 1946 and by the Roman Life Exhibition of 1952.

Another interesting development was the revival of the Sixth Form Literary Society. Members paid regular visits to the theatre in both Bath and Bristol, entertained debating teams from other local Schools and, most impressively, held an annual dinner at the Red House with eminent guest speakers drawn from the literary world. The School had suddenly opened its eyes to areas beyond the City of Bath and, in the words of Mr. Porter, had 'started to become mobile'. Mr. Brewer pioneered the foreign holiday by taking a party to Paris in 1947. School visits to places of educational interest in England also became a regular feature from 1948.

There were other outward changes, too, in the life of the School during this period. Full School uniform was first introduced in 1952. It consisted of a medium grey flannel suit, a grey or white shirt, a School tie, black shoes and a School cap. Founder's Day Service was instituted in 1949 at the suggestion of The Ven. E. A. Cook, Archdeacon of Bath, Rector of the Abbey and Governor of the School. Thereafter the School assembled annually in the Abbey, on or near 12 July (the date of the granting of the School Charter), to commemorate the Founding of the School and to remember its benefactors. The House System was re-organised. In 1945 the four old Houses, which took their names from the Housemaster currently in office, were abolished and three new ones created. These were named after benefactors—'Osric' (after King Osric, whose gift of land for the nunnery in Bath provided the basis for the School's endowment in 1552); 'White' (after Edmund White, who left money to provide the

School with scholarships and prizes); and 'Commans' (after Robert Dyer Commans, whose family donated money for exhibitions).

Certain elements in the School routine, of course, continued much as ever before. Bill Currie recalls the traditional nature of morning assembly in Big School—the formal procession of

Big School.

Photo by T. C. Leaman

Headmaster and Staff, the ritual calling of the roll by a Prefect (each boy answering his name with the word 'adsum') the standard readings and collects. Boys sat for assembly in the long desks and benches which filled the whole room right up to 1960 (see photograph). These, apparently, were so old that they suffered from two main disadvantages—they were badly affected by 'metal fatigue' tending, therefore, to collapse during lessons; and the benches were roughened with age, causing boys to acquire splinters in the most uncomfortable places. The four most senior staff, (Mr. Porter, Mr. Willett,

Mr. Brewer and Mr. McKee) occupied the four old high chairs and desks, one of which was situated along each wall of the room. Once a fortnight the Headmaster read out the mark order. Discipline continued to be strict, although schoolboys were not totally inhibited from taking part in pranks. One boy, allegedly, half-sawed through the whole stock of Mr. Porter's canes, causing the Headmaster at the next beating to gaze in wonder at the effects of his own strength. Staff detention, which was held on three evenings each week after School, was well patronised. Shortly after his arrival at King Edward's, Bill Currie found no fewer than 130 boys waiting for him to supervise. The Prefectorial system, too, continued to flourish with eight senior boys on average holding office each year. Prize Giving, which of course retained its status as a major event in the School calendar, remained in the Banqueting Room of the Guildhall until 1960 (after which numbers became too great).

One further change of considerable significance was the decision made in 1945 to make all games compulsory. Until that date, games had been played each week during two half-days holidays on a purely voluntary basis. (The younger boys had actually been timetabled to play games under a master's supervision from 1923). This system had inevitably undermined all hopes of producing School teams which were consistently skilful and successful, particularly in view of the small size of the school itself. Consequently, in spite of the dedicated labours of a few enthusiastic staff over the years, King Edward's School had dismally failed to establish any noticeable tradition in sport between 1870 and 1945—a period which, in other public schools, saw the rise of the playing field to a place of honour and importance. In Bath, an air of defeatism pervaded the scene; mediocre results were greeted with ecstasy. This pessimistic attitude is well illustrated by the tone of comments in the 'Rugby Notes', published annually in *The Edwardian*—'The matches have gone much as expected. We have been defeated in most games' (1946); 'There was no reason to be very optimistic about the season ahead' (1949); 'We have suffered a good deal from nerves and a kind of inferiority complex' (1951).

Under Mr. Porter games assumed a far greater importance.

All boys were now expected to play sport every week and to learn the rudiments of the major games. To improve matters even further, the timetable was revised in 1951 to enable compulsory games to be played by all pupils on two after-noons (Tuesdays and Thursdays) instead of just one. Previous frustrations, caused by the inadequacy of the School's playing facilities on the Recreation Ground, were finally solved later in the same year when twenty acres of land were purchased at Bathampton. The Governors fully intended that this should not only be the site of the playing fields, but also eventually of the new school buildings. The playing fields, meanwhile, came into full use in January 1952 with six Rugby pitches (instead of the two previously available on the Rec). Although a pavilion was constructed on the site, visiting teams changed at School where tea was also now provided. Showers had been installed at long last in the basement in 1951 for use after gym periods, runs and matches. In spite of the fact that a bus service was in theory arranged to convey boys out to Bath-ampton for mid-week games periods, Bill Currie remembers how in practice things were somewhat different. Boys were frequently required to change at school, to walk through town to the end of Pulteney Street, to run from there to the playing fields, to play their games and then to run back.

Before his retirement in 1961, Mr. Porter was to witness some of the first fruits of this new attitude to sport. Certainly the 1st XV in 1957 recorded 'the second most successful season since the school turned to Rugby in 1922'. They won twelve and drew one out of the fourteen matches played, scoring 175 points against a mere 39. The 1st XI, too, enjoyed an extremely good year, winning ten out of the thirteen games completed. By 1960 morale was riding high through School sport generally. In that year G. P. Frankcom, while still at School, was picked to play Rugby for Somerset against Gloucestershire; J. F. R. Edwards captained Somerset boys over-15 cricket team in seven matches; B. J. Castle repre-sented Somerset in athletics; and G. A. F. Culting was selected to compete for the western counties in the English Schools Swimming Championships. Much credit for this success and for the growth of spirit on the sporting scene was undoubtedly due to the enthusiastic lead given by Mr. H. C.

P. Burden, the Master-in-Charge of Games who, from 1954, had been responsible for both cricket and rugby.

Meanwhile, one further change had appeared on the sports field. In 1946 hockey had been introduced as the School game for the Spring Term. Rugby in future would only be played before Christmas. Although coaching commenced immediately under Mr. Willett's direction, the first hockey matches against other schools were not played until 1949, when the School won two out of its five games. Nevertheless, by 1956, hockey had not only established itself as a major sport, but had also proved the wisdom of introducing a 'non-contact' game in a comparatively small School. In that year, for instance, it was possible to boast that the 1st XI had won ten out of its eleven matches and that the junior team had been unbeaten for five years.

Minor sports also continued to flourish. Life-Saving Instruction, under the supervision of Mr L. G. W. P. Jones, was particularly successful. To the regular annual crop of individual awards was added the shield of the Bath Humane Society, which was won by the K.E.S. team in 1956. Tennis, too, became more prominent as a school activity. 'Non-cricketing members' of the 5th and 6th Forms were permitted to play on games afternoons, in the words of *The Edwardian*, 'amid the leafy freshness of Alice Park'. Summer Term ended with a tournament played for the Blackmore Cup. The average boy was certainly not forgotten. Standard tests were re-introduced in athletics in 1952 to encourage moderate performers to gain points for their Houses. Gymnastics for most boys returned to the Y.M.C.A. Gymnasium (under the instruction of Mr. Parsons) on the closure of Captain Olsson's Gymnasium in The Paragon in 1953. Boxing staged something of a revival from 1952 thanks to the enthusiasm of Mr. Dowson and Mr. Parsons. Fittings were placed in the walls and floor of the Dining Room to support the ropes of a boxing ring, which could easily be dismantled. *The Edwardian* outlined the justification for the sport:

'Quite apart from the merits of the game for its own sake, boxing serves a definite purpose. Because of the small size of our school, the standard of the individual at sport must be high so that we may hold our own in inter-school games. We need to acquire all the courage, self-confidence and stamina we can, and what can help us to achieve this more than boxing?'

Boxing certainly caught the imagination for a while and was still going strong in 1959 with matches against other schools.

One school activity, of course, continued to prosper throughout this period—just as it had prospered ever since its foundation in 1900. The Junior Training Corps (previously the Officer Training Corps) became a part of the new Combined Cadet Force (C.C.F.) in 1948. King Edward's School quickly realised its inability to establish 'Royal Navy' and 'Airforce' Wings of the movement and therefore opted to confine its attention to an 'Army' Wing. Little really changed. It is true, however, that Sergeant A. Cadby, the School caretaker and Sergeant-Instructor of the J.T.C., resigned in 1946 and was replaced by Sergeant-Major E. G. Dodge. It is also true that Lieut.-Col. J. C. McKee resigned as Commanding Officer in 1954, having held that position for twenty-two years. Awarded the Coronation Medal in 1953, he was also awarded the Order of the British Empire (Military Division) in 1954 in recognition of his magnificent services to the contingent. He was succeeded by Capt. (later Lieut-.Col.) W. T. Currie, who had been a glider pilot in the Second World War. Under his leadership numbers rapidly grew. By 1956 the establishment had been increased to a new record of five officers and 170 cadets.

Quite apart from their regular annual camp, from 1954 the C.C.F. began to pay visits to the IXth Lancers in Germany—trips were both profitable and enjoyable. The new Commanding Officer also introduced the ranks of Senior Junior Under-Officers for his most senior N.C.O's in 1957 and the first of many Adventure Training Schemes on Dartmoor in 1959. Although post-war rationing had ended the social side of Inter-Platoon Day (with tea parties on the Recreation Ground for Parents), the event itself still continued with enthusiastic competitions for squad drill, turnout, section leading, arms drill and shooting. Indeed, the revival of shooting was one of the most marked features of C.C.F. life during this period. Under the keen training of Sergeant-Major Dodge, the Shooting Team scored a major triumph in 1958 by winning the Country Life Cup (last won as long ago as 1920).

To emphasise their growing prominence in this sport, they added to their success by gaining second place in this same national competition both in 1959 and 1961.

One of the other most prominent features which had been associated with King Edward's School throughout most of the century had, however, run into more difficult times. The activities of the Old Edwardians' Association had been badly disrupted by the war. Many of them were never revived. The Tennis Club, for instance, was finally disbanded in 1949. Nevertheless, the Rugby Club was successfully re-formed in 1946, playing its matches at Rainbow Wood Farm on Claverton Down. The Annual Dinner, the New Year's Ball and an occasional supper at The Christopher now provided the normal extent of the annual programme. It is true that the Association celebrated its Fiftieth Anniversary with a Special Dinner in 1956, that the London Branch of the Association was revived in 1954 and that an inaugural dinner was held in 1961 to launch the Cambridge Branch (the first of an un-broken series of Oxbridge Dinners). But the golden days of the Association, as witnessed in the 1920's and 1930's, were over.

Nevertheless, Old Edwardians turned up in force to cele-brate the Fourth Centenary of the Foundation of the School in 1952. A beautifully printed brochure had been specially prepared by Mr. F. H. Ledbury to commemorate this mile-stone in the School's history. The proceedings began on Friday, 11 July, with a Dinner at the Guildhall, arranged by the Old Edwardians' Association. Among the chief guests was His Grace the Duke of Somerset as Founder's Kin, being a descendant of the Uncle of Edward VI, the Lord Protector Somerset. Also present was Mr. N. V. H. Symons, C.I.E., M.C., J.P., late of the Indian Civil Service, the only surviving son of the former Headmaster. This dinner was followed on Saturday morning, 12 July (the exact date of the granting of the Charter) by a Founder's Day Service and Commemora-tion of Benefactors in Bath Abbey. The Service was conducted by the Archdeacon of Bath, The Ven. E. A. Cook, M.A., a Governor of the School, and the preacher was the Bishop of Bath and Wells, The Rt. Rev. H. W. Bradfield, D.D. In the afternoon, the celebration continued at Bathampton with a cricket match between the School and the Old Edwardians.

Tea was provided for visitors, Staff and boys in a large marquee. The Centenary was concluded on Monday, 14 July in the School playground at Broad Street. There Mr. N. L. Shackell, President of the Old Edwardians' Association, unveiled the War Memorial Tablet dedicated to those Old Boys who had lost their lives in the Second World War. This tablet was to form part of the War Memorial Library, established in

The Unveiling of the War Memorial Tablet, 14 July 1952; (left to right on the platform) The Rev. C. G. Jones (O.E.), Mr. H. M. Porter (Headmaster), Mr. N. L. Shackell (President of the Association of Old Edwardians).
Photo by T. C. Leaman

1952 as a result of an Appeal launched by the Old Edwardians. Equipped with elegant chairs, tables and bookshelves, it provided much-needed accommodation for Sixth Form private study.

By 1952 space had actually become available to house this new War Memorial Library. This was made possible by an enterprising piece of opportunism by the Governors in 1949. They had managed to use their influence to secure the lease of

St. Mchael's School buildings in Milsom Street. These buildings, which in former years had housed a parish school, had more recently been used by the Admiralty as a printing centre. After a certain amount of redecoration and conversion work, the premises were available for use as an annexe of King Edward's in the Spring Term of 1950. The building was light, airy and quiet. Its yard was separated from the Broad Street

The new Physics and Biology Laboratory, 1950.
Photo by T. C. Leaman

playground only by a narrow passageway. The four main rooms were converted into a good Physics and Biology Laboratory (top floor), a Sixth Form room and a Fourth Form room (first floor) and a Fifth Form room (ground floor). New modern individual desks and chairs were purchased to replace the long communal desks and benches, which boys in the Fourth and Fifth Forms had previously been using. As Mr. Porter recalls: 'This addition to our accommodation was a truly immense benefit. It did not allow us to increase the number of boys in the Upper School, but it did enable us to take all teaching away from the three excessively noisy and cramped classrooms facing the street.' The War Memorial Library was eventually situated in the two rooms on the first floor previously occupied by the Fifth Form and the Junior Science Laboratory. The old Sixth Form room was now converted into a Staff Common Room.

The Move to North Road

In spite of the welcome relief provided by the acquisition of St. Michael's School buildings, the real problem of accommodation had not yet been solved. The Inspectors who visited the School in 1956 were full of praise for the substantial progress which had been made by the School, under Mr. Porter's leadership, in both the academic and social spheres. But they remained severely critical of the basic conditions under which the School was obliged to operate:

'In spite of these improvements the buildings fall much below acceptable standards and there are serious deficiencies which affect adversely the work in several subjects and almost every activity of the School. There is no gymnasium, no handicraft room, no art room, nor in fact any specialist teaching rooms except the laboratories, and all three of these are below standard. Some of the classrooms are small or awkwardly shaped and one is accessible only through another. . . . Altogether, the premises of both the preparatory department and the senior school make a very poor impression; they are old, shabby and rather untidy, and it is surprising that the school manages as well as it does in them. Added to this, the desks and other furniture are obsolete and in bad condition, the blackboards small and broken, and there are some shortages in teaching material.'

Nor was it simply a question of uncomfortable conditions. The physical limitations of the Broad Street site imposed serious restrictions on the size of the School, which in turn reduced the number of subjects on offer to boys by a relatively small staff. Mr. Porter had done his best to improve matters with the resources available. Music had been extended up to the Fourth Form (1946); Handicraft had been introduced to the Second Form (1947); Biology became a Sixth Form option in 1949, Geography in 1951 and German in 1956. The choice system for School Certificate had also been amended in 1947. In future boys on entering the Fourth Form would choose between Latin and Chemistry, thus ensuring that everyone studied Physics for at least five years. Nevertheless, in spite of these modifications, the Inspectors remained critical. 'The effect,' they argued, 'of the simple one-stream organisation in the School is to impose a narrow curriculum in which the whole aesthetic side of the boys' education tends to be neglected and in which few alternative courses are offered . . . With a small school of this size alternative courses are bound to be costly, but H.M. Inspectors felt that the intellectual quality of boys entering the School and the high proportion taking advanced courses and going on to universities would justify the introduction of further such courses.'

There was no doubt in the Inspectors' minds that the School had now reached a critical moment of decision. Academic standards had been revived; competition for places was mounting; the road to university was open once more; ambition had returned. The School was poised to resume again 'a position worthy of its traditions and of the place which it ought to occupy in the City of Bath'. Only one barrier to progress remained—the cramped nature of the Broad Street site. Stung by the sharpness of criticism, the Governors gave their minds yet again to the familiar theme of a possible move. From 1951, it had always been their intention to build a new school at Bathampton on the three acres of land, which they had purchased, immediately adjacent to the new playing field. In 1958, therefore, an architect was appointed to draw up plans for a two-stream school, which could be completed in stages as funds became available. By the Spring of 1959, however, all such schemes had been abandoned.

It was just at this moment of despair that the long-awaited miracle appeared quite out of the blue. In the words of Mr. Porter—'After half-a-century of worry and argument and hopes deferred, the problem of a new site and new buildings was solved in less than a week.' Mr. Edward Pryor, the Headmaster and owner of St. Christopher's Preparatory School in North Road, was forced to retire owing to ill health. He offered the Governors the first option to purchase the property, which consisted of an old Regency building called

'Nethersole', purchased in 1959.

'Nethersole' set in extensive grounds. Mrs. Maw, a Governor of the School and Chairman of Bath Education Committee, saw great possibilities in this, and put forward a scheme to a special meeting of the Governors on 2 April, 1959. At the end of the meeting, the Governors visited North Road, inspected the site and immediately decided to start negotiations. A few days later, they decided unanimously to purchase the buildings and grounds for a sum of £32,500, hoping to complete the

whole scheme of development for a total of no more than
£100,000. As Mr. Porter himself admits: 'This assumption of
liability for a scheme costing so much was an act of very great
courage on the part of the Governors, who had managed for
years on a very slender revenue.'

Detailed plans were quickly formulated. It was decided that
the Preparatory School should be moved from 20 Belmont in
September 1959 to occupy the Nethersole building at North
Road for a period of two years. During that time it would aim
to double its numbers in readiness for its eventual re-housing
at Broad Street in 1961. In future it would be styled 'King
Edward's School, Bath, Junior School', (instead of King
Edward's Preparatory School). The Master-in-Charge would
henceforth be called 'The Head of the Junior School', but
would remain responsible to the Headmaster of the entire
School. The first person to hold this new title was Mr. W.
Paterson, M.A., who had been appointed to succeed Mr. R.
Strickland as Master-in-Charge of the Preparatory School in
1958. To Mr. Paterson, an Oxford graduate, fell the task of
guiding the Junior School through these years of transition.
When he had arrived at Belmont in 1958, the Preparatory
School had numbered 77; when he left North Road to return
to Broad Street in 1961, the Junior School had become a
two-stream School with 117 boys on the roll.

Meanwhile, a scheme had been worked out to create a
two-stream grammar school on the site at North Road, ready
for opening in the September of 1961. In preparation for this,
an additional First Form was to be recruited at Broad Street
in both 1959 and 1960. The Governors appointed Mr. T. W.
Snailum, F.R.I.B.A., as the architect for the new site. It was
decided that the lower floors of Nethersole should house the
Headmaster's Study, the Secretary's office, the Staff Common
Room, the Bursar's office, the dining room, the Kitchen and
one classroom (which later became the Geography Room).
Dormitory and bedroom accommodation on the upper floors
would be converted into an Art Room, a Library and teaching
rooms for Sixth Form sets. The new buildings would consist of
seven classrooms, two Physics Laboratories, two Chemistry
Laboratories, and a large Assembly Hall/Gymnasium complete with stage and changing rooms. It was also hoped to

build within the grounds a miniature range and parade ground (with War Office assistance), and to convert an existing hut into a Music Room.

Raising the money for this new enterprise, of course, proved a trifle more difficult than agreeing to the actual plans. Three main methods were eventually used. First, the Governors launched an Appeal for £30,000 at a meeting on 17 July, 1959.

The first Summer Fair, held at Broad Street in 1959.

Photo by P. J. C. Harbutt

This became the responsibility of an Appeal Committee with Dr. A. H. Ashcroft (Vice-Chairman of Governors) as Chairman, Mr. J. R. Pearson (Old Edwardian) as Treasurer and Mr. D. N. Mackay (a member of Staff) as Appeal Organiser. This, in Mr. Porter's words, 'marked a quite new era of parental co-operation'. From this moment, fund-raising was to become part of the life-blood of the school. A Ladies' Committee of parents was immediately formed, under the chairmanship of Mrs. J. H. E. Brown, with the task of organising a series of events. The first major Appeal function was the inaugural Summer Fair, which was held in the playground at Broad Street and raised over £500. This was followed by a great variety of other happenings—a car treasure hunt, a tennis tournament, a bonfire party and barbecue, a gift auction, coffee mornings, whist drives, cheese and wine parties, concerts and dances. The ladies worked with great determination and enterprise, raising a considerable amount by their efforts. The overall response to the Appeal, however, was somewhat disappointing—especially in the vital area of covenants. By the summer of 1962, when the Appeal was re-launched in an attempt to boost support, the figure collected stood at about £15,000.

Secondly, the Governors decided to sell off most of the School's main assets. The three acres of land at Bathampton, which were now surplus to requirements, were sold to a developer. Similarly, the former premises of the Preparatory School at 20 Belmont were sold to St. John's Roman Catholic Junior School. But perhaps the most dramatic decision involved the sale of the School's entire Endowment Property (with the exception, of course, of the land on which the School stood in Broad Street—formerly the site of the Black Swan Inn). This mainly consisted of houses and flats, which had become extremely expensive to repair, but which, with the removal of rent restrictions, were now attractive to purchase. The sale was only made possible by a reversal of policy by the Ministry of Education, which previously had frowned on the disposal of charitable endowments for the purpose of raising capital. Permission was finally granted on 11 December, 1959, after a visit to London by Mr. E. A. Merrifield (Chairman of the Governors), Colonel C. Stewart (Governor) and Mr. J. B. Taylor (Clerk to the Governors). The eighty properties were sold in March 1960 for a total of £55,000.

Thirdly, Mr. Merrifield, who was also Manager of the National Provincial Bank in Milsom Street (the School's Bankers), agreed to negotiate a loan for £45,000. This finally enabled the Governors in February 1960 to authorise the signing of a contract with Messrs. F. J. Amery and Sons Ltd. to construct the new building and to modify Nethersole. This task had virtually been completed by the summer of 1961. The actual move of furniture and equipment, which took the

Junior School down to Broad Street and the Senior School up to North Road, was organised in August. This was directed by Lt.-Col. R. Langrishe, who had been appointed Bursar and Clerk to the Governors in 1960. In Mr. Peter's words, he 'planned the move with the precision of a military operation'. The Junior School re-opened at Broad Street on schedule (12 September). By then, of course, the Governors had terminated their lease of the St. Michael's buildings, which were shortly

First Day at North Road, 1961.

to be demolished to create more space for a car park. The opening of the Senior School was delayed for a week to enable the completion of alterations to Nethersole. But, at 9.55 a.m. on 19 September, two double-decker buses arrived at North Road packed with pupils. A new era in the history of the School had begun.

The Retirement of Mr. Porter, 1961

In March 1961, Mr. H. M. Porter informed the Governors that he wished to retire at the end of December. When he left, after exactly one hundred terms spent in the service of the School, the Governors presented him with a clock at a Special

THE BOARDING HOUSE IN 1926 Back row (from left): E. G. Wakefield, E. W. Hurst, F. J. T. Dobbs, J. H. Wakefield, F. J. Goddard, J. S. Bolton, D. L. Moore, E. W. Pring, E. W. Morris, G. Walters. *Third row*: R. Say, Sawyer ii, S. Penney, –. Rees, Sawyer i, A. C. Shearn, W. G. Edginton, J. Davies, –. Clark, R. M. Fairfield, J. E. Underdown. *Second row*: Miss Hillman, S. G. Alexander, A. D. Pyster, C. George, Mrs. Langley, Mr. E. T. Langley, G. Robinson, R. S. Low, A. G. Firmin. Mrs. James. *Front row*: J. F. Langley, J. B. Scammell, G. Morris, –. McDonald, K. E. Langley, R. A. Henson, R. N. L. Matthews, A. F. Shearn, D. F. C. Burton, L. E. Leavy, C. Runciman.
Photograph provided by Dr. R. A. Henson

Dinner held in his honour at Fortt's. The Staff and boys gave him a leather-topped, knee-hole writing desk. The handsome cheque presented to him by the Old Edwardians' Association was invested in 'a sumptuous armchair' and a holiday in Luxembourg. *The Edwardian* paid this tribute to his personal qualities as Headmaster:

'He has been careful to uphold the reputation, which boys of K.E.S. have always enjoyed, for good manners, character and a sense of responsibility. He has always demanded good, forthright effort—nothing but the best of which a boy has been capable; and he has never failed to voice his displeasure with the slacker, the litter-lout, the untidy and the dishonest in his determination to promote every quality that goes towards the making of a useful citizen. Strictly just, genuinely interested in and well acquainted with all his pupils, encouraging to his utmost Games and all out-of-school activities, he has enjoyed the respect of every boy and has fostered in the School an extremely happy and friendly atmosphere. The equally warm relationship which exists among the masters also owes much to the unfailing support, kindness and thoughtful consideration he has shown to every member of the Staff Room.'

The new School entrance at North Road, 1961.

It is easy, in the light of subsequent developments and dramatic growth, to underestimate the progress achieved by the School during Mr. Porter's period in office. But when the history of King Edward's is closely examined, it is difficult to find many Headmasters who have contributed so richly or who have gained so much success in so modest a manner. Without the substantial foundations laid by him during the years 1945 to 1961, the sort of expansion witnessed at North Road in later years would never have been possible. Under his leadership, the School had been given a new sense of purpose and direction; a closely-knit community had been created; academic standards had been restored to something like their original level; the Sixth Form had been properly born; ambition again stalked the corridors of Broad Street; the Oxbridge tradition became once more a source of pride; numbers had been increased from 228 to 377, with more clamouring at the door; a new school had been built and its old reputation in the City of Bath revived. He had, like all great leaders, a simple secret of success. A man of vision and a scholar in his own right, he knew from the outset exactly what

he wanted for the school. He achieved it by means of his
boundless energy, his infectious enthusiasm and his endless
determination. Nor had he confined himself merely to the
Broad Street scene. He was much respected as a member of
the South-West Division of the Headmasters' Association and
for a time represented this Division on the Council of the
H.M.A. The Governors, under whom he worked, had displayed real wisdom in making the appointment in 1945, just as
they showed great courage and foresight in taking the School
to North Road in 1961.

CHAPTER SIX

North Road—Years of Expansion, 1961–1982

'No wonder we are known locally as the "school on which the cement never sets!"'
(Mr. Holbeche's Report at Prize-Giving, 1977.)

Mr. B. H. Holbeche: The Age of Rapid Growth

The man appointed to succeed Mr. Porter as Headmaster in January 1962 was Mr B. H. Holbeche, M.A. He had been educated at Wyggeston Boys' Grammar School in Leicester and at the Northampton Polytechnic on a Naval commissioning course. During the Second World War he served for six years in the R.N.V.R., first as a Petty-Officer Electrical Engineer in the Submarine Service in the Mediterranean and then as an Officer in the Fleet Air Arm. After the War he entered St. Catharine's College, Cambridge, read Mathematics for a year and then gained a double First in the English Tripos, Parts I and II, for which he was offered a retrospective Scholarship by the College. Before joining King Edward's, he taught for four years as an Assistant Master at Kingswood School, Bath, and for eight years as Senior English Master and Housemaster at St. Peter's School, York.

To Mr. Holbeche, therefore, fell the task of building on the excellent foundations already established by his predecessor. The continued revival of the School's academic reputation and the completion of the School's physical expansion became matters of supreme importance during the ensuing years. In reality, the actual growth—after one and a half centuries of decline and stagnation—was even more dramatic than had ever been originally envisaged. Before the purchase of the North Road site (in 1959), numbers at King Edward's had remained fairly static—190 boys in the Senior School and 74 boys in the Junior School, a total of 264. By the Spring of 1962

Mr. B. H. Holbeche, Headmaster from 1962.

(with the second stream already in the Third Form), the figures had increased to 261 boys at North Road and 117 boys at Broad Street, making a total of 378. After this second stream had worked its way through the School by the Summer of 1966, numbers had again levelled out to produce a rough annual total of 570 (414 Seniors and 156 Juniors).

This pause in the growth-rate, however, soon proved to be nothing but a temporary respite. Faced with ever-increasing competition for places at the annual Entrance Examination, the Governors decided to enlarge the School even further by adding a third stream to their intake from September 1972. This decision was also brought about by their desire to enlarge the teaching staff, thus providing greater flexibility in the range of courses on offer to examination candidates in senior forms. The eventual effect of this change was to raise total numbers to a new all-time peak of 795 in September 1981, with 618 boys in the Senior School and 177 boys in the Junior School. The staffing situation, too, was transformed during the same period. Whereas, in 1958, there were 10 Senior School Staff and 3 Junior School Staff, by 1981 there were 35 full-time staff at North Road and 8 staff at Broad Street (plus various other part-time helpers).

Expansion on this scale, during such a comparatively short period of the School's history, inevitably created problems. The most obvious and immediate of these was the sheer physical problem of accommodating additional numbers together with new subjects, which increasingly appeared on the timetable (see below). Throughout the course of the century, successive Inspectors had heaped criticism on the lack of facilities for the creative arts. The North Road site now provided an excellent opportunity to correct this omission in the area behind Nethersole, overlooking the terraced playing field. In 1961 an existing hut, which had previously been used by St. Christopher's School as an Assembly Hall and Gymnasium, was converted into the 'Music Room,. Two years later, it also became known as the 'Art Room', doubling up in its function on the appointment of the School's first full-time teacher of Arts and Crafts (Mr. P. Aldren).

This, of course, could only provide a temporary solution. Separate facilities for the teaching of music could not be long delayed. Practice rooms for instrumental tuition were first provided in 1964 at the far end of a 'Recreational Hut', later to be refurbished and upgraded as a Lecture Theatre. It was, however, the arrival of a full-time Music Master (Mr. I. D. C. Phipps) in 1966 that heralded the building of a special Music Room in the following year. At the same time the new Art Master (Mr. S. Williams) inherited a freshly-constructed General Workshop, Art Store and Photographic Dark Room.

The Pottery, opened in 1974.

Photo by T. C. Leaman

In later years the size of this timber-built 'Arts Complex' was further increased by the building of a Music Store and Practice Rooms as extensions of the Music Room (1972); the installation of a pottery kiln and pottery to coincide with the appointment of a second Art Master (1974); the conversion of the old 'Sixth Form Centre' hut into a Print-making Room (1974); and the transformation of the old Lecture Theatre into a second teaching space for class tuition in musical instruments (1977). All these areas eventually combined to provide boys with a rich diversity of opportunity in the creative arts. It became possible to receive instruction in painting, drawing, etching, print-making, photography, pottery—and in no fewer than thirteen musical instruments.

Meanwhile, the other basic requirements of an expanding school had not been neglected. There was, for instance, a growing need for additional classroom space with a particular emphasis on the teaching of specialist subjects. The development of courses in Liberal Studies and General English for all 'A' Level candidates in a rapidly enlarging Sixth form, necessitaed the provision of a Lecture Theatre in 1964. This was capable of seating (at a pinch) fifty boys. Further additions quickly followed. A Biology and General Science Laboratory, built at a cost of £10,000, was opened by Professor B. Perry of Bristol University in September 1965; a new Geography Block, with two classrooms, was erected in 1971; the old 'potting shed' was converted into a C.C.F. and Biology Lecture Room in 1975; and a Mathematics Block was finally completed in 1977. Quite apart from the requirements of teaching, private study accommodation also became something of a problem. The large room on the first floor of Nethersole, which now housed the War Memorial Library, quickly proved inadequate. In 1968, therefore, a Private Study Room, suitably equipped with study desks, was established on the top floor to function as a 'Library overflow'. This was not a great success. Three years later, the Library itself was extended into a neighbouring classroom to create more reading space. Shortly afterwards, a second classroom was opened up to complete this process of expansion. In an attempt to ensure quieter conditions for study, staff supervision was provided in the Library from 1970.

Academic needs were not allowed to swallow up the entire quota of funds available for building projects. Social and recreational facilities were viewed with equal importance in a school that prided itself on the development of a boy's full personality. As early as 1964, an old derelict stable near the Parade Ground had been converted into two 'Middle School Common Rooms'. At the same time, a 'Recreational Hut' (later to be transformed into the Lecture Theatre) had been provided for the Sixth Form, which also enjoyed common room space in an adjoining hut next to the Art Room. This hut was itself later converted into a more ambitious 'Sixth Form Centre', complete with coffee bar and snooker table, which was opened by Col. C. J. Stewart (Chairman of Governors) in 1968. The Sixth Form, however, were obliged to wait until 1974 before they moved into more adequate facilities. Then with the removal of the dining facilities into the Multi-Purpose Hall, a new Sixth Form Centre was established in the basement of Nethersole. Consisting of a

The Sixth Form Centre in the basement of Nethersole, opened in 1974.
Photo by T. C. Leaman

Quiet Room, a Coffee Bar and two small Games Rooms (for darts and a football machine), it increasingly provided a base for evening discos, parties and social activities.

Sport and other extra-curricular activities also received their fair share of embellishment as the expansion continued. The Combined Cadet Force, with considerable help from War Office funds, steadily enlarged its own little empire along the bottom boundary of the site. Gradually a cluster of huts and concrete buildings was constructed on two sides of the Parade Ground, which had been surfaced in 1961. These included a Miniature Range and Stores (1962); a Company Office and

Signal Store (1964); an Armoury (1968), a C.C.F. Lecture Theatre (1975); and a canoe store (1980). The sporting side of school life also received its first major boost in the same geographical area. In 1963 three hard tennis courts were installed for general use on the Parade Ground, which was suitably enclosed with wire netting. Seven years later, in 1970, provision for games enthusiasts was further enhanced by the construction of an all-weather playing surface on what was then called the 'Lower Level'. This enabled the Ground Staff to establish three tennis courts in summer and a practice hockey area in winter. Eventually this was extended, in 1975, into a magnificent full-sized hockey pitch, which could be converted in autumn into three six-a-side soccer pitches and in summer into six tennis courts with additional space for cricket nets and athletics coaching.

Later additions at North Road have included a Volleyball Court, constructed behind the Music Room in 1976, an Adventure Play Area (1977), first-class long jump pits (1980), and a Fitness Area, splendidly equipped with 'multi-gym' apparatus (1980). Meanwhile, at Bathampton, a new pavilion had been opened in 1966 by the School's first-ever Rugby international, Geoff Frankcom. This was, in effect, a somewhat miraculous transformation of an old tractor shed which had previously been used by Pinchin, the groundsman. A fine central area was subsequently extended in 1971 by the addition of two wings which served as tea-rooms after matches. Nor had the original cricket pavilion been forgotten. First showers were added, then toilets in 1975 and, at long last, electricity in 1981. Field events facilities for athletics had been vastly improved in 1973 by the construction of concrete throwing circles, all-weather run-ups for the long jump area and a tartan take-off for the high jump circle.

A growing school creates pressure not only on classroom space and sporting facilities, but also on administrative resources. When Colonel Langrishe retired as Bursar in 1963, his successor (Mr. F. W. Goodbody) inherited a small office in Nethersole and the services of a secretary. He was later to be joined by an assistant (Mr. L. Collins). Together they coped with an increasing volume of work, which included responsibility for the maintenance of the grounds and fabric, the

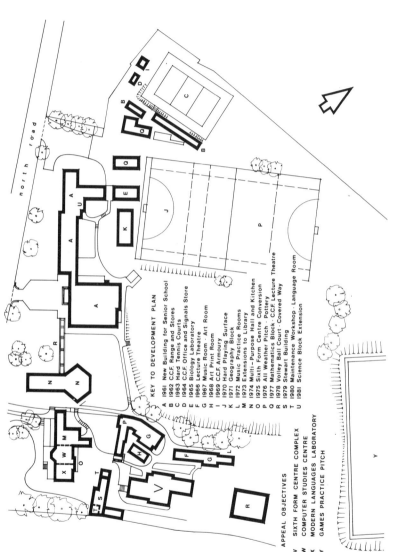

KEY TO DEVELOPMENT PLAN

A 1961 New Building for Senior School
B 1962 C.C.F. Range and Stores
C 1963 Hard Tennis Courts
D 1964 C.C.F. Office and Signals Store
E 1965 Biology Laboratory
F 1966 Lecture Theatre
G 1967 Music Room - Art Room
H 1968 Art Print Room
I 1969 C.C.F Armoury
J 1970 Hard Playing Surface
K 1971 Geography Block
L 1972 Music Practice Rooms
M 1973 Extensions to Library
N 1974 Multi-Purpose Hall and Kitchen
O 1975 Sixth Form Centre Conversion
P 1976 All Weather Pitch - Pottery
Q 1977 Mathematics Block - C.C.F. Lecture Theatre
R 1978 Volley Ball Court - Covered Way
S 1979 Stewart Building
T 1980 Maintenance Workshop - Language Room
U 1981 Science Block Extension

APPEAL OBJECTIVES

V SIXTH FORM CENTRE COMPLEX
W COMPUTER STUDIES CENTRE
X MODERN LANGUAGES LABORATORY
Y GAMES PRACTICE PITCH

Stages of Development at North Road, 1961–1982 (including plans for the 1982 Development Appeal).
Drawing by Mrs. P. A. Fereday

supervision of non-teaching staff and the control of all financial aspects of school business. Although additional space was
provided in 1968 by the conversion of a small cottage behind
Nethersole into a proper Bursar's Department, physical help
was not forthcoming until after the retirement of Mr. Goodbody in 1977. A man of great integrity, who had previously
enjoyed a distinguished career with the Civil Service in
Kenya, he had served the school with tremendous dedication
and loyalty, as Bursar and Clerk to the Governors, often
remaining at his desk until long into the evening. The extent
of his contribution was finally recognised by the appointment
of *two* men to undertake his duties—Mr. A. Francis (subsequently to inherit the title of Bursar and Clerk to the
Governors) and Mr. P. Falla (subsequently to be styled school
Accountant). By 1981 the Bursarial Staff consisted of five
full-time members—and a computer! Their situation had
been made considerably more comfortable in 1979 by the
transformation of the adjoining Old Coach House (more
popularly known as the 'bike shed') into a splendid new
administrative block. Consisting of two seminar rooms, a
school shop, a medical room, an archives room and additional
office accommodation, it fully connected on both levels with
the Bursar's cottage. Officially named as 'The Stewart Building', the whole complex was formally opened by Col. C. J.
Stewart on his retirement as Chairman of the Governors.

But without question, the physical expansion of the School
reached a memorable climax with the opening of the Multi-
Purpose Hall on 8 March, 1974. The cleverly-designed octa-
gonal building could be adapted for a great variety of
functions converting at speed into a dining room, a chapel, a
science demonstration room, a lecture theatre, a centre for the
showing of films and slides and a base for social events
(parents' evenings, dinners, parties—or weddings). Its fur-
nishings included a piano, given in memory of Major S. G.
Alexander, and a Communion table, donated in memory of
F. H. ('Dick') Ledbury. Adjoining the hall were two spacious
serveries to accommodate the large numbers of boys who now
stayed for lunch, and a large modern kitchen. The development was finally completed in 1976 with the building of a
'covered way' (to protect boys from the elements as they

queued on the steps for lunch) and a small toilet block (a clear indication of the hall's growing popularity for social events).

Quite apart from the flexibility which was brought to school life by the M.P.H. (as it affectionately now became known), dining facilities were at once transformed and civilised. Whereas previously boys had endured a set menu which had been served at table (often unfairly) by senior boys in what was commonly called the 'family system', they were now presented with a choice of food as they carried their own trays through the 'cafeteria system'. Whereas previously they had suffered long waits in crowded conditions in the basement of Nethersole, enviously eyeing the sumptuous food served on a special menu to staff, they now dined in spacious surroundings sitting in comfort with friends of their choice—or even with members of Staff, who had voluntarily opted to surrender their former privileges. When, therefore, the Right Honourable Mrs. Margaret Thatcher, M.P., officially opened the hall, a new era had begun in the social life of the School. Mrs. Thatcher, who had recently served as Minister of State for Education in Mr. Edward Heath's Government, graciously addressed the whole school in the Gymnasium before speaking to parents and friends in the M.P.H. She was supported at the ceremony by the Mayor of Bath, the Bishop of Bath and Wells and the Member of Parliament for Bath, Sir Edward Brown.

The Age of Self-help

The years 1962 to 1982, which could with justification be called the 'Age of Expansion', had therefore witnessed a remarkable development of the North Road site. Numbers had trebled. Buildings had multiplied. King Edward's had become in the Headmaster's own words at Prize Giving in 1977, 'the School on which the cement never sets'. Future observers could well ask the question, 'How was all the growth and activity made possible—and how was it paid for?' The answer, in effect, was really quite simple. For if this was the 'Age of Expansion', it was also the 'Age of Self-Help'—the Age of the Ladies Committee, the Pioneers, the Headmaster's slide-rule, the Budget Sub-Committee and Mr. Socha's cement mixer. Under conditions which affected all Direct Grant

Opening of the Multi-Purpose Hall on 8 March 1974. The photo shows (left to right): The Right Worshipful the Mayor of Bath; Sir Edward Brown, M.P., the Rt. Hon. Mrs. Margaret Thatcher, M.P.; the Bishop of Bath and Wells; the Headmaster.

Photo by Roland J. Prosser

Schools, King Edward's was not permitted to make building costs a charge on fees to parents. The money required to construct this large-scale development of premises at North Road was of necessity, therefore, found from other sources. Those sources were created by toil, sweat and enterprise.

In all this activity the Headmaster himself played a major rôle. From the start he displayed a great interest in buildings. His enthusiasm for constructional projects great and small became almost legendary. It was largely through his own drive and energy that the physical expansion of the School continued at such a pace. Actively involved in every operation, he became his own clerk-of-works. Old Edwardians of the 1960's even nicknamed him 'The Dynamo.' With great skill be saved money on numerous occasions by the modification of existing buildings to cater for ever-changing needs and fancies. Old huts were restored and converted; rooms were enlarged by the removal of walls; spaces were divided by the erection of screens.

Costs were always minimised by the use of internal resources. Professional advice and active assistance were frequently sought from highly-qualified friends whose good will to the School was immeasurable—parents, Old Boys, Governors and former parents. The contribution of this unseen army cannot be over-estimated. Nor can the on-site labour of the School's own workforce. Tasks, which many establishments would have farmed out to expensive contractors, were tackled, in what can only be described as a unique manner, by Gunther Richter (the caretaker, who brought supreme skill and painstaking care), by Stefan Socha (the gardener, who offered boisterous enthusiasm and irrepressible humour) and by Michael Cavill (the groundsman, who added enormous strength and massive weight).

Of perhaps even greater significance, was the mobilisation of the boys themselves to contribute to this development. The Pioneer Corps was therefore established in 1962 to provide an alternative activity for boys who were not involved in the C.C.F. This group met initially during the two allocated periods on Saturday mornings, but eventually extended their operations to holidays. Directed by Mr. A. J. Bright, they showed surprising practical skill in laying concrete paths and decorating rooms. By 1963, they had even progressed to much more ambitious schemes such as the conversion of the old 'Potting Shed' into the Middle School Common Room. Although the original Pioneer Corps eventually lapsed with the abolition of Saturday morning school, a new tradition was started in 1974 at the suggestion of the Second Master. Fifth Formers, after the completion of their 'O' Level Examinations, were henceforth required to offer their services for the period of one week in what became known as 'Fifth Form Pioneers'. Directed from the outset by Dr. F. R. Thorn, closely allied with Mr. R. J. Gay, successive groups accomplished a great variety of major projects—the widening and extension of tarmac paths around the school, the construction of the Volleyball Court, the building of concrete steps, the extension of carparks, the erection of wooden fences and seats. All-in-all, vast sums of money were saved by the systematic use of internal resources.

Money, however, was nevertheless needed in increasing amounts to provide those luxurious extras which an ambitious School like King Edward's now required. This is where the parents themselves lent a hand in a most remarkable manner. The Ladies' Committee, which had been established in 1959 to raise money for the Development Appeal, continued its excellent work after the move to North Road. Under a series of dynamic Chairmen (Brenda Brown, Christina Harbutt, Mary Sheppard, Cynthia Mumme, Gill Austwick, Avril Sloper, Elizabeth Blackman and Sylvia Popham), it raised considerable sums of money annually through its social events. Summer Fairs, Christmas Markets, Jumble Sales, Wine-and-Cheese parties, Valentine Dances, 'Nearly-New' stalls, Car Treasure Hunts, and many more enterprising ideas all contributed richly to the funds. Meanwhile, the Fathers' Committee had been launched in 1963 essentially to provide back-up and muscle for the Ladies. Gradually, however, the initiative of an enthusiastic succession of Chairmen (Desmond Cooper, Bill Holtham, Tom Young, John Adams, Gerry Bartlett, Don Bateman and Bill Howe) extended the involvement of this Committee by introducing specific events of their own—Whist Drives, excursions to York and Chester on specially-chartered trains and informal dance evenings.

Together these Committees provided a great wealth of equipment to stimulate and encourage both classroom studies and out-of-school activities: record players, cricket nets, athletic equipment, a trampoline, a cine camera, tents, sleeping bags, tympani, a sight screen, table-tennis tables, a public address system, projectors, sculpturing equipment, a switchboard for the stage, a minibus, language laboratory listening booths and many other items. Quite apart from their major support of the 1971 Development Appeal (see below), the Ladies Committee also raised money for the building of the first phase of the All-Weather Pitch in 1970 and the equipping of the new Medical Room in 1979. One later off-shoot from these two Committees was the Former Parents Association, which was formed in 1980 as a way of maintaining close links with the school.

To give greater unity of purpose to the School's various support groups, a new Committee, known as 'The Friends of King Edward's School' was established in 1964. According to *The Edwardian*, this fulfilled a need 'for an organisation to support the School on a long-term basis'. Composed of representatives from the Governors, the Staff, the Old Edwardians' Association, the Fathers' Committee and Former Parents, the Friends Committee launched its work with an inaugural dinner at the Red House. Its first Chairman, F. H. Ledbury, was succeeded in 1968 by W. P. Sheppard. Gradually this Committee assumed overall control of all fund-raising activities, taking ultimate responsibility for the Development Appeals of 1971 and 1982.

The 1971 Development Appeal, launched on 8 October with a dinner at the Guildhall, aimed to provide a new multi-purpose hall with dining facilities, completion of the All-Weather Pitch and improvements for the Junior School. The target was £120,000. Brilliantly conducted by the Appeal Director, Mr. W. E. Willett (who had been seconded for the task from his work as Second Master), the campaign was an outstanding success, eventually realising £129,000. No praise can be too high for the unstinting effort made by Mr. Willett in the service of the School. With little secretarial help, he organised the massive operation of individual visits by a team of helpers to all potential supporters, thus securing large

The 1971 Development Appeal; a model of the proposed new building. The photo shows (left to right) the Headmaster, Mrs. C. Harbutt, Mr. W. E. Willett (the Appeal Director) and Mr. W. Paterson (Head of the Junior School).

Photo by Bath Evening Chronicle

amounts through covenanted donations. The boys of the two schools were also mobilised to raise money through fund-raising events of their own. Of these the most memorable without question were the Sponsored Walk to Bradford-on-Avon and back by the whole School in 1971 and the Sponsored Marathon of 1974. In the latter teams of runners between them covered the distance between Land's End and John O'Groats—all on the back field at North Road! Quite apart from all the money collected through these various activities, the Development Appeal certainly drew the School and its supporters closely together, giving them a clear sense

The Sponsored Walk to Bradford-on-Avon, 1971.

of purpose. The Social life of the parents, too, was greatly enhanced by such annual gatherings as the May Ball, started in 1973 by Mr. Paul Buckley, a master at the Junior School.

During this stirring period of self-help by the community at large, one other small group of individuals made a major contribution to the financial affairs of the school. The Budget

Sub-Committee of the Governing Board, chaired first by Mr. J. B. (later Judge John) Taylor and then by Mr. H. H. Cork, brought professional expertise and objective judgement to the whole area of economic strategy. Their patient efforts, often unsung and largely unseen, helped to ensure that King Edward's remained financially stable at a time of rapid expansion. The ever-changing scene was a constant challenge in itself. New buildings, additional staff and extra equipment all demanded careful costing. Loans were frequently required. But this was not all. The whole *scale* of the operation had changed in a most dramatic manner. Whereas the annual turnover of the School had been £4,831 in 1920 (with fees for senior boys standing at £15 a year), even by 1956 it had only risen to £20,102. By 1982, however, it was approaching the staggering total of three quarters of a million pounds (with fees reaching a new peak of £1,083 a year). The School, whether it liked it or not, was now involved in big business.

Throughout all this activity, ready support was always available from a loyal group of local Old Boys. The Old Edwardians' Association itself tried hard in the 1960's to revive its social life through various experimental ideas—the monthly 'Club Night', skittles matches, basketball tournaments, shooting evenings, cocktail parties and outings to Harvey's or Dyrham Park. Their links with the School were certainly heightened by the establishment of the Leavers' Tea and Old Boys' Day. This consisted of Founder's Day Service in the Abbey, a cricket match against the School and a reunion supper or lunch. The Rugby Club, too, grew in strength and welcomed recruits from the Sixth Form into its second or third teams. This liaison became even easier in 1962 with the transfer of playing facilities from Rainbow Wood Farm to Bathampton, where the Club leased a pitch from the Governors. Major events in the O.E.'s year consisted largely of the Annual Dinner at Fortt's in November, the Oxbridge Dinner in February and, from 1979, a revival of the New Year's Eve Ball. Perhaps no individual typified the dedication and loyalty of 'the few' than Jack Hayward, who retired in 1970 as Secretary of the Association after thirty-three years of sterling service.

The Enlarged School: Problems and Possibilities

One of the most important first-fruits of the School's expansion and new image was undoubtedly the election of its Headmaster onto the Headmasters' Conference (the H.M.C.) in 1964. Membership of this body, which had been established in 1869, not only gave the school official 'Public School' status, but also brought it into contact with every major

Presentation by the Association of Old Edwardians of a new Headmaster's Chair to commemorate the School's election to the Headmasters' Conference in 1966. Mr. H. M. Porter (President of the Association and former Headmaster) is standing on the Headmaster's right.

school in the country. As Col. C. J. Stewart wrote in *The Edwardian*: 'Membership of the Headmasters' Conference is restricted and very highly prized . . . Our membership is not only a source of great satisfaction, but also provides a challenge to maintain and improve our standards in the future'. The School's growing involvement in the world of education outside Bath, together with the gradual improvement of its academic standards, helped to revive something of the national reputation which King Edward's had enjoyed in the eighteenth century.

Membership of the H.M.C. and of the H.M.A. (the Headmasters' Association) began to involve the Headmaster in an increasing amount of time-consuming committee work. Indeed, during this period, Mr. Holbeche rapidly made a name for himself in the wider world of education. Elected on to the Executive Committee of the H.M.A. in 1966, he became Chairman of its Parliamentary Committee in 1967, National President of the Association in 1970 and Honorary Secretary in 1971. Nor was he idle meanwhile in the ranks of the Headmasters' Conference. He became Chairman of the Direct Grant Committee of H.M.C. in 1972 and in this capacity a member of the central Executive Committee of the Conference, a member of its Academic Committee in 1976 and its representative on the Governing Council of the Schools Council in the same year. He was also a member of two important working parties—on the Plowden Report on Primary Education in 1964 and on the James Commission on Teacher Training in 1971. Mr. Holbeche contributed a number of papers on various aspects of education—'The Problems of Transition from School to University', 'Problems of Timetabling', 'The Four Term Year', 'The Sixth Form of the Future', 'Authority and Participation in the Schools' etc. For all these services to education, he was awarded the C.B.E. in the Queen's Birthday Honours List of 1972.

As a result of this growing demand for the Headmaster's services on the national scene, routine organisation and daily control of the School passed increasingly to a hardworking and loyal team of Senior Staff under the leadership of the Second Master. Indeed, one of the features of this period was the gradual de-centralisation of authority and decision-making. This was, of course, made necessary by the rapid growth in the size of the School. From 1974, when Mr. J. P. Wroughton succeeded Mr. W. E. Willett as Second Master, a new structure of pastoral and academic responsibilities slowly evolved. By 1981 the 'pastoral' team consisted of the Senior Sixth Form Tutor (Dr. F. R. Thorn, who took over from Mr. H. C. P. Burden, the original holder of that office), the Middle School Tutor (Col. W. T. Currie) and the Lower School Tutor (Mr. L. D. L. Jones). They each had responsibility for social and behavioural problems of boys within their sector, co-ordinating the work of the Sixth Form Tutors and of the Form Masters of the Fifth Year and below. A separate 'academic' team of senior staff operated in parallel, not only monitoring the academic progress of individual pupils but also controlling the sphere of internal examinations. This was led by the Director of Studies (Mr. H. H. Kenwood), who was closely advised by the Assistant Director of Studies (Mr. R. J. Rowe—with special responsibility for Forms 4 and 5) and the Academic Tutor (Mr. R. K. Pollard—with direct control over forms 1, 2 and 3). Their work was supplemented by a Careers Master (Mr. J. D. Fletcher) and a team of other Staff with particular responsibilities for advice on admission to universities, polytechnics and Colleges (Mr. G. M. Staley, Mr. B. Heywood and Mr. P. Murphy); G.C.E. examinations (Mr. A. P. Rouse); and timetabling (Mr. M. J. Sledge).

During this same period of administrative reform, the function of the full Staff Meeting was somewhat modified. Whereas previously it had been the one and only council for the discussion and formulation of policy, from 1971 much of its work was delegated to sectional groups or sub-committees (most of which were chaired by the Headmaster). Thus, by 1981, the following groups had been formed to deal with specific aspects of School life and to report their recommendations to the full Staff Meeting for approval—Heads of Department, Sixth Form Tutors, Form Masters, House Masters, Games Policy Committee and Curriculum Sub-Committee. Policy, therefore, tended to be originated at lower levels and to involve all members of Staff. Short Common Room meetings, chaired by the Second Master, were also instituted on a weekly basis from 1977.

This search for a 'consensus of opinion' spread at least slightly in the direction of the boys. Although no attempt was made to set up a democratic School Council (briefly fashionable in certain schools of the period) pupils were certainly given a real opportunity to express themselves. This was achieved partly through the weekly 'Form Period' and partly through the establishment of the Improvements Committee in 1977. Chaired by the Second Master, this Committee consisted of two representatives from each Form. These carried on a weekly dialogue between the Committee and the individual Forms, making suggestions and raising complaints. Their constructive approach led to a series of welcome improvements, including an adventure playground, a water fountain, a drinks machine, wooden seats around the grounds, the Lime Grove Project (which gave active support to disabled children of a local school) and an increase in the number of 'chip' days! Meanwhile, the Sixth Form Centre Committee, founded in 1974, became responsible for the control of its own common room affairs, including the management of its coffee bar and the organisation of a series of discos.

The School's long tradition of placing opportunities for leadership into the hands of senior boys was well maintained. By 1981 there were 5 Senior Prefects (who played a major part in the daily organisation and control of the School); 30 Prefects (with two allocated to each Form) and 37 Monitors (who were responsible for assisting Staff in a great variety of areas around the School, including the Library, Stationery Store, Careers Room, Art Room, Second Master's Office, Lost Property Store, Stage, Fitness Room, etc.) Great thought was given to the training and consultation of these young administrators. In 1974, the Second Master inaugurated an annual Leadership Conference for newly-elected Prefects, a weekly meeting for Senior Prefects and a fortnightly briefing for Prefects. These gatherings not only provided scope for continuous in-service training, but also gave an opportunity for the boys to air their own views. Election of Prefects continued to be the responsibility of the full Staff Meeting, although an 'Opinion Poll' of the boys in the School was always brought into consideration. This was taken after a period in the Spring Term when each Lower Sixth Former had completed a trial spell as a 'Deputy Prefect'. Younger and middle-school boys were also expected to play their part, on a rota basis as 'Duty Form', by assisting with administrative chores (moving of furniture, enveloping of circulars, collecting of litter, etc.)

Parents , too, became much more involved in the life of the community and in the process of consultation. Annual meetings for the parents of each year group, which commenced in 1962, provided an opportunity for staff to discuss on an individual basis the academic and social problems being encountered by boys. Parental involvement showed itself, too, in the occasional use of questionnaires (e.g. on School uniform) amd in close consultations made on 'O' Level choices. The growth of social activities, of course, greatly helped the

Senior Prefects with groups of new boys on Induction Day, 1975.
Photo by T. C. Leaman

freedom with which parents felt able to contact Staff. This development was also assisted by the setting up of separate offices for the Second Master (in 1972), the Senior Sixth Form Tutor and the Director of Studies (in 1974). The installation of a telephone for their use (in 1974) and the appointment of a

Staff Secretary (in 1978) made it much easier for interviews to be arranged, letters to be written and verbal queries to be answered.

Communication with parents on a variety of matters was of prime importance. From 1962 the publication of a termly School Calendar provided a most useful summary of forthcoming events for both the boys and their parents. The School magazine, of course, continued to provide accounts of activities and achievements. Printing costs, however, eventually brought about its reduction, in 1971, from a termly to an annual publication. Nevertheless, *The Edwardian* took on a new format in that same year under its new Editor (Mr. E. H. Bungay) and expanded its scope to feature original articles, poems and artwork. The gap in between issues was, by the late 1970's, increasingly filled by the Headmaster's termly Newsletters, sent out to parents in duplicated form. So great, in fact, became the volume of duplicated material from School itself as well as from the Ladies' and Fathers' Committees that a systematic distribution became necessary. From 1979, therefore, the Second Master organised a monthly issue of enveloped circulars with the help of his 'Admin' Monitors and the Duty Form.

Life Inside the Classroom

Life inside the buildings of King Edward's School changed almost as much as the buildings themselves. The arrival of two streams of entry in 1959 and of three streams in 1972 soon caused anxieties to be felt about the method of division. Originally the intake was divided into 'A' and 'B' Forms, based on the ability of boys in the Entrance Examination. Gradually, however, the disadvantages of this system were realised. Its lack of flexibility took no account of the varying aptitude of boys for different subjects; its rigidity condemned boys for ever to the 'B' Form, where attitude and behaviour rapidly deteriorated in consequence. A start on de-streaming was made in 1965, when the new intake was classified alphabetically into 1A and 1 Alpha. It was not, however, until 1969 that the idea was extended to the Forms above. Henceforth boys were taught in forms for certain subjects, but progressively setted by ability in others. The arrival of the third stream of entry in 1972 again caused long heart-searchings about nomenclature. Eventually it was decided to style future Forms 'P', 'Q' and 'R' in order to stress the unstreamed nature of the division.

These changes also coincided with the introduction of what was called 'peripatesis' in 1967. Throughout the entire previous history of the School, boys had been based in their own Form Rooms, where they stored their books and were taught for the majority of their lessons. However, with the development of new teaching methods and the fashionable growth of visual aids, there was now an ever-rising demand for the establishment of 'subject rooms'. By 1967 these already existed in Physics, Chemistry, Biology, Art, Music, History and Geography. To this list were now added English, Modern Languages, Classics and Mathematics. This became, therefore, the age of blackout curtain, pinboard display areas, tape recorders, projects and film strip projectors. Both boys and Staff suddenly became mobile, struggling in between periods along crowded corridors and steep flights of steps with arms full of books or bags crammed with equipment. Form Rooms were restyled 'Registration Rooms', where Form Masters and Form Prefects met briefly with their boys before Assembly. Because desks were no longer accessible to pupils at will, the advent of lockers in corridors could not be long delayed. The era of locker keys, tied for safety round the necks of younger boys, had arrived. So, too, had the era of lost property.

This period also witnessed the appearance of a host of new subjects in the curriculum. Even as late as 1965, the younger boys were still following a purely traditional course of study in English, Mathematics, History, Gorgraphy, French, Latin, Greek, Physics, Chemistry, Art, Music, Religious Instruction and Physical Education. Although German and Biology had made a somewhat limited appearance on the horizon, little else had changed for generations. The ensuing years, however, were to produce not only the full establishment of those two subjects on the timetable, but also the introduction of a wide range of others—Economics (1965), Nuffield Latin (1970—as a replacement for Greek, which disappeared completely), Craft (1974), Local Studies (1974), Citizenship (1975), Commerce (1977), Pottery (1977), British Industrial Society

(1980) and Computer Studies (1981). Woodwork remained, as it had done from the middle of the nineteenth century, high on the agenda of subjects to be added sometime in the future! Meanwhile, modern syllabuses and teaching methods were particularly evident in the audio-visual French course (which paved the way for a Language Laboratory, listed as a target for the 1982 Development Appeal), Foreign Exchange visits, the Mode III English Language Course, 'Field Studies' in Geography, Economics and Biology), the 'Modern Mathematics' Course and the new Television and Video Room (opened in 1975).

The introduction of new subjects inevitably posed a problem of choice, particularly at the 'O' Level stage. Until this point, the School's policy had been firmly set against early specialisation and had been more inclined to that of 'keeping all doors open'. Faced increasingly, however, with the problem of overloading (which produced an inevitable decline in performance), the School introduced its first real choice system in 1969 with three compulsory subjects at 'O' Level and four chosen from a range of options. This scheme was soon rejected as unsatisfactory. It was essential to stretch the able, while not overloading the weak; to maintain the balance in boys' choices between Sciences, Languages and Humanities; and to produce teaching sets of similar size. Eventually, after two further experimental schemes in 1970 and 1972, the so-called 'Delta Choice Scheme' was devised in 1974. This proved most satisfactory, clearly benefiting from the greater flexibility available with increased numbers and additional Staff. By 1982 it consisted of the following range of subjects:

THE 'DELTA' CHOICE SCHEME FOR 'O' LEVEL

CORE SUBJECTS   (taken by all): English Language, Mathematics, French

OPTIONS   (boys choose one subject from each line):

Line A: Biology I, Geography I, Art I, Traditional Latin
Line B: Nuffield Latin, Art II, Geography II, Physics I.
Line C: Chemistry I, History I, Physics II, Geography III, Music
Line D: History II, Chemistry II, German, Citizenship (C.S.E.)
Line E: Chemistry III, History III, Biology II, British Industrial Society

By this time, too, Mathematics and English Language could be taken early at the end of the Fourth Form by the more able boys, who were thus enabled to study Additional Mathematics and English Literature as extra subjects in the Fifth Form. The 'Delta' Scheme introduced a new idea of consultation in depth and over a long period with parents and boys before decisions were finally made. It was very much the creation of the Curriculum Sub-Committee, an off-shoot of the Heads of Department Meeting. Between 1974 and 1981, when it was disbanded, this Sub-Committee, chaired throughout much of this period by Mr. H. C. P. (Bill) Burden, was responsible for a series of major reports on the curriculum and the introduction of new subjects.

The Sixth Form, too, witnessed a number of modifications as the enlarged entry made its way up the school (reaching the very top in 1978). In 1969 the Liberal Studies Course was re-shaped with the appearance of outside lecturers, who contributed to such themes as 'The World of Personal Affairs', 'The World of Leisure' and 'The World of Industry', the latter being supplemented by a two-day Conference organised by the Industrial Society. Shortly afterwards, in 1970, the old 'Form' divisions of Upper Sixth Arts, Upper Sixth Science, Lower Sixth Arts and Lower Sixth Science disappeared to be replaced by Tutor Groups, each consisting of about a dozen boys. Form Masters were superseded by Sixth Form Tutors, who became responsible for the pastoral welfare and academic progress of their boys in a much more personal way. At the same time, boys entering the Sixth Form were expected to sign a 'Code of Conduct', promising to conform to basic standards of work and behaviour, and to attend an Introduction Course, designed to introduce them to the problems of working at a higher level. These moves helped to counter the rebellious teenage spirit, which was clearly evident in Society during the early 1970's. The School successfully avoided the worst manifestations of this period of long hair, scruffy appearance and drugs.

Much more attention was also given to the task of helping pupils to prepare for further education or for careers after leaving school. A Careers Room had first been established in 1962. Guidance received there from a vast range of literature was initially supplemented by visits from the Public Schools' Appointments Board and the Careers Advisory Service of the Ministry of Labour. The whole work was co-ordinated by a Careers' Master, who did what he could to assist in the little time he had available. Biennial Careers Conventions, at which boys and their parents could receive personal consultations with representatives from industry and the professions, first appeared on the scene in 1974. Similar guidance was also offered over the problem of selecting courses of study at universities and polytechnics. By 1967 two members of Staff (an Artist and a Scientist) shared the responsibility for advising boys on applications and conditions for entry. In the same year the School also started its 'Pre-University Course', arranging a series of visits to Universities and a number of talks by Old Edwardian undergraduates. Nor were boys who underperformed in the G.C.E. Examinations neglected in their moment of despair. From 1976 a special 'surgery' was arranged during August to assist boys who needed help or advice after the publication of 'O' and 'A' Level results.

That few boys ever needed to avail themselves of this 'Surgery' is a tribute to the remarkable growth of academic success during this period. The Headmaster himself contributed to this in three ways—by his pains-taking selection of boys after the annual Entrance Examination, which ensured that the right sort of academic material was available; by his detailed and thorough work on University (U.C.C.A.) testimonials, which ensured that the ability and personality of each boy were fully recognised; and by the energetic lead he gave to the coaching of Oxbridge candidates. Much credit must also be given to a talented and dedicated senior Staff, who sacrificed considerable time and effort in successfully raising teaching standards in their own particular Departments. Several achieved academic distinction in their own right through research, writing or examining for the G.C.E. Boards. In 1979, for instance, no fewer than six members of Staff were working on books for publication. As early as 1972 a collection of scholarly essays, written by seven talented Oxbridge candidates and edited by the Senior History Master, had been published under the title of *Bath in the Age of Reform, 1832–1841*. In the twenty years between 1962 and 1982 a total of 134 boys had gained entry to Oxford and Cambridge. Of these 18 had been awarded scholarships and 23 Exhibitions spread over a wide range of subjects. This tradition was further stimulated by the annual Oxbridge Dinners, which were held in College Halls and alternated between the two universities. Nor was academic success merely confined to the most able. By 1981 the subject pass-rate at 'O' Level had reached a new peak of 87%, while that at 'A' Level was averaging 86%.

This clearly emphasised the fact that expansion had not been accompanied by a decline in academic standards. Indeed, it became noticeable that the recruitment of additional staff had brought with it far greater flexibility on the time-table, a wider range of subject choices and much more varied contributions to Liberal Studies and extra-curricular activities. The most promising boys on the Science side were increasingly encouraged to take Mathematics 'A' Level in the Lower Sixth (where many of them were awarded a Grade 'A'), before going on to take the Oxbridge Scholarship Examination in the first term of their Upper Sixth year. No fewer than 70 per cent of Sixth Form leavers on average made their way to university—a far cry from the situation in Capt. Annand's day!

This period also brought the last official Inspection by the Ministry of Education (1966); the transfer of Prize Giving from the Pavilion to the Assembly Hall at North Road (1972), followed by a reception for invited guests in the Multi-Purpose Hall; the end of Saturday morning school (1969); and the arrival of the School's one-and-only female pupil (Miss G. Wrigley) who came as an Oxbridge candidate for three months in 1972.

Life Outside the Classroom

Extra-curricular activities flourished and diversified. In spite of ever-increasing problems of long-distance travel, brought about by the extension of the catchment area into the remote villages of Wiltshire, boys showed little reluctance to stay behind after School to pursue their interests. Extensive use was also made of the lunch hour to promote Societies and to

Prize-Giving, 1980. The photo shows (standing from left to right) Mark Williams, Andrew Ridyard, David Sloper, and the Headmaster; (sitting) Lt. Col. John Blashford-Snell, the explorer, who presented the prizes.

Photo by Bath Evening Chronicle

accommodate rehearsals. Without question, one of the most dramatic developments during these years was the growth of an impressive tradition in Music. Almost the first action taken by the Headmaster in 1962 was to establish a School Choir under Mr. B. J. Maslen. By the end of that year, the Choir had performed in the first Carol Service held in St. Mary's, Bathwick, a House Music Competition had been organised and, of even greater significance, violin classes had been started in the Junior School. There was, however, no short cut to the establishment of a School Orchestra. Nevertheless, partly as an interim measure in the development of School music, the C.C.F. came to the rescue by reviving the C.C.F. Band in 1963. In what was nothing short of a miracle, Mr. Alan Tongue (with the help of Tim Sylvester, a senior pupil) set about the seemingly hopeless task of training musicians from scratch. *The Edwardian* describes one other difficulty which faced them—the lack of instruments:

> 'The next problem was to find brass and woodwind instruments for these volunteers. The Headmaster and Mr. Tongue promptly entered the second-hand market and scoured the country for cheap low-pitch instruments. The greatest windfall came from the cellar of a Drill Hall in London—almost a complete set of brass instruments triumphantly retrieved by Major Currie in the back of his car and disinfected in Mr. Tongue's kitchen. By Easter the School possessed some thirty-five instruments for a total outlay of £180'.

Nevertheless, in spite of these problems, within six months the Band had given its first concert in the Hall. By the Spring of 1964, it had also combined with the School Choir to perform in what could certainly be regarded as the forerunner of the Choral and Orchestral Concerts. Although the C.C.F. Band had virtually collapsed as an effective unit by the end of the year, its place was taken by the formation in embryo of a proper School Orchestra with considerable Staff support . It was not, however, until the appointment of Mr. I.D.C. Phipps, as the first full-time Director of Music in 1966, that further progress could be made. Under his guidance the standard of music quickly advanced. By 1972, there were 90 boys receiving instrumental tuition from six peripatetic teachers, 44 boys in the Senior Orchestra, 30 boys in the

Carol Service in St. Mary's, Bathwick, conducted by Mr. B. J. Maslen, 1963.

Photo by T. C. Leaman

Junior Orchestra and 73 boys in the Choir. The Choral and Orchestral Concerts, which had moved to the Assembly Rooms in 1969, became increasingly ambitious. Such was the strength and confidence of the Music Department that the School was able to stage a home-grown musical production in 1976, entitled *For God and Parliament*, with music by Ian Phipps and Glenn Tommey and words by two Old Boys (Paul Johnson and Philip Smith). This was followed in the next year by another musical *Oh, What a Lovely War*.

Meanwhile, the dramatic tradition of the School had also been developing in a lively manner. A succession of producers (Trevor Rhymes, John Lornie, Ewart Willett, Michael Rogers, Lawrence Meering and Jonathan Chambers) staged a variety of plays in a most professional manner. Illustrating the sheer diversity of their programme, this list is only a small selection of the total sequence—*Hamlet* (1965), *She Stoops to Conquer* (1962), *Caucasian Chalk Circle* (1971), *Under Milk Wood* (1970) *The Devil's Disciple* (1978), *Murder in the Cathedral* (1964), *Forty Years On* (1979) and *The Magistrate* (1981). The latter years also saw the emergence of the revue—at first in the form of *The Long John Silver Show* (1974) and *The Rhubarb Tart Spectacular* (1975), both fully staged and directed by senior pupils; then, later still, the more informal and highly popular *Sixth Form Revues*. The School Play (in December) certainly became one of the major events in the Calendar, along with the Carol Service in St. Mary's Bathwick (December), the Choral and Orchestral Concert in the Assembly Rooms (March), Founder's Day Service in the Abbey (July) and Prize-Giving in the Hall (October). To this list was also added in 1978 the annual Arts Festival. The brain-child of Mr. I. D. C. Phipps and Mrs. J. Gilligan, it consisted of a series of lectures, recitals, poetry-readings, art and photography exhibitions and a 'Mastermind' Competition, culminating in the forementioned large-scale Choral and Orchestral Concert in the Assembly Rooms.

Boys at School during this period could not complain that life was dull. Quite apart from music and drama, they were presented with many opportunities to express their personality through a wide range of Clubs and Societies. Some of these quickly came and went, according to current interests of

'The Man Who Came to Dinner', 1980. The photo shows (from the left) David Abbott, Toby Longworth (without the hat) and Debbie Hogg. During the 1970's it became customary to invite girls from Bath High School to perform the female parts in School plays.

Photo by Wessex Newspapers

masters and boys. The Vecturian Society (which studied modern transport), the Pears Society (for Sixth Form lectures), the Kinematograph Society (for cine film enthusiasts), the Polemics (a lunching and discussion society), and the Europa Film Club all served a usefulness in their time. Other Societies weathered the storm of fad and fancy, and survived virtually unscathed through these twenty years —the Junior History Society, the Stamp Club, the Badminton Club, the Model Railway Society, and the Christian Union. Perhaps the most unusual activity of all was the formation in 1970 of Alexander Popham's Bath Regiment, which became affiliated to The Sealed Knot, a national society for the re-enactment of the battles of the English Civil War. *The Edwardian* commented:

'The top level this term has echoed to the beat of Roundhead drum and the stamp of Pikeman's feet. Alexander Popham's Bath Regiment has been making its preparations in winter quarters for the new campaigning season. Buff coats, grey tunics, green caps and stockings, yellow sashes have all been improved to meet the Commander's high standards. Meanwhile, the regiment's funds have been built up by a 'weekly assessment' and other Scrooge-like methods devised by our Treasurer-at-War. Pikes, halberds, partisans have been assembled, together with the regimental standard and drum, to do battle next Spring at Cheriton, Warwick Castle, Ludlow Castle, Marston Moor etc. A regimental news-sheet, *Mercurius Politicus*, will from time to time keep our supporters informed of what is astir. A rush of volunteers in the Autumn increased our numbers to thirty-five (including a large proportion of stout rugger men).

In November the regiment's inaugural banquet was held when, under the flag of truce, local Royalists were entertained in lavish style. The Lord of the Manor, who graced us with his presence, had not only loaned his splendid baronial hall for the occasion, but had also offered hay and stabling for our horses. The good Mistress Ruddick had, with Mistress Richter, provided a most sumptuous feast .of Queen Henrietta Maria's Morning Broth, charr fish in sweete sauces, game pie, half chickens with manchets, West Country dumplings, Eliza Acton's gingerbread biscuits, dough cake, Bath buns, Banbury Cakes, jellies, fruit and coffee. Roundhead cadets (who resem-

bled at times an Under-15 Rugger team) performed efficiently
as waiters and tapsters.

Meanwhile, the official military training unit (the C.C.F.)
had continued to provide a regular programme of annual
camps, arduous training exercises in the Black Mountains and
Brecon Beacons, field days, inter-platoon competitions and

Alexander Popham's Bath Regiment marching into action, 1971.

night schemes. The Shooting Team, under Lt. M. Hunt and
C.S.M. E. G. Dodge, steadily built on the long tradition of
success by competing annually at Bisley for the Ashburton
Trophy. The climax came in 1966 when the School won *The
Country Life* competition for the third time in its history (the
previous occasions being in 1920 and 1958). Increasingly,
parties of cadets were also taken much further afield—to
Ireland, Germany, Denmark, Malta and Norway. During
most of these years, the C.C.F. was commanded in enthusiastic style by Lieut. Col. W. T. (Bill) Currie. His long service to
the Cadet Force, both in the School and in the country

(where, from 1977, he became Chairman of the Somerset Schools C.C.F.), was rewarded by the award of the Cadet force Medal in 1964 and the Queen's Silver Jubilee Medal in 1977. When he retired in 1978 to hand over the command to

The Field Studies Group engaged in geological studies in the Massif Central, 1964.

Photo by P. M. Gayton

Maj. I. D. C. Phipps, he had had the satisfaction of being in office at the time when the C.C.F. celebrated its 75th Anniversary with a dinner at The Beaufort Hotel.

From 1964 boys who were not keen to join the C.C.F. were in future given the option of either working with the Pioneers (see above) or of accepting a more personal challenge with the

Duke of Edinburgh's Award Scheme. Originally started under the direction of Mr. J. Ockenden, the Scheme continued successfully throughout the majority of this period under the control of Mr. R. J. Gay. Opportunities for foreign travel were slowly extended with the gradual removal of restrictions during the post-war years. Parties visited Italy, Switzerland, Spain and Greece for sight-seeing and recreational purposes. However, the establishment of the Field Studies Group by Mr. P. M. Gayton in 1963 pioneered new ground by offering the notion of a study/adventure holiday. Expeditions of this nature, therefore, were subsequently despatched by minibus to the Central Massif, Lappland, Ireland, the Netherlands and Scotland. Much in the same vein, archaeological work camps were organised at Cirencester (1966) and Durrington Walls (1967). Students of Biology and Economics were also given similar opportunities for field work at residential centres during the 1970's.

Perhaps one of the most noticeable features, however, was the development of a programme of Outdoor Pursuits. This evolved slowly at first through the enterprise of individual staff. The Ski Club, which had been formed in 1967 by Mr. M. J. Allen and Mr. J. P. Wroughton, continued to cater annually for an increasing number of members with visits to Norway, Italy and France. Similarly, the Rambling Club, re-founded in 1972 by Dr. F. R. Thorn and Mr. B. A. Watson, developed an insatiable appetite for day rambles, supplemented by longer stays in Wales and periodic visits to the mountains of France and Spain. With the establishment of the Canoe Club (1978) and the Rock Climbing Club (1980), it became evident that some co-ordination was necessary. In 1979, therefore, Mr. M. A. Cunliffe was appointed as the School's first Director of Outdoor Pursuits to plan a programme of outdoor education throughout the School. One outcome of this was the inauguration, in 1980, of an annual camp for Second Year boys, at which training was given in hill-walking, canoeing, rock-climbing, orienteering, pony-trekking and camping.

Sport at King Edward's received a considerable boost in 1961 with the appointment of Mr. L. D. L. Jones as the School's first full-time Master-in-Charge of Physical Education. The games field was in consequence dominated, throughout this entire period, by his ebullient good humour and his tireless enthusiasm for rugby, cricket and athletics. There was a large number of individual and team successes. Boys, at varying times, were called upon to represent county teams in rugby, hockey, cricket, athletics, swimming, badminton, tennis and chess; Geoff Franckom, who was awarded his Rugby Blue at Cambridge, went on to play for England on a

The School's Under-16 Badminton Team, 1980—Avon County Champions; (from the left) Ian Eldridge, David Buck, Neville Walker, Martin Eldridge.

Photo by Wessex Newspapers

number of occasions from 1965; Trevor Rhymes brought honour to the School in 1977 when he was elected National President of the Amateur Swimming Association; Mike Robinson was placed third in the 80m. Junior Hurdles Final at the All-England Schools' Championships of 1974; the Senior Badminton team won the Avon Schools' Premier League in 1980 and 1981; the Chess Team emerged victors in the F. J. Pierce Rose Bowl Competition and reached the zonal final of the *Sunday Times* Knock-Out Tournament in 1981; the Under-15 Rugby team, in 1971, not only won all eleven of its matches, but scored 477 points with only 6 points being awarded against it; the 1st XI Hockey team, unbeaten in 1980, went on to become champions of Avon in 6-a-side tournaments both indoors and outdoors. There were disappointments, of course, such as the occasion in 1969 when, in the Bearwood Festival, the 1st XI Cricket team found itself bowled out by Sebright for just two runs!

The Under-15 Rugby Team, 1971.
Back row: G. A. J. Webb, T. G. Towler, J. A. Carling, P. E. Martin, P. M. Scott, P. M. Branson, D. C. K. Herapath, P. J. Collett, R. H. Bowles, Mr. J. P. Wroughton (coach).

Front row: G. A. Dobie, A. M. Prosser, A. J. Wakefield (Capt.), L. E. Hubbard, S. B. C. Jones, B. A. Maunder (*absent* A. R. M. Mills).
Played 11, Won 11, Lost 0, Points for 477, Points Against 6
Photo by Bath Evening Chronicle

Sport was certainly played and enjoyed by a large number of boys. Fifth and Sixth Formers were increasingly given a wide range of options from which to choose on their games afternoon. With the opening of the Bath Sports Centre, it became possible to offer (in addition to the major games) soccer, badminton, squash, table-tennis, swimming, basketball, golf, cross-country, tennis and social service. Yet, in spite of all this interest and involvement, sport at King Edward's remained something of an enigma. The high level of success fervently desired by a large number of dedicated games coaches on the Staff, was seldom achieved. It proved difficult to compensate for the lack of tradition; it proved impossible to compete with boarding schools in terms of time made available for training. The spectre of defeat continued to haunt as, with the rise of large comprehensives, the School remained comparatively small. No-one, however, could blame the

The School Hockey Team, 1980: unbeaten in school matches and winners of the Avon Under-19 6-a-side tournaments (both indoors and outdoors).
Back row: Jim Thomas, Peter Hatherley, Neville Benbow, Chris Langley.
Front row: David Holman, David Paige (Capt.) Mark Holness.
Photo by Wessex Newspapers

Headmaster for lack of encouragement. Week after week, whatever the weather, he unfailingly provided School teams with vocal support and touchline enthusiasm. In the bleak winter months, his Russian-style fur hat became a familiar sight at Bathampton—as did his award of wine-gums to try-scorers on Monday mornings.

Nevertheless, sport did play a major part in the life of the boys, thanks partly to the House System. This had been modified in 1962 with the addition of a fourth House (Symons). At the same time, further incentive was provided by the award of three new House Trophies—the Games Shield for sport, the London Cup for other competitions (e.g. Music, chess, arts, etc) and the Work Shield for academic perform-ance. By 1981 the House System was as strong as ever, with competitions in 5-a-side football and basketball joining those in the major sports. The system itself had undergone some-thing of a transformation in that year with the re-organisation of the boys into three Houses aligned with the three streams ('P', 'Q' and 'R') so that Form and House Spirit would reinforce each other. The new Houses were named Parry, De Quincey and Rosewell (after distinguished Old Edwardians).

Continuity and Change

In a scene that was always changing, the School found it reassuring during this period to retain a few of its traditional links with the past. Perhaps the most important of these were the Broad Street premises, which continued to house a thriving Junior School. Mr. W. Paterson had been appointed to be in charge of the Preparatory Department during its last year at 20 Belmont in 1959. It then consisted of 74 boys and three Staff, taking its lunches in Big School and its gymnastics at the Paragon. In 1959, Mr. Paterson was joined by Mr. T. Elsom-Rhymes as part of the planned expansion. The 'Junior School', as it was now styled, was accommodated on a temporary basis in Nethersole during the building of the Senior School at North Road. By the time Mr. Paterson and his charges returned to Broad Street in September 1961, he had 117 boys under his control. Numbers thereafter continued to rise steadily until they reached a new peak of 177 in 1981.

The buildings themselves were gradually modified and adapted to cater for yet another role in their long history of change. In 1973, for instance, the underground play area was converted into a dining room. Lunches there were eventually supplied by the new North Road Kitchen, from which they were delivered in insulated containers. The same year also saw the building of music practice rooms and store rooms. Probably the most dramatic transformation was reserved, however, for the Summer Term of 1978. On a brilliant May morning the Mayor of Bath, Councillor Ken Holloway (himself an Old Edwardian), unveiled a plaque to commemorate the cleaning and restoration of the Georgian facade. Money for this work had been raised partly by means of a 'miniappeal' and partly by a grant from the Bath Town Scheme. The visual effect was remarkable. Two years later, in 1980, the interior of the Junior School was also treated to an equally

The Opening of the Junior School's new Art Room by Mr. H. M. Porter, 1980.

Photo by Bristol United Press

impressive transformation. In a scheme[1] costing nearly £50,000, a new Art Room was created by amalgamating three smaller rooms at the top of the building; a new Library and Television Room was established in the basement; a new internal staircase was ingeniously inserted as part of a major plan to ensure conformity with modern fire regulations; and a complete electrical rewiring was undertaken throughout the entire building. It was totally fitting that the whole project

1 Devised by Mrs. P.H. Fereday, mother of an Old Edwardian. She also supervised the restoration of the facade, in her capacity as Architectural Consultant to the School.

was officially opened by the former Headmaster, Mr. H. M. Porter.

Life in the Junior School also flourished during these years of physical growth. The 'Parents' Day', first held in 1962 as a means of communicating progress, had by 1969 developed into regular Parents' meetings. Increased attention was also given to the enlargement of personality in each individual boy. Hobbies groups, the Puppet Theatre, educational visits, Field Studies and Outdoor Activity Weeks all in turn contributed richly to this process. Horizons were further extended by nine ski-ing holidays in Austria (1967–1975) and an educational cruise to Scandinavia. Nor was the cultural side of life neglected. Music and drama played an increasing part in the School calendar with (from 1962–1963) the establishment of a choir, a recorder group and violin tuition. To the annual Harvest Festival was added, in 1972, the first public Carol Service (held in St. Michael's) and the first Junior School Concert. Sport, too, was beginning to assume a new prominence, which was rewarded in 1969 with the winning of the Bath Schools' Cricket and Swimming Cups. By 1974 the Soccer Team had also tasted success by reaching the Final of the Bath Schools' Cup and gaining third place in Division One of the League.

Links with the past were also forged through the long-standing service of a number of individuals who retired from office during these years. Both Mr. W. E. Willett and Mr. H. C. P. Burden had worked in the school under Mr. Porter and therefore brought with them to North Road some of the traditions of Broad Street. When Ewart Willett retired in 1974, he had served the School for 29 years, including twenty-four as Second Master. No contribution could have been more varied. He had, in his time, been Head of the Classics Department, Editor of *The Edwardian* (1945–65), First Form Master, Play Producer, Master-in-Charge of Hockey, Tennis and Badminton, Leader of Expeditions abroad and Campaign Director of the 1971 Development Appeal. His kindly personality, complete integrity and uncompromising standards gave stability both to the School in general and to the Staff Room in particular during this era of change. Equally representative of all that was good in the 'old' School, was Bill Burden, who had first joined King Edward's as a Prep School boy in 1926. After working his way through the School under Capt. Annand, he eventually returned in 1946 to work under Mr. Porter as a teacher of French, Latin and Religious Education. His later service was to include responsibility as Master-in-Charge of Cricket and Rugby, Senior Sixth Form Tutor (from 1974) and Head of Religious Education and Liberal Studies. A man of great dignity and moral stature, he shared with Mr. Willett the reputation of being a complete gentleman.

Mention must also be made of two other characters who helped the School to weather the storm of change. Col. C. J. Stewart, who had succeeded Dr. Ashcroft as Chairman of

Colonel C. J. Stewart (centre), shown at the opening of the Stewart Building in 1979, with the Headmaster (left) and Mr. M. Rutherford (right).

Governors in 1963, was himself the nephew of a former Chairman—thus helping again to ensure continuity of purpose. When he retired in 1979 (to be succeeded by Mr. M. Rutherford), Mr. Holbeche paid him this tribute: 'There can be very few records of service to match Col. Stewart's in the

annals of the School; his leadership and foresight, his judgment and financial acumen, his broad humanity and his
single-minded devotion to the best interests of the School, all
these qualities have been an inspiration to us all during a
unique and exciting period in the history of this ancient
foundation.' Equally loyal and spanning almost exactly the
same term of service, was Miss Margaret Boulton, who retired
in 1978 after $15\frac{1}{2}$ years as Headmaster's Secretary. To her had
fallen the task of holding together the 'administrative services'
during this crucial period of expansion. Her success was
largely due to her great strength of character, her unique
improvisation and style, her tremendous dedication and her
cheerful efficiency.

All these personalities added richly to the course of human
life and provided, at the same time, a rock on which the new
developments could thrive. Change of a more unwelcome
kind, however, was thrust upon the School in 1976. The
Donnison Commission, which had reported its findings in
1970, had recommended that Direct Grant status should be
phased out from the country's secondary schools. Although its
Report had subsequently been ignored by Mr. Heath's Con-
servative Government, the victory of the Labour Party in the
elections of 1974 sounded the death knell. The new Government immediately announced its intention to abolish the
Direct Grant System, a threat which had been accomplished
by the summer of 1976. Schools such as King Edward's were
forced to choose between complete independence and integration into the State sector. The Governors, with full backing
from both Staff and Parents, decided to go independent. This
meant that, although government grants were guaranteed for
boys who were already in the School, pupils entering from
September 1976 would be required to pay the full fees. In
order to offset the harshness of this situation for parents of
able boys with limited means, the Governors established their
own Bursary Scheme. Thus, from the limited funds available,
some fifteen per cent of the first independent intake received a
certain degree of financial assistance. Fears that the removal
of the Direct Grant would inevitably reduce the number of
applicants and dilute the level of academic ability had, by
1982, proved totally unfounded.

Footnote

It is not the function of a historian to prophesy the future or to comment critically on a period of history in which he himself has been an active participant. Some statements can, however, be made on the basis of historical fact. First and foremost, the period 1961–1982 was one of the most momentous and exhilarating periods in the long history of the School. It was as if the Governors in 1959, by the sudden opening of a valve, had unleashed a great torrent of force, the pressure of which had been building up for over a hundred years. A School, which had been physically confined and stunted in its growth, now became expansive in attitude as it spread its wings over the fine new site at North Road. A School, which for 150 years had been unambitious and introspective, now assumed a dynamic and confident air. Its local reputation and national fame, shattered by the mindless folly of nineteenth century philanthropists, were restored in full measure. The name of King Edward's, Bath once more returned to the lips of Oxford dons. Its growing repute took the Headmaster up to London to join the inner councils of the educational elite— and a future Prime Minister down to Bath for the opening of the School's new Hall.

Secondly, there can be no doubt that this remarkable achievement was based on the joint efforts of the wider School community, epitomised by 'The Friends of King Edward's' Committee. No praise can be too high for the courageous and ambitious attitude of the Board of Governors throughout this entire period—or for the support and interest tirelessly offered to the School by two successive Chairmen, Col. C. J. Stewart and Mr. M. Rutherford, equally enthusiastic and encouraging in their approach. It is, perhaps, significant that the School has only tended to prosper during those periods of its history when Governors and Headmaster have worked closely together. These were certainly years of prosperity. For his own part, the Headmaster himself, Mr. Holbeche, must take major credit for physical expansion and numerical growth over twenty years. His inventive mind and relentless determination ensured that 'Plans for Development' appeared without respite as an item on the agenda at most Governors' Meetings.

Furthermore, he successfully carried out the very difficult exercise of staffing this expansion by recruiting the right teachers at the right time. It was essential, but extremely difficult, to balance out the additional requirements of each subject, without creating a wasteful surplus of manpower, and to balance out the needs of the community by employing Staff who could also make rich contributions to the life of the School. On a broader front, he set about the task of gaining publicity for the name of the School through his work nationally on educational committees. At the same time, his involvement locally (as a Magistrate on the Bath Bench and as Chairman of the Everyman Arts Club) helped him to promote the reputation of King Edward's in the world beyond North Road.

But in a community which became increasingly democratic, decisive contributions were also frequently made by senior staff to a whole range of vital developments in social, organisational and academic matters. Their dedication, enterprise and loyalty, like that of their predecessors over the whole history of the School, must never be underestimated. Nor, indeed, must the hard work of that new phenomenon in the affairs of King Edward's—the parents themselves. The Ladies' and Fathers' Committees, backed by hundreds of covenantors who gave so sacrificially, funded the structural developments which made the period so exciting. This 'Age of Self-Help' was truly the 'Age of Total Involvement'. Therein lies the secret of the School's success.

That success, both striking and real, *has* been achieved during these twenty years cannot be disputed. Even as early as 1966, the Inspectors stated in their official Report that the School was 'barely recognisable as the same institution' which had been visited ten years earlier. It had 'successfully negotiated the years of rapid expansion' and had 'emerged as a two-form-entry school with standards raised and prestige enhanced'. They praised its 'vigorous corporate life' and its 'staff of quality', which was 'admirably led'. If these Inspectors had visited the School again in 1982, they would certainly have noticed that the second phase of the expansion had been completed with equal efficiency. They would possibly have commented that the School had at last achieved the objectives set by their predecessors in the Inspection Report of 1927—a new school site, better facilities, a highly-qualified team of specialist Staff, a fully-fledged Sixth Form, high academic standards and strong links with the universities. They would surely have concluded that the School, just 55 years later, had risen once more 'to a position worthy of its traditions and of the place which it ought to occupy in the City of Bath.'

The Spring of 1982 sees storm clouds gathering yet again. Threats, which contain varying degrees of venom, have recently been made by a Labour Party pledged to abolish independent education. The student of history and the reader of this book can therefore take comfort together in the sound knowledge that King Edward's School, Bath has shown a rare capacity for survival. Over the 430 years of its existence, crisis has followed crisis—the dispersal of the School in 1644 during times of Civil War; the misappropriation of the School's Endowment by the Corporation in the Seventeenth century; the public row over the Mastership in 1754; the ruining of the School's academic reputation by the admission of free Foundationers in 1822; the public protest of parents in 1830; the disastrous effects of the 1849 Scheme; the collapse of discipline under Mr. Fagan; the School's relegation to Second Grade Status in 1872; the sacking of Mr. Sanderson in 1896; the scathing Inspection Report of 1927; the Direct Grant battle of 1946 and the loss of Direct Grant Status in 1976.

The School has weathered each storm in turn, showing enormous resilience in times of stress. Today, King Edward's is far more buoyant and confident than ever before. The new Development Appeal, launched in February 1982, seeks to raise £200,000 for the creation of a Sixth Form Centre complex, a Computer Studies Area, a Language Laboratory and a rubberised surface for the Junior School playground. There is little doubt, given the optimism and total-involvement which now exist, that these targets, in the short term, will be achieved. Will the School, in the long term, manage to survive? It *is* possible for the discerning mind to learn a few lessons from history. The next chapter should be well worth reading.

Postscript

This present chapter of the School's history was brought to a sudden and tragic end two weeks after the typescript of this book had been delivered to the printers. On 17 February, 1982, Mr. Holbeche was killed in a road accident near Taunton on his way to a regional meeting of the Headmasters' Conference. The news stunned not only the School itself, but also the City of Bath and the wider world of education. Representatives from all walks of life and Headmasters from a long list of distinguished schools joined Governors, Staff, Boys, Parents, Former Parents and Old Boys to pack Bath Abbey on 5 March for a most moving Memorial Service. At the express wish of his widow, Mrs. Philippa Holbeche, the 1982 Development Appeal continued without delay. Launched in the Banqueting Room of the Guildhall on 20 February (just three days after the Headmaster's death), it now became a memorial to his work and achievement at the School over twenty years.

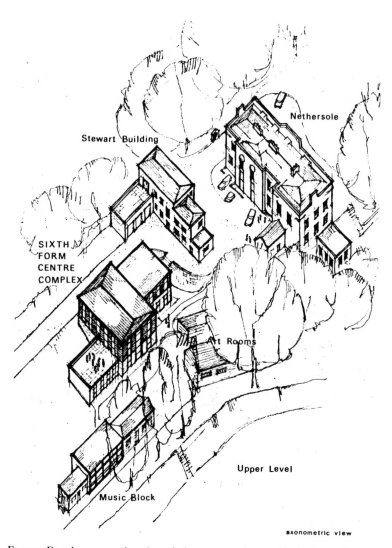

Future Development: the site of the proposed new Sixth Form Centre Complex, one of the targets in the 1982 Appeal.

Line drawing by Mrs. P. A. Fereday

Bibliography

Primary and Unpublished Sources

Bath City Archives

Bath City Council Minute Books.
Chamberlain's Accounts of the City of Bath.
The 1641 Survey.
Various leases in Furman's Repertory.
The Wiltshire leases and the Plan of Ruth Wiltshire, 1768.
Papers relating to repairs of property, 1823–1830.
Correspondence regarding the complaint about the management of the School, 1930.
The School Scheme of 1847.

British Museum—State Papers Room

Charity Commissioners' Report: Vol. 4(1820), Vol. 5 (1821), Vol. 8 (1822).
School's Inquiry Commission Report, 1869.
Secondary Schools' Commission Report, 1895.

King Edward's School Archives

The School Charter (with a translation by Dr. F. R. and Mrs. C. M. J. Thorn).
Scheme for King Edward's School, Bath, 1872.
Scheme for King Edward's School, Bath, 1914.
King Edward's School Governors' Minute Books, 1872–1981.
King Edward's School 'School Committee' Minute Books, from 1872.

Board of Education Inspection Reports, 1904, 1914, 1920, 1927, 1939.
Ministry of Education Inspection Reports, 1956, 1966.
School Prospectuses, 19–20th Centuries.
Old Edwardians' Society: Inaugural Dinner Brochure, 1907.
Tercentenary Festival Brochure, 1853.
Third Centenary Brochure, 1853.
Fourth Centenary Brochure, 1952.
Headmaster's Prize-Day Reports, 1921–1981.
Notes on King Edward's School, Bath, 1921–1961 by H. M. Porter.
Notes on the Laurence Family by G. F. Laurence.
Various Scrapbooks, Photograph Albums and miscellaneous correspondence.

Miscellaneous

Bath Charity Trustees' Minute Books, 1853–1870.
The Index of Old Bath by Miss E. Holland.

Printed Sources:
Bath and Cheltenham Gazette.
Bath Chronicle.
Bath Guide, 1810.
Bath Herald.
Bath Journal.
H. C. Barnard: A Short History of English Education, 1760–1944 (1947).
Robin Davis: The Grammar School (1967).
Joseph Farington: The Farington Diary, Vol. 1 (1922).
Levi Fox: A Country Grammar School—A History of Ashby-de-la-Zouch Grammar School through four Centuries, 1567–1967 (1967).
John Haddon: Bath (1973).
P. R. James: The Baths of Bath in the Sixteenth and Early Seventeenth Century (1938).
George Monkland: Literature and Literati of Bath.
H. A. Page: De Quincey's Life and Writings, 2 Vols. (1877).

Edward Parry: Memories of Rear-Admiral Sir W. Parry (1858).

D. E. Regan: Local Government and Education (1977).

(Rosewell) The Arraignment and Tryal of the late Rev. Mr. Thomas Rosewell for High Treason (1718).

Katharine E. Symons: The Grammar School of King Edward VI, Bath and its Ancient Foundation (1934).

Katharine E. Symons: The Endowment of King Edward's School, Bath (1938).

John Wood: Essay towards a Description of Bath.

John Wroughton: Bath in the Age of Reform, 1832–1841 (1972).

John Wroughton: The Civil War in Bath and North Somerset (1973).

The Edwardian: 1909–1981.

Appendix

Chairmen of the Governing Board

1872–1874:	Rev. C. Kemble, M.A.
1874–1879:	Sir J. Murch, J.P.
1880 :	T. Gibbs, J.P.
1881–1888:	Sir J. Murch, J.P.
1889 :	C. F. Marshall, J.P.
1890–1899:	R. D. Commans
1900–1936:	E. A. Bagshawe, M.A., J.P.
1937–1956:	R. C. L. Fuller, J.P.
1956–1962:	E. A. Merrifield
1963 :	Dr. A. H. Ashcroft
1963–1978:	Col. C. J. Stewart, O.B.E., T.D., J.P., D.L.
1979– :	Mr. M. Rutherford.

Presidents of the Association of Old Edwardians

1906–1924	W. B. Odgers, M.A., LL.D., K.C.
1925–1933:	Rev. D. B. Hooke, D.D.
1934–1937:	W. F. Long
1938–1939:	Sir S. Williams, K.B.E.
1940 :	H. F. Hammermeister
1941–1942:	W. P. Jones
1943–1944:	G. J. W. Vezey
1945–1946:	K. W. Calvert
1947–1948:	L. A. Wilson
1949–1950:	F. H. Ledbury
1951–1952:	N. L. Shackell
1953–1954:	J. J. Hayward
1955–1956:	R. A. Henson, M.D., F.R.C.P.
1957–1958:	J. B. Taylor, M.B.E., LL.B., J.P.
1959–1960:	Sir George Beresford-Stooke, K.C.M.G.

1961–1962: G. H. Moore, M.Sc., F.P.S., F.R.I.C.
1963–1964: F. G. Coles
1965–1966: H. M. Porter, M.A.
1967–1968: B. E. Ireland, J. P., M.I.C.E.
1969–1970: G. A. Young
1971–1972: K. E. Langley, J.P.
1973–1974: T. C. Leaman
1975–1976: W. P. Sheppard
1977–1978: J. R. Pearson, F.C.A.
1979–1980: W. E. Willett, B.A.
1981–1982: R. A. Henson, M.D., F.R.C.P.

King Edward's School Song

Now let us lift our voices,
  With one consent to sing.
Long live the name of Edward,
  Our founder and our King!
Who would not join this chorus
  Is either rogue or fool,
Long live the name of Edward!
  God bless the brave old School!

Chorus Long live the good old School, boys,
  Let all good fellows sing!
Long live the name of Edward,
  Our founder and our King!

We sing our great departed,
  Whom none may disallow,
Strong souls whose tasks are ended,
  Brave voices silent now;
Their memory leads us forward,
  To fight an upward fight,
To strike a blow at baseness,
  And make the right our might.
        Chorus

Old time is on our track, boys,
   And seas may soon divide
The voices now united,
   The friends now side by side;
But whereso'er we carry
   The pride of Edward's name,
Let each forget himself, boys,
   And strive to play the game.
        Chorus

Index